LA CRISTIADA

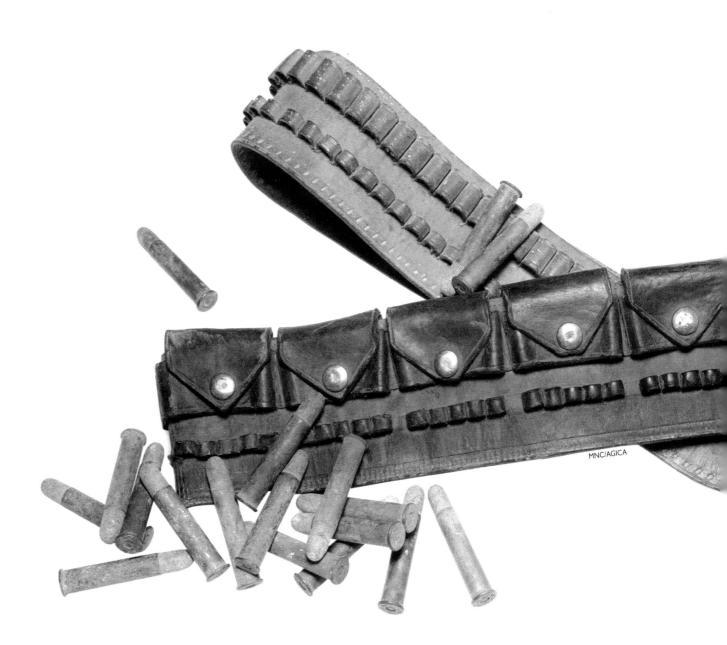

LA CRISTIADA

THE MEXICAN PEOPLE'S WAR FOR RELIGIOUS LIBERTY

JEAN MEYER, PhD

SQUAREONE
PUBLISHERS

COVER DESIGNER: Jeannie Tudor
COVER PHOTO: From the Jean Meyer Archive
TRANSLATOR: Luis Villares
EDITORS: Maureen Walther, Jennifer Daigle, and Marie Caratozzolo
TYPESETTERS: Jeannie Tudor and Gary A. Rosenberg

Square One Publishers
115 Herricks Road
Garden City Park, NY 11040
(516) 535-2010 • (877) 900-BOOK
www.squareonepublishers.com

Library of Congress Cataloging-in-Publication Data

Meyer, Jean A., 1942-
  La Cristiada : the Mexican people's war for religious liberty / Jean Meyer.
      p. cm.
  Includes bibliographical references and index.
  ISBN 978-0-7570-0315-8 (pbk.)
 1. Cristero Rebellion, 1926-1929. 2. Cristero Rebellion, 1926-1929—Pictorial works. 3. Church and state—Mexico—History—20th century. 4. Freedom of religion—Mexico—History—20th century. 5. Catholic Church—Mexico—History—20th century. I. Title.
  F1234.M68326 2013
  972.08'2—dc23
                            2012010568

Printed in India

10   9   8   7   6   5   4   3   2   1

For Don Aurelio Acevedo,
who fought on the battlefield,
and his son Cristobal,
who have been instrumental in
preserving the history of the Cristero cause.

UNITED STATES

State capital
Federal District

BAJA CALIFORNIA

Mexicali

SONORA

Hermosillo

CHIHUAHUA

Chihuahua

COAHUILA
DE ZARAGOZA

Gulf of
California

BAJA CALIFORNIA SUR

SINALOA

NUEVO
LEÓN

Monterrey

Saltillo

DURANGO

Central Plateau

Culiacán

La Paz

Durango

ZACATECAS

SAN LUIS
POTOSÍ

TAMAULIPAS

Ciudad
Victoria

AGUASCALIENTES
Aguascalientes

Zacatecas

San Luis Potosí

QUERÉTARO
Querétaro

NAYARIT

Mexico

Islas
Marías

Tepic

JALISCO

Guadalajara

GUANAJUATO
Guanajuato

HIDALGO
Pachuca
de Soto

TLAXCALA
Tlaxcala

Xalapa

COLIMA
Colima

MICHOACÁN

Morelia

MÉXICO

Toluca
de Lerdo

Mexico City

VERACRUZ

Puebla

PUEBLA

MORELOS
Cuernavaca

GUERRERO

Chilpancingo

OAXACA

Pacific Ocean

Sierra Madre del Sur

Oaxaca de Juárez

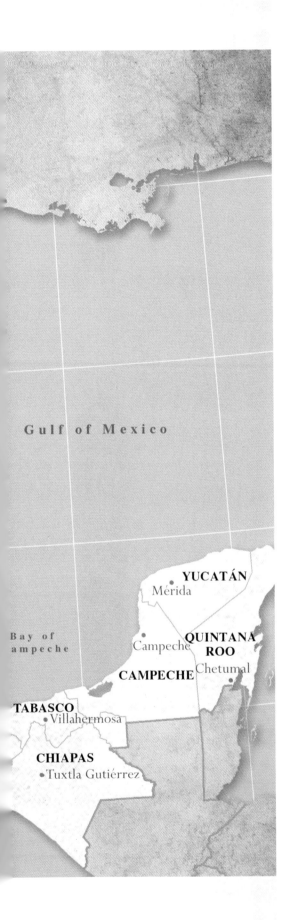

Gulf of Mexico

Bay of ampeche

Campeche

YUCATÁN
Mérida

QUINTANA
ROO
Chetumal

CAMPECHE

TABASCO
Villahermosa

CHIAPAS
Tuxtla Gutiérrez

Contents

Acknowledgments

In my research throughout the years, I was privileged to hear the Cristiada's history directly from the voices of those who lived through it. But in offering this history to a new audience through the printed word, so much depends on photographs and artifacts, which can uniquely—and perhaps more fully—bring this remarkable time to life. In this area, special thanks go to the Archivo General del Instituto Cultural de Aguascalientes, for so generously providing a large number of the photographs in this book. Many of the photographs are iconic in their own right, and it is truly an honor to be able to bring to the United States these and numerous other images of this hidden war, which shaped so many families in both countries.

Publishing the text in the United States provides another opportunity to highlight the existence of Cristero artifacts in this country. Here, special recognition goes to the de la Torre Family collection at the University of Arizona Special Collections Library, and the Knights of Columbus Archives, among others, whose significant pictorial contributions served to more dramatically capture this period in Mexican history.

From research to translation to editing, *La Cristiada* could not have come to be without the contributions of numerous other individuals. In this, my gratitude extends in a special way to the Cristeros and their families, who in charity and service to the truth shared original stories and personal testimonies, giving voice to a once silenced time; to the staff at Square One Publishers, especially Rudy Shur and Marie Caratozzolo, who believed in this project and so painstakingly guided the process of editing and publishing this book; and finally, to Carl A. Anderson, Supreme Knight of the Knights of Columbus, and others at the Knights of Columbus—especially Maureen Walther and Jennifer Daigle, who edited the text; Susan Brosnan and Leith Johnson, who provided much-needed information and photographs; Luis Guevara and Andrew Walther, who helped guide this project to completion; and so many others, including Maria Garcia-Arteaga, Cecilia Castillo-Urriola, Mary Lou Cummings, Loreto Thompson, Michelè Nuzzo-Naglieri, Brian Caulfield, Charles Lindberg, John Cummings, Justin Perillo, and Matt Duman—for faithfully helping to bring this story to an American audience.

Foreword

Few periods in history have been more forgotten than the Mexican people's struggle for religious freedom in the 1920s. It is remarkable that less than a century later, this story is virtually unknown in both Mexico and the United States, despite the fact that the issue was—just a few generations ago—a lightning rod in both countries.

At the time, the Mexican government seemed intent on stamping out the Catholic Church in a country where nearly everyone was Catholic. Priests and lay people were martyred. Bishops were exiled.

In the United States, the Ku Klux Klan and Margaret Sanger, among others, encouraged Mexican President Plutarco Elías Calles in his crackdown on the Catholic Church. At the same time, the Knights of Columbus, the U.S. bishops, *America* magazine, and others stood in solidarity with Mexican Catholics on the side of religious liberty. The Knights raised more than $1 million for peaceful relief efforts for those affected by the persecution and for the education of the American public on the reality of the situation in Mexico. Then-Supreme Knight, James Flaherty, also met with President Coolidge and urged him to find a solution to the violence.

Hundreds of thousands of refugees flooded north to escape this persecution, seeking safety in the United States. And thus the story of the Cristiada also became the story of many Americans, who—like the first settlers of America's thirteen colonies—came as immigrant refugees suffering from religious persecution.

As the violence escalated and public awareness of the situation increased, the American government did finally pressure Mexico to stop its violent campaign against the Church, and though imperfect, things began to improve in 1929. Then came the Great Depression and World War II, and soon the world had forgotten Mexico's war for religious liberty. In Mexico, as well, few wanted to remember this terrible period. It was expunged from the national memory and omitted from the educational curriculum.

The suppression of history has happened in other countries as well. When he was awarded the Nobel Prize in Literature in 1970, Alexander Solzhenitsyn—who was himself censored, forced into labor camps, exiled, and targeted for assassination due to his criticism of Soviet Russia—described what had happened in his own country as "a closing, a locking up, of the national heart, amputation of the national memory." He warned that when this happens, "nationality has no memory of its own self. It is deprived of its spiritual unity. And even though compatriots apparently speak the same language, they suddenly cease to understand one another."

In the case of Mexico, the point of revisiting this period in history is not to reopen the wounds of a past conflict, but to learn the lessons of history, to promote reconciliation, and thereby to build a future in which all people—whatever their political or religious affiliation—can work together for the good of their country. This was the lesson of Nelson Mandela's Truth and Reconciliation Commission in South Africa. And though the events it addressed were more recent than those in Mexico, both truth and reconciliation should always be welcomed.

This book—and the film on the same subject *For Greater Glory*—are important steps in restoring the national memory of Mexico and the continental memory of North America. The Mexican people fought for their freedom with weapons of war, while many Americans supported the cause of liberty by waging battles in the political arena and court of public opinion. For both nations, this book marks an important moment in the restoration of the spiritual unity of those who have for too long been deprived of their voice.

Today, we understand human rights in the context of a broad, international consensus. The world has adopted a Universal Declaration of Human Rights, of which Article 18 specifically protects freedom of conscience and religious freedom "in public or private," and guarantees to each person the right "to manifest his religion or belief in teaching, practice, worship and observance."

Given this context, many American readers may be shocked that such events could have occurred so close to home and less than a century ago. But beyond

shock, this historical episode should inspire gratitude that they live in the United States, in a country ruled by law, where differences are decided in courtrooms and with ballots, and where the only solutions even contemplated to disputes over religious liberty are peaceful in nature.

We should be grateful, too, that we have seen in the past few decades the effectiveness of a peaceful approach to securing religious liberty—an approach championed and lived out by Blessed John Paul II, whose visits to Mexico and Poland helped usher in a new era of religious freedom for both countries—and, indeed, for all of Eastern Europe.

Whether Mexican, American, or Mexican-American, each of us has a need and a duty to know the story of the struggle for religious freedom and to work to keep that freedom alive today.

This book helps us understand the greater context of the quest for freedom on this continent, and serves as a reminder of the sacred importance that the right to religious freedom holds for the people of this continent.

It is our hope that this book will bring to a general audience the groundbreaking work on this period done by Professor Jean Meyer in his 1976 book published by Cambridge University Press. In doing so, we trust that this book will make an important contribution not only in this regard, but also in spurring further research and discussion on this important period of history.

Carl A. Anderson, Supreme Knight
Knights of Columbus

Introduction

From the persecutions against Christians in ancient Rome to the numerous struggles in Mexico over the centuries, there have been many conflicts throughout history between Church and State. None, however, was like the bloody, dramatic conflict explored in these pages—a conflict about to age beyond the memories of its last living witnesses.

In 1926, this violent chapter of Church-State conflict in Mexico began: the Cristiada. For three years, a vast segment of Mexico's Catholic population rose up against the Mexican government, which was led by President Plutarco Elías Calles.

It was an epic conflict in Mexico's history on par with the *Iliad*—an uneven war, a David-versus-Goliath struggle. It was the moving story of a people penalized for their faith and who, as a consequence, challenged an iron-fisted government and an army that was far superior to its own in every way but one: the willingness to sacrifice. The magnitude of the ensuing tragedy convinced both the State and the Church to put an end to the confrontation, which contradicted the goals pursued by both institutions: peace, development, justice, and the right of all men to live in liberty and in conformity with their conscience.

Just as when reading the *Iliad*, one can view the story from the side of the Greeks or the Trojans, so it is with the Cristiada. Mexican Catholics, facing what they saw as a great unjust restriction of their religious practice codified in the laws of a new regime, stood up and challenged the government. The government, on the other hand, seeing decades of dictatorships and revolutions, and fearing the Catholic Church's influence in the lives of Mexico's citizens, sought to bring religious institutions firmly under its control.

Surprisingly, the Cristiada is not well-known. For many years following the war, there was almost a conspiracy of silence to steer clear of the Cristiada as a subject matter, despite the fact that the civil war mobilized hundreds of thousands. From 1938 to 1980, the conflict and its consequences were practically taboo subjects in Mexican historical and political study, as well as literary circles. The Mexican literary critic Adolfo Castañón once noted how much of "the literature produced by Cristero war participants has been passed over and avoided by our measly literary history." Even to this day, existing literature tends to mostly ignore this period in silence, or dismiss it using a few defamatory lines. As I began researching the Cristiada, I encountered this silence personally, even within the Catholic Church and the State. The reason that this epic struggle had been so quickly forgotten was explained to me in 1965 by the Archbishop of Mexico City Miguel Darío Miranda (who later became a cardinal). Telling me why the archives would be closed to my research efforts, he said, "The tragedy is too recent, the ashes are still hot and we do not want the fire to burst again."

For that reason, the Cristiada's events survived almost exclusively in the accounts of those who lived through them. For some who participated, the war's abrupt ending—at the peak of the insurgents' formidable momentum—left a sense of shock, and for the rest of their lives they attempted to understand and restore the unique event that the Cristiada actually was. For years, the veterans of the Cristiada were very silent, waiting and hoping that someday historical justice might present their honorable yet ignored fight.

The silence thawed only gradually. My part in the process began in the mid-1960s, some forty years after the Cristiada began. At first, some time was needed to locate those who would bring their comrades forward and overcome their reticence. A memorable opportunity took place on Cubilete Hill at the annual meeting of Cristero fighters, fittingly held on the feast day of Christ the King ("Cristo Rey," the inspiration for the name "Cristeros"). Key in arranging this interview was a man to whom the Cristeros—and, arguably, all who enjoy religious freedom in Mexico today—owe a debt of gratitude: Aurelio Acevedo. He stood out among the Cristero survivors as one of the first rebels to take up arms in 1926. Beginning with just a dozen comrades, he disbanded at the end of the war in 1929 with as many as 2,000 combatants on his side. Remaining underground as an active member of the resistance until 1940, Acevedo continued the battle by publishing *David,* a small periodical that contained documents and firsthand accounts, and that served as a vital link among the old Cristeros.

With Acevedo vouching for me, I found a remarkable willingness among the veterans to speak about their experiences. They brought with them personal treasures of a time that has since been largely lost and forgotten: private archives, school notebooks filled with handwritten material that was as reliable as it was rustic, documents once folded and carried in pockets, photographs

stored in old cracker boxes, and personal memories of an aging generation. It was the latter that was especially telling and which made a shorthand expert out of this historian, forcing me to take up the tape recorder as they told their stories. These were indispensible testimonies, especially considering the relative deficiency of existing written records, the unwillingness of State and Church officials to allow access to archives, and the insufficiency of foreign diplomatic files. What remained were the characters who played their roles on either side of the conflict, and the witnesses of that period.

These interviews brought out the unique insights of historians of the people for whom recounting the truth of that period was a hallowed and sacred task. "We are here to tell the pure truth . . . for God is watching us anyway," said former Cristero leader Ezequiel Mendoza Barragán. Memories went together with reflection, searching for meaning. Because it was these aged survivors and not I who lived through this time, I will try to give the reader a taste of this, too—their experience of the conflict they could only interpret as being the revelation of God through history—through their own words, drawn from their testimonies and written accounts.

Studying their written testimonies alone, this period and culture takes on an epic nature. This fact is illustrated in the literary critic Castañon's reflections upon reading Ezequiel Mendoza Barragán's *Testimonio Cristero:*

> [A]s I read his book, I like to imagine [Mendoza] tracing lines on the paper with his rough rancher's and natural captain's hand, and I almost see him writing and enunciating the words that bring about a joyful smile or a grimace, as the thread of ink rips his memory. I see him setting his sight on the horizon with a gaze of Homeric wisdom, the eyes of an old military man who has the graciousness of recognizing the virtues and weaknesses of Tyrians and Trojans, of Federals and Cristeros.

This war was the confrontation of a Maccabean people against their leaders—their State and its army. And in this dramatic history, the truth is humble but undeniable: the string of preventable errors and unchecked aggression that took place in the summer of 1926 ultimately resulted in the deaths of at least 200,000 people, civilians and combatants alike.

The best way to acknowledge their contribution is to give a voice to those who were crushed by the tragedy, to those who had to remain silent to survive or who simply preferred to remain silent out of modesty and humility. So as the last living memories age and fade, I present to the readers a taste of this episode in Mexico's history in the spirit of objectivity and reconciliation, publishing for the first time in English this pictorial presentation of some of the greatest moments of this dramatic and tragically human history.

Each section presents a vital element of the history: the conflict over freedom of religious practice; the military uprising; the Cristero culture and support systems that sustained the war; the Cristeros' faith and those martyred for it; the Cristeros' independent self-governance; the rise of Cristero leadership and turbulence in the Mexican presidency; the United States' influential role in negotiations; and the final resolution. Sadly, a last chapter must be added to this history: the 1930s reprise of restrictions on religious practice and a new, but much smaller, uprising.

Each section of this book comes out of decades of research; but, this book, being more of an introduction than a comprehensive treatment of the conflict, is in no way exhaustive. In order to receive the treatment it deserves, this nearly unknown epic would require numerous volumes just to present the documents and testimonies that are not accessible to the public. For a more detailed scholarly treatment of the rebellion, I refer the reader in particular to my previous books, including *The Cristero Rebellion: The Mexican People between Church and State 1926–1929* (Cambridge University Press, 1976).

The Cristiada changed the face of Mexico, shaped the United States' population through refugees and diplomacy, and brought a new focus to religious freedom in the Americas. Regardless of one's preconceptions, the faces and voices of those involved in the event can be moving. They have the power to evoke deep emotions in anyone who explores these pages of blood and glory written by the people of Mexico.

The "Capitals" of Church and State.
Encircled by the National Palace, Federal District buildings, and the Catholic archdiocesan cathedral, the Zócalo (or main square) in Mexico City exhibits the two pillar institutions of Mexico—the Catholic Church and the government.

Our Lady of Guadalupe.
Devotion to Our Lady of Guadalupe was strong among the Cristeros,
and remains the most popular devotion in Mexico, from where it has spread
throughout the Americas and the world. She appeared to an indigenous convert
in 1531, imprinting an image of herself on his cloak. The cloak with the image is
housed in Mexico City. (Artist: Juan Correa, oil on canvas, c. late 17th century)

1.

The Church-State Conflict

A CENTURY OF TENSIONS

Mexico in the 1920s was a Mexico shaped by revolutions: the war for independence from Spain (1810–1821); the war against American incursion in the Mexican-American War (1846–1848); the revolution against French intervention and Maximilian's Empire (1861–1867); and the Mexican Revolution, which took various forms and opponents over a thirty-year span from 1910 to 1940. The latter period was a time of intense civil war from 1910 to 1920, followed by years of civil and political unrest, including the Cristero rebellion—the subject of this book.

Like those living in 1920s Mexico, we cannot view this history exclusively as a series of battles fought between opposing political groups, resulting in mere secular power shifts or change in civil authorities. We have to remember the role played historically by the Roman Catholic Church and the Catholic faith, since it was the Church's teachings, legacy, and influence that so shaped the lives and minds of those involved in the persecution and the Cristero rebellion.

For centuries, the Catholic Church was the most advanced social institution in Mexico. It placed at the country's service an unrivaled administrative network, including hospitals, schools, universities, banking, and civil registry. During the Spanish colonial period in the sixteenth and seventeenth centuries, the Church often assumed the role of peacemaker, mediating in class conflicts and tensions between the people and the State. As a strong institution, it could lend support—and even affirm legitimacy—to those in power, and at times was pressured by the State in their close collaborations with each other.

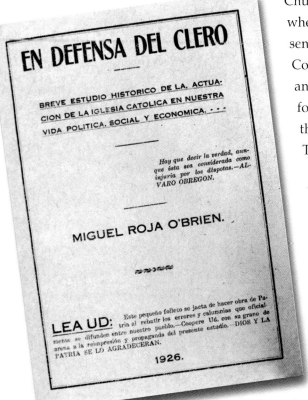

In Defense of the Clergy.
This 1926 booklet examines the historical record of the Catholic Church's many contributions in Mexico over the centuries.

But in the late eighteenth and early nineteenth centuries—in the spirit of the French Revolution—the Bourbons in Mexico tried to weaken the Church and replace it with the State. This secularization continued even when Spain regained control of Mexico from the French. It sparked dissent among many clergy, leading some priests (like Miguel Hidalgo y Costilla and José María Morelos) to later join with revolutionaries and play a decisive role in Mexico's break with Spain and in the wars for independence. Eventually the revolutionaries achieved victory, thereby freeing Mexico from Spanish control with the signing of the Treaty of Córdoba in 1821.

But victory came at a great cost. The new State felt threatened by the clergy, which it saw as exerting immense influence over the people. At this point, a crucial pattern emerged—from 1857 through 1917, every revision of Mexico's constitution intensified its restrictions on religious practice, particularly regarding the clergy.

Pitting liberals against conservatives, the civil wars of the period helped to further politicize the submission of the Church to the State. Thus, in the decades leading up to the Cristiada, religious freedom and social issues became entangled. The liberals wanted economic reform—to change the means of production and restore free trade and free movement of the people. But from there, they sought to take away the Church's property and abolish religious orders. They also wanted to eradicate religious "fanaticism" and recover "freedom of thought," which they felt the Church threatened.

In the ensuing clash, however, the Church proved to be an unyielding opponent. From 1890 to 1910, social Catholicism developed rapidly in Mexico, beginning with the labor and farmer movements and leading to the creation of the National Catholic Party in 1911. Through this movement, Christian

State expropriation.
Pictured here is a Federal camp established in a Mexico City monastery in 1914.

Altar of Santa Dregeda Church.
This church in Mexico City was looted by mobs during the Mexican Revolution in April of 1915—more than a decade before the Cristero rebellion.

teaching was proposed as a solution to many of the problems facing the Mexican nation and people, and Catholic identity was expressed in one's social, political, and economic involvement. With the breadth of this movement, social Catholicism became one of the principal agents in public life.

These victories in social justice and political involvement soon faced new difficulties: from 1910 through 1920, Mexico suffered yet another civil war. Fought to end the long dictatorship of Porfirio Díaz, this war shaped many of Mexico's future presidents, generals, and civil leaders of the Cristiada era.

The father of this revolution, Francisco Madero, won the support of many Catholics, but his followers ended up on the losing side when Madero was assassinated. Mexico's leadership traded hands repeatedly between the multiple factions, until Venustiano Carranza won decisively in 1917—to the detriment of those hoping for easement of religious practice.

Most important, under Carranza, a new constitution was drafted in 1917, containing even more restrictions to religious practice than before:

■ Article 3 restricted religious education;

■ Article 5 outlawed monastic orders;

■ Article 24 banned worship outside the confines of the church building;

■ Article 27 turned Church property over to the ownership of the State;

New president, renewed anticlericalism.
President Carranza, engineer of the 1917 Constitution,
with his entourage aboard the presidential train in 1920.

A celebration in honor of Christ the King.
Such common public religious celebrations, such as this one in San Marcos, Jalisco, were penalized by the articles of the constitution.

■ Article 37 revoked citizenship should anyone be found disobeying the constitution due to the influence of a clergy member;

■ Article 55 forbade priests from holding public office;

■ Article 130, among other things, banned foreign-born priests; gave the government the authority to determine the number of clergy in each locality; took away the clergy's right to vote, assemble, and speak freely against the government; subjected the establishment of any new church to State review and approval; prohibited religious publications from commenting on public affairs; banned any group of a religious nature from involving itself in politics; restricted clergy inheritance and ownership; forbade the wearing of clerical garb; and rescinded the right to a trial by jury for any infraction of the law on these religious issues.

Obviously, the Catholic Church disapproved of these articles. Carranza and his successor President Álvaro Obregón (1920–1924) left the constitution's articles unsupported by regulations, hence avoiding the outrage that strict enforcement could have provoked. There was no lack of mutual recriminations and incidents, but conciliation was a daily practice. President Obregón even initiated discreet contacts in Rome to explore the possibility of diplomatic relations with the Vatican, and Rome put its faith in the future reform of the Mexican constitution.

Three presidents, three revolutionaries.
Adolpho de la Huerta (left) stands with Generals Obregón and Calles. All would serve as Mexico's president in the years following the Mexican Revolution.

AGICA

ACJM members.

Founded in 1913 during the Mexican Revolution, the ACJM (Catholic Association of Mexican Youth) provided Catholics with a place to grow in the faith among friends, despite growing hostilities toward Catholicism. This 1922 photo was taken during the presidency of Álvaro Obregón.

1926 ACJM membership card for Alfonso de la Torre.

Alfonso, along with his father and siblings, became involved in the Catholic resistance. The back of his membership card is signed by the founder of the ACJM, Jesuit Father Bernardo Bergoend.

This relative peace enabled the rebirth of Christian unionism and the rise of Catholic organizations like the Catholic Association of Mexican Youth (ACJM), founded in 1913; the Knights of Columbus (K of C), an American organization that blossomed in Mexico in the early 1920s; and Catholic political groups like the Unión Popular (UP).

Thus, Mexico at the time of the Cristero rebellion in the 1920s was uniquely shaped by both powerful government and powerful religion. The very government was born out of the victory of one rebel group over others. Unsurprisingly, "revolutionary" was applied proudly to the 1920s government and its political leaders, who adopted as their agenda a program of "progress" and "modernization."

Considering this status quo from unenforced laws, the question of religious liberty was, generally speaking, not the main topic of the day. One must ask, why did religious freedom come back into the spotlight in 1926 with such ardor and violence?

A NEW CAESAR AGAINST THE CHRISTIANS

This uneasy equilibrium changed when a friend of President Obregón came into power as his successor: Plutarco Elías Calles (1924–1928).

Looking back at the impact made by this controversial Mexican president, the veteran politician of the Mexican state of Guerrero, Rubén Figueroa Figueroa, once remarked, "And let me tell you something. There has never been another man like Plutarco Elías Calles. And to this day, he has been denied the recognition he deserves." In many ways, Rubén Figueroa Figueroa was right. There has never been another man like General Calles. He boasted an impressive résumé, including work as a military general; governor of Sonora (1915–1919); Secretary of Industry, Commerce, and Labor (1919–1920); Minister of War and Navy (1920), and finally, Minister of the Interior (1920–1923) under President Obregón, who arranged for Calles to succeed him in 1924. He established the political party—the National Revolutionary Party (PNR), which would later become the *Partido Revolucionario Institucional* (PRI)—that would dominate the Mexican presidency for decades. He would reform economic and social institutions that had remained in disrepair from years of civil unrest and warfare. He would go on to maintain a new level of diplomacy with other nations, truly putting Mexico on the political map.

Presidential duo.
Newly sworn-in President Calles (at right) and his predecessor Obregón (center) exit the inauguration ceremony.

In many ways he was great—so great that he brings to mind one of the greatest of the Roman emperors, Diocletian, who was the savior of the empire and, at the same time, a tremendous persecutor of the Christians.

Indeed, one large issue complicated Calles's achievements: his troubles with the Church. Calles's hostility toward the Catholic Church began before he became president. As governor of Sonora, he sought to provoke a schism and establish his own church by expelling Catholic priests and replacing them with priests willing to form a new religion.

But Calles was not alone in seeking to weaken Church authority. In 1925 and 1926, the *Confederacion Regional Obrera Mexicana* (CROM)—the official central labor union and the most powerful one of the era, headed by Luis Morones—struggled with other labor organizations, including the Catholic unions. In 1925, the CROM committed the "error" of founding a schismatic church of its own to weaken the Catholic Church. On February 21, 1925,

President Plutarco Elías Calles.
During his early presidency, Calles faced various difficulties, including reconstruction after years of revolutions and the fear that the United States' recognition of his administration might be withdrawn.

Católicos, : alerta!

La CROM, instrumento ciego del Gobierno en la persecución religiosa, ha ordenado la hechura de 800 sotanas.

¿Con qué objeto ha mandado hacer esas sotanas?

¿Es para continuar la ridícula mascarada del cisma, porque ya el infeliz Patriarca Pérez haya habilitado a cien agentes de la policía reservada como sacerdotes?

¿O es que se va a disfrazar a algunos de la CROM, presentándolos con el traje eclesiástico para sorprender al pueblo, agitarlo y llevarlo al motín, culpando después a los verdaderos sacerdotes?

Todo puede y debe temerse de quienes lo mismo se prestan para formar la Orden de los Caballeros de Guadalupe e ir a asaltar el templo de la Soledad, capitaneados por el hoy Secretario General de la CROM, que para fungir de espías y denunciar señoritas como propagandistas contra el boycot.

Pueblo, no te dejes sorprender.

Si el Patriarca Pérez, a sueldo de Morones, fabri ca sacerdotes, YA SABES QUE NO LO SON.

Ne los escúches ni pongas el pie en los templ

A la vuelta

priests from this new "Mexican Catholic Apostolic Church" attempted to seize Soledad Church in Mexico City. The operation was protected by the Knights of Guadalupe, another pseudo-Catholic organization that was filled with CROM members and led by CROM Secretary-General Ricardo Treviño. Within days, Catholics of the district rioted, killing one and injuring three. It was stated in *The New York Times* that later, the CROM-founded Knights of Guadalupe even went so far as to petition the State to turn over the Basilica of Our Lady of Guadalupe to the control of the nationalist "Mexican Church," with the intention of making the basilica "the Vatican of Mexico." [Note that this organization of the Knights of Guadalupe is completely unrelated to the modern organization with the same name.]

These actions failed on many levels. Instead of weakening the Church and Catholic devotion, they stirred up more hostility towards CROM policies and plans. Moreover, since the nationalist "Mexican Church" was allowed to take possession of half a dozen churches with the support of the government, many people suspected Calles's complicity or outright support of CROM's activities, and became further enraged against the Calles administration.

Pro-CROM labor rally.
Workers converge at the
CROM building in Mexico
City on May 1, 1924.

Luis Morones.
Shown speaking at a CROM
banquet, Luis Morones (standing)
sought to unify all of Mexico's labor
parties under the CROM's banner.

Morones's attempt to create a schism through the CROM failed. But it did provoke a defensive reaction from Mexican Catholics. On March 14, 1925, the Catholic Association of Mexican Youth (ACJM) banded together with Catholics of other organizations to form the National League for the Defense of Religion (the *League,* as it will be called henceforth). Shortly after, the name of this organization was changed to the National League for the Defense of Religious Liberty. Initially, the League sought to mobilize Catholics in a peaceful civil struggle. Directed by militant youth from *Acción Política* (Political Action) and composed largely of individuals from the middle class who willingly abandoned their support of the State's revolutionary cause, the League would become a leader in stirring up and mobilizing the people against the government.

For Calles, there quickly arose the problem of situating the Church in a society that the State wanted to control completely, with the Church and the State in confrontation on all fronts. The controversies over the clergy (the "black

Protest of Catholic workers, Mexico City, 1926.
The National Catholic Labor Confederation, formally accepted by the bishops in 1920, quickly rivaled the CROM, with around 80,000 members to the CROM's estimated 100,000 members in 1922.

threat"), over the State's secularist mission, and over the proper place for the Church prompted the sentiments of the 1917 Constitution: "acts of war," according to writer and political journalist Walter Lippmann, "conceived to crush counterrevolutionary agitation." Calles's followers were nationalists and for them the "black party" was totally beholden to the pope, a "foreign sovereign." The phrase was written and spoken: "Expel the foreigners. Mexico for the Mexicans!" There were denouncements about the plot by the clergy, untiringly schemed by counterrevolutionary agents and that, according to many, loomed over the country in 1925 and 1926.

LIGA NACIONAL DEFENSORA DE LA LIBERTAD RELIGIOSA.
"Dios y mi Derecho"   ¡Domingo 31 de octubre de 1926!
¡FIESTA DE CRISTO REY!

En los últimos días del año santo su Santidad Pío XI instituyó la fiesta universal de "CRISTO REY" para el último Domingo de octubre de cada año. ¡Todas las Naciones libres del Mundo la celebrarán públicamente vitoreando a CRISTO REY por plazas y calles! México, que no es un Pueblo Libre, no podrá hacer cosa semejante; pero sin embargo; ¡México ofrecerá a Cristo Rey un Trono Pobre! ¡el trono de nuestras miserias, de nuestros sacrificios por su Santa Causa! ¡Trono regado con la sangre de nuestros mártires!...
Estamos seguros que Cristo lo aceptará, porque Cristo es el emblema de la pobreza, del sacrificio y del martirio:......! ¡Vayamos a ofrecérselo el domingo 31 a la Villa, por intercesión de la VIRGEN DE GUADALUPE y pidámosle por nuestra Patria.
La Liga invita a todo el Distrito Federal a que organice peregrinaciones a pié, de Peralvillo a la Villa, cada hora, de las 6 a. m. a las 6 p. m. del domingo 31.

☞ ¡QUE NO FALTE NINGUNO DE SUS SOCIOS! ☜
CADA MEDIA HORA SE REZARA EN LA BASILICA LO SIGUIENTE:
1º—Consagración del género humano al Sagrado Corazón. *Fórmula de SS. León XII.*
2º—Credo. (*de pié*)
3º—Plegaria a Cristo Rey por México, [*Fórmula del Ilmo. Sr. Valverde y Téllez.*]
4º—Tres Padres Nuestros y Ave María, [*en cruz.*]
5º—Consagración a la Santísima Virgen de Guadalupe.
6º—Salve Regina ¡VIRGEN DE GUADALUPE! ¡Sálvanos!

The League celebrates the Feast of Christ the King.
On December 11, 1925, Pope Pius XI instituted the international feast day of "Christ the King." A year later, the feast was celebrated in Mexico during the Cristiada. *"Cristo Rey"* would be taken up by the Cristeros, who made it their battle cry for religious freedom.

In Focus
Protests in the Zócalo

Civil protests were an essential course of action in the years leading up to and after the Calles Law took effect. These photographs offer a glimpse into a Catholic demonstration that was held in the Zócalo—Mexico City's central square. Home to the city's main Cathedral and Federal offices, the Zócalo was a very symbolic location for protests to take place. These photographs also show some of the tactics employed by police and firemen to disperse the religious demonstrations. When civil servants proved insufficient during protests, the military was often brought in as well.

Demonstration at the Zócalo.
A large crowd protests the religious restrictions in the central square in Mexico City. One banner mentions the 1917 Constitution, which significantly limited how clergy, religious groups, and churches functioned. On another banner, the word *socialista* ("socialist") is visible, perhaps harkening to the government's growing control over many elements of Mexican life.

Silenced—at least for the moment.
A group of firefighters and policemen stand in front of the Cathedral in the Zócalo after dispersing a religious demonstration.

**Quenching
resistance.**
These photos of the
demonstration capture
the chaos as protesters
are dispersed by both
police and firemen.
Firemen hose the
protesters, who can be
seen in the distance.

THE RELIGIOUS CONFLICT

A relic of precarious religious freedom.
In this March 1926 flyer, Bishop Miguel de la Mora announces a public Mass in San Luis Potosí that was made possible through a "peaceful arrangement" with the governor. He asks everyone to "avoid any public demonstration . . . that might harm the arrangements made."

In some ways, it was a newspaper that lit the spark of revolt. After Calles publicly declared a series of regulations to enforce the constitution and sought extraordinary power to amend the penal code, the Mexican newspaper *El Universal* initiated a campaign to raise public awareness and stir agitation. On February 4, 1926, it ran a controversial interview that had taken place nine years earlier with the Archbishop of Mexico City, José Mora y del Río. In that interview, the archbishop criticized Articles 3, 5, 27, and 130 of the constitution for their anticlerical content. Disastrously, the newspaper published this years-old declaration as if it had just been issued—as if it were a new voice from the clergy that was entering the fray and criticizing the State.

The incident afforded an opportunity to justify more restrictions. Calles closed more Catholic schools and convents, expelled foreign priests, and limited the number of priests in each state. Other civil leaders followed suit. Adalberto Tejeda, who had been appointed Minister of the Interior after Gilberto Valenzuela was found to be too moderate, ordered Archbishop Mora y del Río's arrest on charges of inciting rebellion against the State. Although the archbishop was later acquitted, the incident escalated the situation.

On February 23, 1926, just six blocks from the U.S. Embassy in Mexico City, government agents occupied La Sagrada Familia Church, claiming that it did not follow the regulations. This occupation inspired a riot in which seven Catholic protestors were killed while trying to prevent the Federal agents from entering and inspecting the church. In response, Mexico's governors received strict orders to "enforce the constitution at all costs." President Calles himself announced that the government would be "inflexible"

San Luis Potosí, June 2, 1926.
A crowd moves toward San Luis Potosí, a place noted for religious protests.

Ceaseless search for resolution.
Apostolic Delegate Jorge José Caruana (left) and Bishop Pascual Díaz pore over pages in a text. Even following their exile, both men played an important role in the ensuing drama and its eventual resolution.

and would "use every facility that the law provides so that this time the problem that has been unsolved will be settled."

The government struggled to instill and enforce respect for the law. In practice, compliance with the laws ranged from "gentlemen's agreements," in which the letter of the law was overlooked (as in Veracruz, Coahuila, Guerrero, Puebla, Oaxaca, Chihuahua, Campeche, Guanajuato, and Zacatecas), to brazen persecution of the Church (as in Tabasco, Jalisco, and Colima). Some places, like Michoacán and San Luis Potosí, were a mix—a tolerable arrangement ultimately giving way to violent confrontation.

The number of conflicts and solutions were as disorienting and divisive to the bishops as they were to the governors. In a cautious move, the Vatican ordered Catholics "to scrupulously abstain from joining any political party," and in March, the Vatican sent a new apostolic delegate, Monsignor Jorge José Caruana, to approach CROM leader Luis Morones. But on May 10, 1926, Apostolic Delegate Caruana became the third papal representative to be expelled from Mexico. Thereafter, the exasperated delegate abandoned his conciliatory approach and advised the bishops to take up a policy of resistance that Rome had previously so feared. Later, the Episcopal Committee was formed, consisting of a majority of the Mexican bishops and chaired by Archbishop Leopoldo Ruiz y Flores of Morelia. Thus, the bishops now had an organization that could more effectively deal with and strategize on the issues at hand.

Monsignor Caruana with Bishop Díaz.
The Vatican's selection of Caruana as the apostolic delegate to Mexico was partly for his successful role in negotiating a past conflict between the government and Church in Guatemala.

As the bishops resisted, it became increasingly clear that many people might do more than just resist; they might fight. However, Calles did not take this threat seriously. He underestimated the strength of the Catholic youth of the ACJM and the League, and disdained the reactions of the masses. In a letter to Archbishop José Mora y del Río on June 3, 1926, Calles

"Services End in Mexican Churches."
The Mexican bishops' decision to suspend worship in churches (see page 24) made front page news, even in regional U.S. papers like the *New Haven Evening Register.*

stated that no agitation inside or outside Mexico "will be capable of changing the firm purpose of the Government strictly to comply with the supreme law of the country."

A crucial development occurred later that month on June 14, 1926, when Calles made firm his promise, signing the "Law for Reforming the Penal Code." This decree caused the final rupture.

Known as the Calles Law, the code enforced the previously unenforced anticlerical articles of the 1917 Constitution by attaching fines, imprisonment, and other penalties to various prohibitions in the articles. Punishment for transgressions ran anywhere from fines of 500 pesos with a fifteen-day jail sentence to much steeper fines, including removal from office (as in the case of municipal governors who were found to be lax in their enforcement of the code) and years of imprisonment.

The Senate deliberated slowly on Calles's decree for two weeks. Then finally, on July 2, 1926, the Calles Law was published in the *Diario Oficial* and became enforceable.

During those days of uncertainty, the bishops remained indecisive. Rome remained silent and tried to find a compromise, something Calles's friend and predecessor Obregón would have favored. But Calles himself was caught in a conflict of interests. On one side, the pro-Church League and its supporters demanded lenient interpretation of the law. On the other side, the CROM's Luis Morones and Minister of the Interior Adalberto Tejeda both demanded harsher measures. Calles likewise anticipated some of the public outrage—particularly in the United States—that the code would provoke, and he even sought to remedy some of this by writing an op-ed piece requested and published by *The New York Times* on August 1, 1926. In the article, Calles defended the penal code and sought to explain some of the controversial elements, ultimately declaring that any deviation from the code "naturally is going to result in the complete defeat of the bad clergy who have forgotten their spiritual function and dream of dominions of a temporal and anachronistic order."

He also defended the Calles Law by denying the obvious anti-Catholic import of the laws, noting that the laws applied to everybody, not only Catholics. However, non-Catholics were a small minority in Mexico, and some of the restrictions—like the ban on priestly celibacy and monastic life—really only applied to Catholicism, since Protestant denominations did not share those religious practices. Furthermore, while the government expelled and banned foreign Catholic priests, Calles favored evangelical proselytism and openly supported the Young Men's Christian Association and Protestant missions. Similarly, the Methodist Bishop George Miller praised Calles's cooperative attitude, and through Episcopalian Bishop Moisés Sáenz, non-Catholic missions were afforded every facility by the government.

Despite public outcry, Calles stuck to his ultimatum: on August 1, the law was to take effect in the country. This erased any last doubts held by the Episcopal Committee. On July 25, the committee published its own highly momentous decision—the bishops announced that from the moment the Calles Law went into effect, all worship in all of the churches in Mexico would be suspended.

At this point, President Calles summed up the situation, declaring, "I believe we reached the point where the sides have been defined forever; the

A Catholic church in Cholula, Mexico.
This was one of many Catholic churches turned over to State control, August 4, 1926. According to the press, the government had taken possession of over 90 percent of the Catholic churches in Mexico just a few days after the Calles Law went into effect.

Government "inventory."
Benches, chandeliers, and other religious items taken from churches and abandoned.

Mexican clergy, with Archbishop Mora y del Rio (center).
While in many ways uncertain of how to proceed, the formation of the Episcopal Committee in 1925 helped to coordinate and consolidate the bishops' efforts and positions, leading to the ultimate decision to suspend the liturgy throughout Mexico.

hour is coming in which the final battle will be fought; we will learn if the revolution has triumphed over reactionaries or if the triumph of the revolution has been ephemeral."

Indeed, the bishops' decision to suspend worship was nearly unprecedented, not having occurred since a Mexican archbishop's conflict with a viceroy centuries earlier. However, it soon made little difference that this suspension came from the Church and not the State. What the Church suspended, the State banned, and as the churches faced the dreaded day, the government responded to the strike on public worship by prohibiting private worship.

In preparation for the suspension of worship and liturgies, priests and bishops were busy with people seeking the sacraments that would be illegal in just a few days. Children were baptized, Masses were celebrated at all hours, and even marriage ceremonies were abbreviated to accommodate the many couples wishing to wed. *Time* magazine even reported that seventy-two-year-old Archbishop José Mora y del Río fainted after confirming 5,000 Catholics in one day, and then after regaining consciousness, he continued to perform confirmations until midnight, despite the suggestions by accompanying priests that he rest.

Cathedral in Mexico City.
Thousands rushed to attend services and receive sacraments here before the Calles Law went into effect. This was especially poignant due to the Cathedral's location—directly across from the government buildings.

At midnight on the night of July 31, 1926, the Calles Law took effect. Bells were silent in all the churches in Mexico and liturgies were suspended. The final ceremonies were celebrated, the lights were put out, and the Blessed Sacrament was removed from the tabernacles. These were hours of agony for many people. The following day, the government sent officials and police to seal the church doors after taking inventory of all the items inside.

In many places, people rioted spontaneously, and blood flowed.

**The United States—
a new home for religious Catholics.**
On August 1, 1926, the day the Calles Law went into effect,
one of the first groups of religious refugees to the United
States—seven nuns—arrived in New York.

MEXICO IN CRISIS

The religious crisis was not the only crisis Calles faced. In 1926, Mexico suffered a general crisis that extended to all areas of life. Economy and oil, diplomacy with America, the Mexican labor movement, and the Mexican railroad system—each area was in crisis, and the violence of the religious confrontation cannot be understood apart from this context.

Beginning in 1925, the Mexican government struggled intensely with the U.S. oil companies, trying to apply national control over them. Part of this was an inherited problem for Calles: for nearly a decade, the United States was particularly upset by Article 27 of Carranza's 1917 Constitution. This article

Meeting at the White House.
Chief Justice William Taft, President-elect Calles, and President Coolidge stand together in this 1925 photo. The sensitivity of relations between the U.S. and Mexico was inadvertently expressed by a joke Coolidge made at the moment this photograph was taken. When the photographer requested that Coolidge and Taft move in closer to Calles, Coolidge declined, joking that it might squeeze Mexico out, which they would "never do."

Volatile labor issues.
The anticlerical articles of the constitution were not the only articles that got attention. Here, one of the signs at a labor demonstration calls attention to Article 123, which involved workers' rights.

gave all oil and mineral findings to the State in an attempt to bring more of Mexico's resources under national control. American businessmen and investors quickly viewed this as a threat to their economic interests in the country, with some going to Washington to pressure the Wilson Administration to address the issue.

Tensions peaked in December 1925, when Mexico's congress passed the first oil laws—the Petroleum Law and the Alien Land Law—which declared that foreign oil holdings obtained prior to 1917 expire after fifty years. It even obliged foreign corporations to waive their right of appeal to their home government. The Alien Land Law further forbade foreigners from owning property in certain coastal and frontier "prohibited zones," to the outrage of American companies that already claimed land within these zones. These laws took effect January 1, 1927—the very day the League would choose for its first mass uprising.

Mexico's international policy also disturbed relations with the United States. Mexico and the United States were both involved in Nicaragua's civil war—but on different sides. President Calles provoked the ire of the United States by clandestinely supporting the Nicaraguan liberals led by

Juan Bautista Sacasa with arms, munitions, and even Mexican soldiers to face the U.S. troops that had landed there to support the conservatives led by Adolfo Díaz. The possibility of a U.S. invasion of Mexico was seriously discussed. Calles himself took the threat very seriously and, rather than see the oil fields fall into American hands, gave orders to prepare for the destruction of the oil wells, saying, "We will light a fire that will be seen as far as New Orleans."

The tension with the United States gave hope to the exiled General Enrique Estrada, a Mexican revolutionary living in the United States who had been defeated in the revolutions and coups from 1911 to 1924. The air was buzzing with plots and intrigue. Rumors indicated that General Estrada was planning an invasion in August 1926, and that the Yaqui Indians, who periodically took up arms against the Mexican government, were also rebelling.

Mexico's primary labor union—the CROM—began a purge of railway workers. This, compounded by job losses resulting from railway reorganization, led to heated disputes and a violent, three-month-long railway strike ending in 1927. Trains were derailed, Federal soldiers sent in, and adversaries of the government executed. Eventually the strike lost momentum in April and May 1927, though the victory for the State was taxing.

Thus the Mexican government was under attack from all sides. It explains why President Calles resented the opening of another interior front—the religious conflict—like a stab in the back while he was patriotically defending Mexican interests against the United States. There was a sense, as some lyrics said, that the American flag flew over Mexico's land and the Vatican flag flew over Mexico's spiritual life. Calles failed to consider the responsibility of those from his own camp who provoked and precipitated a crisis that could have been avoided.

Looking back, a question persists: why this persecution of his own peo-

Building lines of communication—literally.
President Calles speaks on the telephone with President Coolidge after direct telephone service was established between both countries.

ple? After all, in the first two years of his presidency, Calles clearly displayed the talents of a great statesman. In fact, seeing his rigorousness, austerity, and impressive tenacity in rebuilding the nation, even "Catholics themselves expected much of Calles," as Jesuit Father Rafael Ramírez later remarked. But persecution did come. In fact, Calles later executed a priest whom Father Ramírez had known while in the seminary— Father Miguel Pro, who was innocent of the crimes for which he was punished. (Father Pro's significant death is further detailed in Chapter 5.)

The persecution cannot be explained as some sudden outbreak of personal cruelty, or by the force of inevitable conflicts. Nor can it be explained away as Calles's concession to political allies, although he undoubtedly felt pressure from the powerful union boss Luis Morones. Calles was not easily manipulated by his allies, and his responsibility for the persecution cannot be denied. Nor can the persecution be attributed merely to other people's actions committed in his name. Even in the case of the unjust execution of Father Pro, Calles would never have denied his responsibility for it, because that would have suggested something had occurred against his will—implying weakness, a diminishment of his power.

El Clero Norte Americano envía una Felicitación a los Católicos Mexicanos. Está firmado por 4 Cardenales, 9 Arzobispos y 51 Obispos reunidos en la Ciudad de Washington.

"El Imparcial" de fecha 22 de Sepbre. de 1926 da la siguiente noticia:

(ASSOCIATED PRESS.) Cablegrama.

"La Jerarquía Católica de los Estados Unidos reunida en la Universidad Católica de Washington, envió un mensaje de simpatía a los católicos de México, firmado por 4 Cardenales, 9 Arzobispos y 51 Obispos reunidos en dicha ciudad. Está enviado a los Arzobispos, Obispos, Sacerdotes y seglares de México. Dice:

"Estáis demostrando ante el mundo entero el verdadero espíritu de los mártires, dispuestos a soportar y a sufrir todo por el amor de Cristo. Os estáis mostrando también como los reales campeones en México, de la religión y de la libertad civil. Esta lucha puede ser larga, puede dar muchos mártires a la Iglesia y a la humanidad; ella terminará solamente con la victoria de la libertad de conciencia.

El sufrido y amante de la paz, pueblo mexicano, emergerá de esta prueba más fuerte y más puro. Fortaleceos, queridos hermanos: Nos, los Obispos y Sacerdotes católicos de América, os acompañamos con nuestras oraciones y nuestra más profunda simpatía en este vuestro honor de sufrimiento.

Con las bendiciones de Dios estaremos con vosotros hasta el fin y hasta la victoria."

Por su parte la Federación Nacional Católica de Francia, por conducto de su representante el General Castelnau, envía al pueblo católico de México un hermoso y sentido mensaje, en el que nos manifiesta la expresión de su FERVIENTE SIMPATIA, DE SU ADMIRACION ARDIENTE y DE SU CONFIANZA INQUEBRANTABLE. Ya se conocerá íntegro dicho mensaje.

¡Animo pues, Católicos mexicanos! no desmayemos un momento; sigamos adelante sin inmutarnos; el mundo entero nos contempla; levantemos sin temor el estandarte de Cristo que, tarde o temprano deberá darnos la deseada victoria.

NO DEJE UD. SU UNICA ARMA: EL BOYCOT.

International notice, international inspiration.
This flyer highlights a letter of sympathy to the persecuted people of Mexico. It is signed by several members of the Catholic hierarchy in the United States, including four cardinals, nine archbishops, and fifty-one bishops.

Perhaps this is the key to the answer—power. Calles, like Rome's Diocletian before him, felt that the State's power was threatened by a dynamic Church with committed Christians. Like Diocletian, he even seemed to see the Church as a conspirator that could ally itself with his political rivals. With this politicized view of Mexico's millions of Catholics, when plans for a political and military coup took shape in Mexico, Calles soon believed that it had an origin within the Catholic Church.

This fear of Church involvement in politics was tragic, but it was not his greatest error in judgment. Calles's greatest lapse was underestimating the popular reaction of the Catholic people, whose faith his laws sought to control and exterminate. Harassed by a thousand enemies, Calles overreacted and gave free rein to the radicals within his own faction, meanwhile handing a great opportunity to the extremists on the Catholic side.

SUICIDIO

Ayer a las 24 horas falleció en el seno de la Sacrosanta, Sapientísima y Bienaventurada beatería, la Santa

Iglesia Católica Romana

Víctima de congestión de sangre herética acumulada desde la Santa Inquisición, y de la contagiosa enfermedad de Estupiditis Letárgica ocasionada por la perpetua embriaguez de vino de consagrar; habiendo expedido el certificado de defunción, el famosísimo médico Don Plutarco quien dió fé que la venerable paciente, en el colmo de la tortura agónica, se suicidó atracándose una gigantesca dosis de Dinero Mexicano extraído del bolsillo de los "Pobres de Espíritu" a base de confirmaciones, bautizos y matrimonios precipitados a última hora.

Su afligido padre el Papa PIO XI, sus adoloridos hijos los Arzobispos, Obispos y demás tonsurados hasta Sacristanes y Caballeros de San Cristóbal, participan a Ud. tan infausto suceso, con el más profundo dolor y la nostalgia del hartazgo y la holganza que terminaron con la infeliz desaparecida, y le suplican eleve al Ser Supremo las oraciones que su piedad le dicte porque la difunta no vuelva a la Tierra a sufrir más "persecuciones."

El duelo se recibe en: Constitución 1917, entre Reforma y Querétaro, y sus cenizas descansarán para siempre bajo el altar mayor del grandioso Templo de la Conciencia Nacional.

Por todos los "Impíos" que chamuscó en la Edad Media, descanse en Paz.

CONSUMMATUM EST

Tampico, Agosto 1º de 1926.

Death of the Church.
This poster by the Mexican government was placed on a church after the cessation of liturgies. Written like an obituary for the Roman Catholic Church, the text describes the bishops' action as an act of suicide.

"Follow the Boycott!"
This pro-resistance poster promotes the boycott to pressure the government, and encourages those who are committed to help those less committed: "You believe in our triumph. Encourage the cowards, support the weak."

¡AL FIN TRIUNFO EL PUEBLO!

El pretendido boycot que el clero romano en su inconciencia, ha decretado contra el Pueblo Mexicano (no contra el Gobierno), ha sido el más estruendoso fracaso. Sus récomendaciones pueriles, se han tomado a burla. El pueblo sabe lo que hace. Ha comprendido que siempre el clero sueña con su perdido poderío de siglos pasados. Se ha dado perfecta cuenta que antes lo obligaban a ser católico con argumentos tan convincentes como el martirio, las hogueras y las persecuciones, y ahora quieren convencerlo por medio del hambre; y para eso, aconsejan a los capitalistas fanáticos, que lo sigan extorsionando, que no den trabajo a los obreros, que maten al pueblo de hambre, que no gasten su dinero, (pero, sí, que se lo den al cura), pero todos han puesto orejas de mercader.

¡Hermanos obreros! ¡Pueblo humilde! ¡Sociedad toda! Los felicitamos sinceramente porque han demostrado con entereza a los eternos enemigos del pueblo: Clero, sacristanes, Caballeros de San Cristobal, y demás cucarachas de sacristía, que el pueblo sabe dar su merecido a quien tan ignominiosamente lo ha engañado hasta ahora, y que a todas sus bravatas y a todas sus pueriles y ridículas recomedaciones, les ha contestado como es debido: con la más completa indiferencia y con el más soberano desprecio.

SAN LUIS POTOSI, SEPTIEMBRE DE 1926.

SE SUPLICA LA REPRODUCCION.

Praising the "resounding failure" of the boycott.
Pegging the boycott on "clerics, sacristans, Knights of San Cristobal" (the Knights of Columbus), and "cockroaches of the sacristy," this flyer calls the failed boycott a movement "against the Mexican people (not against the government)."

GRASPING FOR PEACE

Some believed that the bishops' decision to cease liturgies would ultimately help to destroy the Catholic Church rather than show the harmfulness of the government's anticlerical policy. President Calles, in a meeting with French diplomat Ernest Lagarde on August 26, 1926, suggested that "every week that passes without religious services will lose the Catholic religion about two-percent of its faithful." Also of this opinion was Minister of the Interior Adalberto Tejeda, who explained, "The Church has exceeded our wildest hopes in decreeing the suspension of religious services; nothing could be more pleasing to us . . . We have got the clergy by the throat and will do everything to strangle it."

Meanwhile, the League organized an economic boycott to pressure the government. It asked the people to restrict their purchases to essential goods while avoiding public schools, dances, theaters, cinemas, public transportation, and the purchase of lottery tickets, fruit, candy, ice cream, newspaper ads, and opposition newspapers. The boycott was published in a circular along with a letter signed by Archbishop Mora y del Río and Bishop Pascual Díaz of Tabasco, giving their wholehearted endorsement of the boycott and recommending that Catholics cooperate fully with the plan.

On August 21, 1926, Archbishop Ruiz y Flores and Bishop Díaz met with President Calles in Chapultepec. The bishops were more than pacifying, praising Calles for his "equanimity" and his "firmness." They offered excuses, asked for forgiveness, and even accepted unfounded criticisms; they went so far as to say that "our people are ignorant," as are the priests. They affirmed that they and the pope had ordered submission to the law. But they could go no further in smoothing the way for Calles, who ultimately rejected their pleading by declaring, "We are wasting time. I will not stray from the road bounded by the law. I will not waver." He then dismissed them, saying, "I have already told you, you have only two roads to choose: subject yourself to the law, but if that is not in agreement with your principles, throw yourself into armed struggle and try to topple the current government."

To this, Bishop Díaz replied, "It has never been our intention to obstruct

Bishop Pascual Díaz Barreto, Mexico City, 1925.
Elected as the secretary for the Episcopal Committee in 1926, Pascual Díaz's involvement would later prove pivotal.

your magnificent work in the government and we want to convince you that we are not fomenting any kind of rebellion." But Calles remained unmoved.

As the first counter-measure to this failed attempt, in September, the League collected 2 million signatures on a petition that was sent to Mexico's congress to reform the constitution. The bishops also presented a petition to congress. But congress rejected these as well, inciting the anger of many over the government's apparent disdain for the peaceful gestures. As Don Ezequiel Mendoza Barragán, a famed Cristero from Coalcomán, Michoacán, said in an interview:

Demonstration in Mexico City.
Protestors march down San Francisco Avenue.

Hundreds of us signed the . . . papers; they were sent to Calles and his minions, but it was all useless. Other letters with different words were written; we signed them and they were sent to Calles, but our complaints were tossed into the wastebasket, and his followers, who thought of themselves as big and powerful, squeezed us tighter, killing people and confiscating the personal property of Catholics.

The continued disappointment echoed among many people, dividing loyalties and building up the resentment that would make armed action attractive, if not inevitable.

The Church was not alone in opposing the Calles Law. In its November 1926 congress, the National Peasants League (LNC) discussed these problems and refused to support the government. Even many who considered themselves defenders of the Mexican Revolution spoke out angrily, calling Calles's policy catastrophic and accusing the government of inventing a conflict to serve as a pretext for controlling the public. After all, how could anyone expect the Church to accept the law that threatened it with death? Many others, including Senator Lauro Caloca, Deputy (Congressman) Aurelio Manrique, and former President Obregón himself, along with the agrarians (or *agraristas*, who favored the government's promised land reform but were also mostly faithful Catholics) saw the Calles Law as particularly dangerous.

Senator Caloca described the State's response as having "the goal of violently stripping the people of their most cherished religious sentiments as a criminal assault." Deputy Manrique denounced and questioned the impetus of "the current, artificially provoked religious conflict, artificially provoked, I repeat, provoked by whom?" In fact, when it was proposed to send a

Pope Pius in Tribute to the Work of Knights in Mexico

(The final paragraphs of Pope Pius XI.'s Encyclical Letter "Iniquis Afflictisque" on the Church in Mexico.)

WE CANNOT praise enough the courageous faithful of Mexico who have understood only too well how important it is for them that a Catholic nation in matters so serious and holy as the worship of God, the liberty of the Church, and the eternal salvation of souls should not depend upon the arbitrary will and audacious acts of a few men, but should be governed under the mercy of God only by laws which are just, which are comformable to natural, divine, and ecclesiastical law

A word of very special praise is due those Catholic organizations which during all these trying times have stood like soldiers side to side with the clergy. The members of these organizations, to the limit of their power, not only have made provisions to maintain and to assist their clergy financially, they also watch over and take care of the churches, teach catechism to the children, and like sentinels stand guard to warn the clergy that their ministrations are needed so that no one may be deprived of the help of the priest. What We have just written is true of all these organizations. We wish, however, to say a word in particular about the principal organizations, so that each of them may know that it is highly approved and even praised by the Vicar of Jesus Christ.

First of all We mention the Knights of Columbus, an organization which is found in all the states of the Republic and fortunately is made up of active and industrious members who, because of their practical lives and open profession of the Faith, as well as by their zeal in assisting the Church, have brought great honor upon themselves. This organization promotes two types of activities which are needed now more than ever. In the first place, the National Sodality of Fathers of Families, the program of which is to give a Catholic education to their own children, to protect the rights of Christian parents with regard to education, and in cases where children attend the public schools to provide for them a sound and complete training in their religion. Secondly, the Federation for the Defense of Religious Liberty, which was recently organized when it became clear as the noonday sun that the Church was menaced by a veritable ocean of troubles. This Federation soon spread to all parts of the Republic. Its members attempted, working in harmony and with assiduity, to organize and instruct Catholics so that they would be able to present a united invincible front to the enemy.

No less deserving of the Church and the fatherland as the Knights of Columbus have been and still are We mention two other organizations, each of which has, following its own program, a special relation to what is known as "Catholic Social Action." One is the Catholic Society of Mexican Youth, and the other, the Society of Mexican Ladies. These two sodalities, over and above the work which is special

to each of them, promote and do all they can to have others promote the activities of the above-mentioned Federation for the Defense of Religious Liberty. Without going into details, with pleasure We desire to call to your attention, Venerable Brothers, but a single fact, namely, that all the members of these organizations, both men and women, are so brave that, instead of fleeing danger, they go out in search of it, and even rejoice when it falls to their share to suffer persecution from the enemies of the Church. What a beautiful spectacle this, that is thus given to the world, to angels, and to men! How worthy of eternal praise are such deeds! As a matter of fact, as We have pointed out above, many individuals, members either of the Knights of Columbus, or officers of the Federation, of the Society of Mexican Ladies, or of the Society of Mexican Youth, have been taken to prison handcuffed, through the public streets, surrounded by groups of soldiers, locked up in foul jails, harshly treated, and punished with prison sentences or fines. Moreover, Venerable Brothers, and in narrating this to you We can scarcely keep back Our tears, some of these young men and boys have gladly met death, the rosary in their hands and the name of Christ King on their lips. Young girls, too, who were imprisoned, were criminally outraged, and

these acts were deliberately made public in order to intimidate other young women and to cause them the more easily to fail in their duty towards the Church.

No one, surely, Venerable Brothers, can hazard a prediction or foresee in imagination the hour when the good God will bring to an end such calamities. We do know this much: The day will come when the Church of Mexico will have respite from this veritable tempest of hatred, for the reason that, according to the words of God "there is no wisdom, there is no prudence, there is no counsel against the Lord" (Prov. xxi, 30)

DI SUA SANTITA

THE VATICAN   November 27th, 1926.

DEAR SIR:—

The copies of magazines and numerous pamphlets of propaganda which the well deserving Association of the Knights of Columbus recently published in defense of the Catholic Religion which is suffering persecution in the Republic of Mexico safely reached me. I humbly placed them before the throne of the August Pontiff, bringing to his knowledge everything done so far for the diffusion of the same. I have the pleasure of notifying you that the Holy Father in accepting the offer of the homage showed himself already fully informed about the activity of the Knights of Columbus in this field; activity that he followed with paternal complacency because it gives great advantage to the Catholic cause in Mexico.

As a proof of such interest and high satisfaction for the merits towards our faith of the Knights of Columbus, His Holiness charged me to let you know that already he spoke highly in the Encyclical Letter "Iniquis Afflictisque" recently published about the Mexican Church.

In notifying you that the Holy Father imparts with all his heart to you and all the well deserving members of your Order the Apostolic Benediction, I take advantage most willingly of the opportunity to confirm myself with the sense of my particular consideration.

Yours,

JAMES A. FLAHERTY
SUPREME KNIGHT
KNIGHTS OF COLUMBUS

P. Card. Gasparri (P. CARD. GASPARRI).

---

and "the gates of hell shall not prevail" (Matt. xvi, 18) against the Spotless Bride of Christ.

Triumph of Church Predicted

The Church which, from the day of Pentecost, has been destined here below to a never-ending life, which went forth into the world, endowed with the gifts and the inspirations of the Holy Spirit, what has been her mission during the last twenty centuries and in every country of the world if not, after the example of her Divine Founder, "to go about doing good"? (Acts x, 38.) Certainly this work of the Church should have gained for her the love of all men; unfortunately the very contrary has happened as her Divine Master Himself predicted (Matt. x, 17–25) would

be the case. At one time the bark of Peter, favored by the winds, goes happily forward; at other times it appears to be swallowed up by the waves and on the point of being lost. Has not this ship always aboard the Divine Pilot who knows when to calm the angry waves and the winds? And who is it but Christ Himself who alone is all-powerful, that brings it about that every persecution which is launched against the faithful should react to the lasting benefit of the Church. As St. Hilary writes, "it is a prerogative of the Church that she is the vanquisher when she is persecuted, that she captures our intellects when her doctrines are questioned, that she conquers all at the very moment when she is abandoned by all." (St. Hilary of Portiers "De Trinitate," Bk. VII, No. 4.)

If those men who now in Mexico persecute their brothers and fellow-citizens for no other reason than that these latter are guilty of keeping the laws of God, would only recall to memory and consider dispassionately the vicissitudes of their country as history reveals them to us, they must recognize and publicly confess that whatever there is of progress, of civilization, of the good and the beautiful, in their country is due solely to the Catholic Church. In fact every man knows that after the introduction of Christianity to Mexico, the priests and religious especially, who are now being persecuted with such cruelty by an ungrateful government, worked without rest and despite all the obstacles placed in their way, on the one hand by the colonists who were moved by greed for gold and on the other by the natives who were still barbarians, to promote greatly in those vast regions both the splendor of the worship of God and the benefits of the Catholic religion, works and institutions of charity, schools and colleges for the education of the people and their instruction in letters, the sciences, both sacred and profane, in the arts and the crafts.

Urges Prayers for Enemies

One thing more remains for Us to do, Venerable Brothers, namely, to pray and implore Our Lady of Guadalupe, heavenly patroness of the Mexican people, that she pardon all these injuries and especially those which have been committed against her, that she ask of God that peace and concord may return to her people. And if, in the hidden designs of God that day which We so greatly desire is far distant, may she in the meantime console her faithful children of Mexico and strengthen them in their resolve to maintain their liberty by the profession of their Faith.

In the meantime, as an augury of the grace of God and as proof of Our fatherly love, We bestow from Our heart on you, Venerable Brothers, and especially on those bishops who rule the Church of Mexico, on all your clergy and your people, the Apostolic Blessing.

Given at Rome, at St. Peter's, on the eighteenth day of November, 1926, the fifth year of Our Pontificate. PIUS XI.
(Translation Ⓒ N. C. W. C.)

The pope's words on the Mexican situation.
In this excerpt, published in the Knights of Columbus magazine *Columbia*,
Pope Piux XI praises the efforts of organizations like the Knights of Columbus
for their support of the clergy and their continued work in Mexico.

Marching for the repeal of the Calles Law.
On October 30, 1927—the Feast of Christ the King—thousands of Catholics gathered in Mexico City's Federal District to march in a peaceful protest against the Calles Law.

AGICA

telegram of support to the government, Deputy Manrique urged that it be rejected, denouncing the government's tactic as a "torturous policy toward the issue of religion . . . its attacks on freedom of thought . . . should be strongly criticized. . . . In Mexico, this freedom does not exist, just as respect for human life does not exist." The laws gave churches the perfect opportunity to condemn the law's injustice from every pulpit, incite resistance, and even justify rebellion.

Rome, too, issued a statement on the matter with the publication of Pope Pius XI's encyclical *Iniquis Afflictisque* on November 18, 1926. In it, the pope lauded Mexico's bishops, clergy, Catholic faithful, and various Catholic organizations in Mexico, including the League, the ACJM, and the Knights of Columbus, for their efforts and continued faithfulness to the Church. At the same time, the pope decried the Calles Law and described instances of its enforcement as "lawless acts" clothed "with the semblance of legality."

Although an agreement would be reached in 1929 between the bishops and the President, it would not be until after an army of untrained Cristero soldiers would directly confront their persecutor, the State, in a bloody war lasting three years, threatening the revolutionary regime and encouraging it to seek recourse.

From far and wide.
From towns large and small, the Catholic faithful—men, women, and children of all ages—traveled for miles to participate in the 1927 peaceful demonstration for religious freedom.

Pre-Cristiada Timeline 1855–1925

THE STATE AND THE CHURCH

1855–1857
"Reform Laws" are passed, restricting Church privileges and enabling government seizure of Church land.

1857
The Constitution of 1857 is put into effect. It includes more religious restrictions.

1861
Reform Laws become national laws as Juárez' liberal regime returns to Mexico City.

1876–1911
The "Porfiriato"—the presidency of Porfirio Díaz.

1910
Mexican Revolution begins. Numerous revolutionaries vie for the Mexican presidency over the next decade.

DIPLOMACY AND U.S. RELATIONS

1859
In an effort to obtain a U.S. loan to fund the Reform War effort, President Benito Juárez signs a law nationalizing all Church properties.

1861
Seeking to recoup unpaid debts and to ward off influence from the largely Protestant United States, Napoleon III of France tries to establish a French Catholic empire in Mexico.

1905
The U.S. Catholic organization, the Knights of Columbus, establishes a council in Mexico.

1914
United States supports the Huerta rebellion, sending troops for the takeover of Veracruz.

CATHOLIC IDENTITY, PROTESTS, AND THE WAR

1855
Archbishop Lázaro de la Garza of Mexico City condemns the Ley Juárez; rebellion in Puebla ensues, backed by many clergy.

1857
General Felix Zuloaga rejects the constitution, initiating the Reform War (1858–1861).

1861–1867
Civil war erupts against French intervention in Mexico, ending with the execution of French-imposed emperor, Maximilian.

1890–1910
Social Catholicism booms, leading to the founding of the National Catholic Party in 1911, and the ACJM in 1913.

1910–1930
To escape the violence of the revolution, 700,000 Mexicans enter Texas.

1914
Enrique Gorostieta, future commander of the Cristero army, becomes the youngest Federal general at age twenty-seven.

Pre-Cristiada Timeline 1855–1925

THE STATE AND THE CHURCH

1915

As governor, General Plutarco Elías Calles expels priests, and wins battles that help secure the presidency for Venustiano Carranza.

1917

Carranza promulgates the 1917 Constitution, which contains several anticlerical articles.

1918

The CROM is founded, led by Luis Morones.

1920

Álvaro Obregón becomes president; anticlerical laws are enforced by various governors.

1924

Plutarco Elías Calles becomes president.

1925

In an attempt to nationalize religion, a government-backed schismatic church is founded, led by Joaquín Peréz.

DIPLOMACY AND U.S. RELATIONS

1915

St. Philip Seminary is established in Texas for seminarians who are unable to study in Mexico due to persecution.

1917

In January, the U.S. State Department responds to pleas from Catholics, and requests that Carranza spare the lives of prelates. Meanwhile, hundreds of clergy continue to flee or are expelled from Mexico.

1923

Bucareli Treaty is signed to protect U.S. owned oil properties and other holdings in Mexico. Shortly after, the U.S. officially recognizes Obregón's administration.

1924

U.S. arms embargo prohibits sale of weapons to Mexico, except for Obregón's administration.

1925

Mexican congress passes oil laws that directly violate the Bucareli Treaty.

CATHOLIC IDENTITY, PROTESTS, AND THE WAR

1915–1920

Emiliano Zapata and Francisco "Pancho" Villa rebel against Carranza; they are supported by many Catholics who were upset by Carranza's policies.

1918

Archbishop Orozco y Jiménez issues a pastoral letter, and is exiled to the United States.

1923

Catholics in Mexico dedicate a monument to Christ the King on Cubilete Hill.

1925

In February, a riot ensues after members of the nationalist "church" seize La Soledad Church in Mexico City. In March, the National League for the Defense of Religious Liberty is founded.

Cristeros under General Elías Vergara.
These volunteer "soldiers" were active in the area between the cities of El Oro, Zitácuaro, and Angangueo. General Vergara (middle row, at left), a man of deep religious devotion, refused to campaign during Holy Week (the week before Easter).

2.

The Unexpected War

THE BIRTH OF A REBELLION

The first uprising erupted on August 1, 1926, the day public worship in Catholic churches was suspended. That month, there were six insurrections; in September, thirteen new centers of rebellion appeared; and a score more occurred in October. In November and December, insurrection spread throughout Mexico's central plateau. By the end of the year, the 59th Regiment, commanded by Federal General Arenas, was annihilated, and twenty municipalities in Jalisco alone were in a state of rebellion, despite the opposition of the archbishop, who discouraged armed confrontation.

Often these early insurrections were directly provoked by specific government actions: the closure of a church, injustices against a local parish priest or lay leaders, the takeover of church inventories. For example, during the first four days of August in 1926, the government's closure of churches for inventory provoked a massive resistance that turned so violent that the police or the army had to intervene at times. On August 15, the arrest and death of the respected priest Father Luis Batís Sáinz (a martyr and now a canonized saint) provoked the uprising in the region of Valparaíso, Zacatecas. Similar events occurred in small towns such as Acámbaro (Guanajuato), Sahuayo (Michoacán), and in cities such as Santiago Bayacora (Durango) and in Guadalajara (Jalisco).

More than collateral damage. Not even Mexico City's metropolitan cathedral was safe. Here, a priest and officers survey the damage to the stone column and the pulpit where the city's archbishop used to preach.

These uprisings, in turn, provoked the government to mobilize more troops and to make a great error in arresting more priests. When the people saw the government actions—the mobilization of agrarian militias, the arrival of troops in places where soldiers had never before been seen, the general disarmament of the rebels, and the first levying of taxes—many were convinced that the days of leniency regarding anticlerical laws were at an end. All acts of authority were resented as acts of aggression.

Initially, these uprisings were not taken seriously. In fact, the first series of failed uprisings was mocked in the Mexican legislature. Deputy Santos read out a list of skirmishes gathered from daily reports from the government posts throughout the country, and quipped that "it is true that they have attempted to carry out a revolution, which has failed because they do not know how to carry out a revolution. They should ask us about it. We could give them revolution classes." Nevertheless, Deputy Santos also warned his fellow senators against underestimating the spirit that inspired the uprisings in the first place.

The face of judgment.
A Cristero commanding officer in a serape and sandals awaits judgment before Federal officials.

Upholding the Constitution.
The 1917 Constitution rescinded the right to trial for those who disobeyed its religious restrictions. Here, Federal soldiers execute Father Francisco Vera in 1927 for celebrating Mass and wearing religious vestments—both prohibited by the constitution. The general who ordered the execution had this photograph taken and sent to President Calles, who passed it along to the press.

FROM ACTIVISTS TO "CRISTEROS"

Within a couple months, many dissenters were primed for more than spo-
radic uprisings; they were ready for organized war. People felt that their
patience, penances, and prayers over a period of five months, from August
to December, had been in vain because "Calles's heart was hardened like
that of the pharaoh," as one account put it in biblical terms. Wherever residents assembled—as they did in Santa María del Valle (Jalisco), or Santiago Bayacora (Durango)—when they asked themselves what they should
do, the answer was the same: "A revolution!" President Calles did not help
the peace effort when he himself laid out two options for the Catholics,
saying, "The law or guns." Victoriano Ramírez ("El Catorce"), who later
became a leading Cristero commander in Los Altos, Jalisco, summed up
the decision for war while in an assembly: "There's no way other than
throwing punches."

What the people needed were leaders to organize
and guide them in the art of war. This leadership
was found in the National League for the Defense
of Religious Liberty. After exhausting peaceful means,
the League decided to imitate the "revolutionaries"—as the comrades of Calles, Obregón, and other
government leaders called themselves—by resort-
ing to armed action. They made this decision in
light of the many small spontaneous uprisings that
had occurred during the previous months. Like
those insurgents, the League was now also convinced
that the government had left them no other option
but war.

"Propagandists."
Just weeks after the League's call for
insurrection, these women were held
by the police for allegedly distributing
League pamphlets in Mexico City.

The League officially sounded the battle cry when it published its manifesto, *A la Nación*. This called for a unified rebellion to begin in January 1927.
There was no turning back. The revolution broke out as the new year began.
Groups of Catholics rebelled against the government to the cry of "Long live
Christ the King and the Virgin of Guadalupe!" Little did the insurgents sus-
pect that the military struggle would be an even slower, more horrific path
to resolution than the civic struggle they had forsaken.

There was nothing official about how these insurrections began. They
started like common news, transmitted by word of mouth from person to
person. The facts of the movements were communicated: "Those from San
José are rebelling, and so are the people from Pueblo Nuevo," "There's fighting going on in Cojumatlán," and so on. But what people shared with one
another was not merely news of an event; it corresponded to a previously felt
certainty, the certainty of a threat felt by all. The suspension of worship
frayed nerves, and Calles's actions seemed to entice them toward war. Peaceful protest, being ineffectual and slow, was becoming an unconvincing

option. For some, there was a feeling that one always had been ready for this, and the hour to stand up had come at last. As the Cristero Luis Gutiérrez would later explain:

> We did not want to abandon the Church into the hands of the military. What would we do without it, without its festivals and statues that patiently listened to our lamentations? The government takes away everything from us, our corn, our pastures, our animals, and, if this were not enough, it also wants us to live like beasts, without religion or God. But they will not see this last thing happen, for we will cry out loud whenever we can: Long live Christ the King! Long live the Virgin of Guadalupe! Long live Unión Popular! Death to the government!"

The insurgents differed from the Federal soldiers in significant ways: they operated spontaneously and without formal organization, causing the American military attaché to observe the "notorious absence of a supreme leader." This was unprecedented, even counter-cultural, considering Mexico's recent history in the revolution from 1910 to 1920; those revolutionaries had leaders with whom subordinates had strong associations, and each movement often took its name from its leader. There had been, for instance, the *Villistas* (following Pancho Villa), the *Zapatistas* (following Emiliano Zapata), and the *Carrancistas* (following Venustiano Carranza).

These insurgents, however, had no such leader. Rather, they called themselves the *Liberators,* the *Defenders,* or, in areas controlled by the Unión Popular, the *Populares.* It was the Federal soldiers who came up with the name *Cristeros*, taken in part from the Cristero battle cry *Viva Cristo Rey!* ("Long

AGICA

Soldiers under General Lauro Rocha.
Several photos of this group exist, thanks to the photographic skills of one of its soldiers, Heriberto Navarette. (See page 50 for more information regarding this photographer.)

AGICA

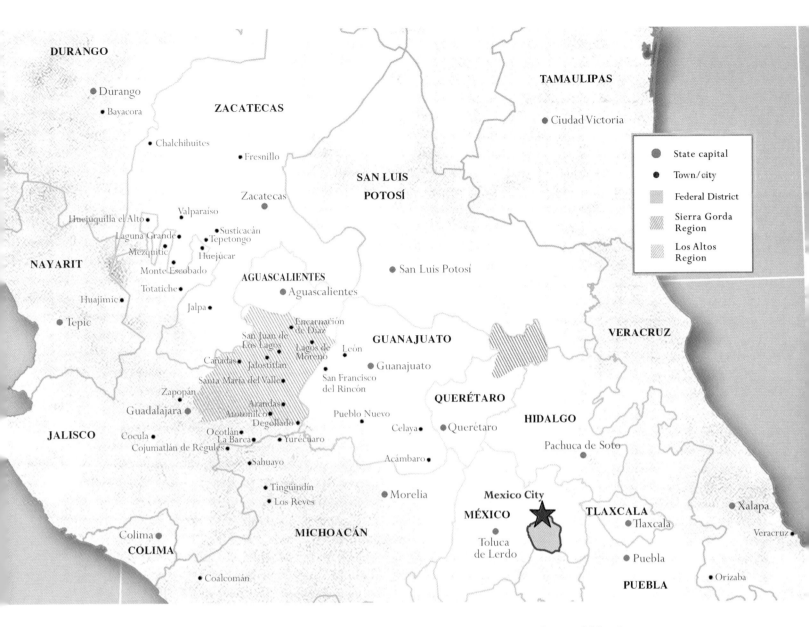

live Christ the King!"). Indeed, as one Cristero said, "This was how I felt: I went out to win over armed people, willing to go to war to defend the freedom of God and my fellow men."

This dramatic evolution of the conflict, the failure of legal efforts, and the spontaneous mobilization of the people all fed the hopes of the League's leaders, who soon desired not only to free the Church of the despised laws through constitutional amendments, but also to bring about the downfall of the Calles regime through seizure of power. Before August 1926, the League would not have even dreamed of such a political hope; but suddenly, anything seemed possible.

Unfortunately, issuing the manifesto was just one of many instances demonstrating the League's military inexperience and its inability to lead the war effort. The League leaders promised an easy and prompt victory, aided with money and arms coming from the United States. But as time would show, none of this happened. With such promises, the manifesto gave false hopes to the leaders of nonviolent, civic resistance, such as Anacleto González Flores, President of the Unión Popular. It also caused many Mexican

General Vega's train raid.
Taken on April 19, 1927, this photograph shows the remains of the train that was attacked and derailed by General Vega's men. Bodies of victims lie along the hill.

Catholics to throw themselves completely unprepared into battles that became massacres.

The insurrection was huge and unanimous in the central-west region, including Jalisco, Colima, Nayarit, and the part of Zacatecas adjacent to Jalisco. The rural masses, whose strength lay only in numbers, were inspired to try to relive the biblical taking of Jericho, a feat impossible without divine assistance. Men, women, and children from various towns and settlements came together, believing they could force the government to surrender by their mere presence. They chose new municipal leaders, and the unarmed crowd threw itself into the war.

Each rebel group, made up of 50 to 100 men, tended its own territory and was involved in its own local battles. Often, in the Zapatista tradition of the peasant soldier, each group simultaneously waged war and maintained its farm. For the first year, the Cristeros—unorganized, ill-equipped, and poorly trained—were sustained only by their belief in the righteousness of their cause.

Armed with makeshift weaponry, what could the Cristero masses really expect to accomplish against trained regiments and battalions? During their first clashes with the army, the Cristero crowds scattered and rarely gained anything for the people. The government remained stubbornly resolute, and the remaining rebels were left with few weapons, little money, and even less organization. In a telegraph to Mexico City, Federal General Ferreira summed up his work in quelling the rebellion, saying, "This is a manhunt rather than a campaign." Heartened by the quick weakening of the movement, President Calles assured the governor of Jalisco that the matter would be resolved in one or two months at most. Knowing the citizens, however, the governor skeptically responded, "As long as it doesn't last two years."

As relieving as General Ferreira's report of victory was, it nevertheless concluded with an alarming observation: "The insurgents are protected by all the inhabitants." Indeed, the Cristeros were irrepressible fighters, and the government's harsh tactics continued to motivate the people, contributing to the spread of rebellion and the development of the war.

The day after the massive January insurrection, former President Obregón tried to reach out once again to President Calles and the bishops, but no resolution was reached. And on April 19, 1927, Calles was handed the perfect excuse to resist Obregón's conciliatory attempts: the Cristero General Father José Reyes Vega and his troops raided a bank train, fought the military escort, and set fire to the train cars, resulting in the deaths of an estimated one hundred soldiers and civilians, including children. The horror of the event shocked the Federal soldiers and Cristeros alike.

Although most bishops opposed violence, Calles used the train attack to expel all of them from the country. This seriously hindered the peace efforts by Obregón and the bishops. On April 21, while some of the Mexican bishops remained in hiding, six bishops were abducted at night from their homes and loaded onto a train bound for Texas. Some, including Archbishop Mora y del Río, who later died in San Antonio, Texas, would never again set foot in their homeland.

AGICA

Retaliation photograph.
The writing on this photograph indicates that these Federal soldiers are posing with religious items picked up from "fanatic assailants" on a train led by "friar-bandits," including Vega. This is a reference to Vega's infamous train raid.

Reforming Mexico's Military College.
Responsible for reforming Mexico's military, General Amaro (center) looks on as Arnulfo Gómez signs the act inaugurating the reforms to the Military College in Mexico City. Although known then to be vehemently anticlerical, General Amaro later returned to Catholicism, and even donated his personal library to the Jesuits.

GENERAL AMARO AND THE FEDERAL ARMY

The Mexican government's military force, called the Armed Forces of the Federation, was more than a mere instrument of national defense at the beck and call of the government. Known popularly as "the Federation," the army was the very backbone of the State and played an active role in the conflict. After all, from 1910 to 1920, Mexico's presidential succession was determined, not by presidential elections, but by military power. From 1920 to 1930, most of the Mexican presidents were generals who had taken part in these and other conflicts. Included among them was Carranza (who was assassinated), Obregón (who repelled a coup by his predecessor Alberto de la Huerta), and Calles (who faced Yaqui rebellions in addition to the Cristeros).

In some ways, the army and the government constituted a single entity that considered the Church its personal enemy, and many of the Federal generals, including Secretary of War Joaquín Amaro, were personally and violently anticlerical. It was not long into the war before stories surfaced about the Federal soldiers, or *Federales* as they were called, that deepened the Cristeros' fears of the government's and the army's agenda. Federal General Eulogio Ortiz shot one of his own soldiers who was bathing in a river just because he was wearing a scapular (a Catholic sacramental). Some officers led their troops into combat shouting, "Long live our father, Satan!" and Colonel Mano Negra, the notorious executioner, died crying out, "Long live Satan, the Great!"

The 70,000-man Federal army was big, well equipped, well organized, and backed by the government. It consumed between 25 and 45 percent of the national budget, and reacted quickly with all the efficiency afforded by its means and the nature of the war itself. Yet it had its drawbacks. With the Mexican Revolution and the Huerta rebellion less than a decade in the past, the Federal army needed rebuilding. In 1925, just a year before the Cristero revolt, President Calles appointed Joaquín Amaro as the Secretary of War and Chief General of the Federal military. From 1925 to 1932, General Amaro worked diligently to strengthen the army so it could better deal with any new threats. By utilizing trains, trucks, aviation, and cavalry, he succeeded in providing the army with great mobility.

Desertion also became an increasingly significant problem. During the Cristiada, the Federal army lost around 25 to 30 percent of its members each year. As one American noted, the high desertion rate was surprising, since a soldier's pay was significantly higher than the pay of a worker. This indicated that there must have been reasons other than poor financial compensation for the soldiers' dissatisfaction. And there were: poor living conditions during a war with no end in sight led to high rates of depression and alcohol and drug abuse. Additionally, unlike the Cristeros who fought for a cause close to their hearts and homes, this was rarely the case for the Federal soldiers.

Victim of Ortiz.
Federal General Eulogio Ortiz ordered Father Mateo Correa Magallanes to hear prisoners' confessions—and then executed the priest for refusing to reveal the details.

Off to war.
Federal troops travel with artillery equipment on the flatcars of a train.

To boost its strength, the army recruited the *agraristas*—who sought land reform—with a promise of land redistribution. This was an enormous gain for the army and a serious blow to the Cristeros, who had hoped from the beginning to have the agraristas on their side. After all, in many ways this group had more in common with the Cristeros than the Federal soldiers. They were peasants who knew the inhabitants and the lay of the land very well. They even dressed more like Cristeros, wearing clothing from their homes rather than military uniforms—a fact that caused friendly fire incidents. Tiny details that differentiated them from their Cristero enemies, like armbands or rolled up sleeves, were not always easily discernable. Most importantly, the agraristas were also practicing Catholics, who were known even to risk their lives rather than give up the locations of priests. So when many of them sided with the State, a resentful enmity arose. Families were split—a father agrarista may have had a son Cristero, or vice versa. In this respect, the agraristas became both clients and hostages of the State, benefitting from land redistribution while being used as instruments of war against their own people.

For their part, the Cristeros were clear that the warfare was provoked by religion, not by agrarian policy. As one said, "We are not against the agraristas. We are in favor of the redistribution of land, but we are against the agraristas when they become soldiers." And indeed, as the war went on, some agraristas—from Zacatecas, Guerrero, and Colima, for example—did change sides and became Cristeros.

A group of agraristas.
Although employed by the Federal army, these men—with their sombreros and varying "uniforms"—look more like the Cristeros. One even wears a jacket and tie.

Nevertheless, the Federal army gained an additional 30,000 men from recruiting the agaristas—roughly one-third of its force. With these auxiliary troops, the army in 1926 was able to crush the isolated resistance groups one by one, as well as those groups coming from Los Altos in Jalisco, and the Sierra Gorda region.

Although the Federal army maintained a degree of success against the Cristeros (making use of the agraristas who were often placed on the front lines of battle), the Cristeros celebrated their own victories in those first war-torn months. The first occurred in September 1926, near the village of Santiago Bayacora, Durango, where one Federal general died and two units were destroyed (one cavalry regiment and one infantry battalion). Another Cristero victory came in January 1927, at the famous battle of San Julián (on the Jalisco highlands). With such small successes, the great Federal effort that took place in January to squash the movement failed; and despite the arrival of three aviation squadrons and six mountain artillery regiments to Jalisco, the situation quickly deteriorated in February.

It became increasingly clear that the Federal military might was not capable of solving the problem. The indifference toward the people's exasperation was intentional, given that the uprisings had been announced beforehand and preventive military measures were taken. The military's reconcentration policy; scorched earth tactics; seizure of civilian property; execution of prisoners; massacre of property; and rape of women—all of these actions confirmed in the Cristeros' minds the evil nature of their enemies and the absolute need for victory.

MOBILITY AND TACTICS

For the first year—from August 1926 to July 1927—the war primarily involved the Cristeros just escaping the enemy. But by July 1927, the resistance had consolidated and the Cristero ranks had swelled to 20,000 combatants—significantly fewer than the Federal army, but still a considerable force to battle. They still operated spontaneously and without any organization, but they were no longer the same untested rebels who escaped from the Federals like helpless little birds, primitively supplied with clubs, rocks, and the charitable support of the population. Though always short of ammunition and money, the Cristeros were well-mounted and better armed with rifles that were taken from the enemy, which was being increasingly worn down by *piquyhuye* (hit and run) warfare. Scattered in the spring of 1927, the Cristero combatants returned as true warriors.

As the war progressed, it became clear that the course of events would be determined by the Cristeros' strategic use of Mexico's topography and by the Federal army's lack of overpowering force, which left it unable to subdue the popular insurrections that broke out in the four points of Mexico's central high plain.

In Focus
The Battle of San Francisco del Rincón

After suffering initial losses in 1926, the Cristeros adopted guerilla warfare as their favored and more effective strategy for the remainder of the war. Pictured here are scenes just before a battle that took place at San Francisco del Rincón, Guanajuato, on April 5, 1929, near the end of the war. They show guerilla warfare at work as the Cristeros used the natural advantages offered by the mountainous terrain to strategically position themselves against the enemy. In this battle, the soldiers were led into combat by Generals Aristeo Pedroza (one of the rare priest-combatants) and Lauro Rocha. Perhaps because of its strategic location near Los Altos, San Francisco del Rincón was the site of several other battles during the war. One of the earliest Cristero victories took place there in February of 1927, under the leadership of Victoriano Ramírez ("El Catorce") and Colonel Miguel Hernández.

AGICA

Battlefield photographer.
Several photographs in this book, including these pre-battle scenes, are the work of Cristero Heriberto Navarrete, shown here with his camera. Battlefield photographs of Cristeros were rare; Cristeros had few cameras, and photographs of combatants—if leaked to the enemy—could endanger those pictured.

AGICA

Guerilla cavalry.
General Lauro Rocha rides with his cavalry to the place of battle. The Cristero cavalry proved vital in employing guerilla tactics.

Combat communication.
The large black banner, which is waved high, served to organize maneuvers.

AGICA

AGICA

General Jesús Degollado Guízar.
Born in Cotija, Michoacán, Degollado
worked as a pharmacist and was active
in the ACJM. In 1927, the League named
him the leader of the armed struggle in
southern Jalisco, Colima, and western
Michoacán.

Unlike the Cristeros, who employed guerrilla tactics from camps spread
far and wide through the country, the Federal troops needed to be central-
ized in populated areas because they depended on their city garrisons for
food, pay, and support. It was impossible for the Federal army to maintain
numerous outposts without dangerously fragmenting the troops, and the
Federal troops could rarely settle down in one place near a rebellious area.
The only available solution—using expeditionary troops—was utilized all
too frequently. Zone leaders came and went and troops made excursions
with their provisions to troubled areas before returning immediately to their
bases of origin.

For example, a headquarters in Colima would learn that a group of Cristeros had taken a town square. Some Federal units would be sent over by
train, while the operational units and garrison would be alerted by telegraph

Captain Alberto B. Gutiérrez.
Captain Gutiérrez (second from left) stands before a pictorial representation of Christ.

AGICA

General José María Gutiérrez.
Before the League recruited General Gorostieta, Gutiérrez served as one of the most prominent Cristero military leaders.

to follow the rebels with forced marches. Once out of danger, with or without actual combat (since the desire to fight was not always present), the troops would return to the city and their quarters because they could not be lodged, paid, or fed in a distant place.

To the Federal army's annoyance, the Cristeros constantly avoided engagement in open combat, instead employing guerrilla tactics to great effect. The Federal soldiers would hear the insurgents' battle horn, and then attempt to engage the rebel group, while being pulled farther and farther into the mountains, where they would typically lose a few men in a small skirmish. Then twelve hours later, they would hear the battle horn again. And each time the Federals would leave an area, the rebels would return again, and the whole cycle would repeat. In this manner, the Cristeros of Santiago Bayacora, Durango, ambushed some 800 Federal soldiers in the Puerto de la Arena canyon. Likewise, under the leadership of Colonel Ezequiel Mendoza Barragán, the Cristeros of Coalcomán destroyed a regiment twice its own size. This took place in an area of the terrible Sierra Madre del Sur called *El Espinazo del Diablo*—a prime strategic area marked by high mountains and deep, narrow canyons.

Such failures of strategy had the unfortunate effect of frustrating and enraging Federal officers—some of whom were ruthless to start with and inclined to take merciless retaliations on civilian populations. Such actions, born of sheer frustration, resulted in destruction without ever restoring peace, spreading war farther away, increasing outrage on both sides, and deepening the resolve of the rebels.

As General Amaro found out, sheer numbers could not solve the problem. The rebels always seemed to be just out of easy reach, leading Amaro to ponder one final deficiency in his troops—a weak cavalry. Amaro had established the Federal army in just a few years. He modeled it after those in Europe and America, where the mobility of the infantry, the so-called "queen of battles," was supported by aviation and artillery in countries endowed with good railroad infrastructure. But this was not the situation in Mexico, where entire regions remained inaccessible to the infantry. Mexico's land required cavalry, and trained horsemen were lacking.

In contrast, the Cristeros had a cavalry far superior to the Federal cavalry, as even the Federal Governor of Jalisco, Silvano Barba González, pointed out. In fact, the Cristero ranks contained a better cavalry than infantry, with many gifted horse riders.

In his attempt to remedy the situation, General Amaro purchased a great number of horses from the United States army; however, the horses were not the best choice for either the cavalrymen or Mexico's hostile natural environment. And even with horses available, training was often no substitute for the experience a soldier brought from his region. For example, the army gained good foot soldiers with the Yaqui Indian battalions and indigenous

Attacks on railroad trains and infrastructure.
For the Cristeros, targeting trains such as these was not only a means of procuring needed resources, including ammunition and money, but also a way to undercut the Federal army's mobility, which was largely dependent upon the railroads.

troops that formed in Oaxaca, Puebla, and Guerrero (including Juchitecos, Tehuanos, and Serranos Indians)—but no cavalry. Good mounted regiments were rare.

To make matters worse for the Federal army, often the population and even local authorities favored the Cristero cause over the government's. With such inconsistent backing, the Federales often faced unexpected difficulties in obtaining food and support. In response, the government developed a reconcentration policy, relocating rural citizens to the more urban areas in the country. Additionally, before engaging in the frantic search for new recruits, the Federal army transformed some haciendas, or large estates, into unofficial military support by excusing some hacienda owners from the relocation program and offering them the means to organize self-defense groups against the Cristeros. This served a dual purpose: it gained troops and also protected the economic interests of the great landowners, who were faithful government allies.

By May 1927, General Amaro's high hopes for victory over the Cristeros were thwarted. Federal units mobilized to Jalisco had to be increased from

Troops among the mountains.
Riders of the Division of the South under the command of General Jesús Degollado are shown on the banks of the Armería river, between Jalisco and Colima.

AGICA

Preparing for battle.
These mounted troops, under the command of General Lauro Rocha, are photographed just minutes before entering combat.

four to twelve, and from four to seven in Michoacán. From the cities of Aguascalientes to Iguala, General Amaro concentrated twenty additional units brought from the north, hastily forming new regiments and battalions. In the meantime, the insurrection doubled in Colima and Guanajuato. Amaro hurriedly formed additional regiments and battalions. Unlike the Cristeros, who were always short of supplies, the main problem for the Federal army was not acquiring weapons, but rather finding men to bear them. In July 1927, an unexpected windfall of troops came when the Yaqui territory was pacified, enabling General Amaro to send twenty additional units to battle the Cristeros: fifteen Federal units who had won the Yaqui rebellion and five Yaqui battalions who had been enrolled after their defeat.

Nevertheless, due to the popular character of the insurrection and the persistence of its motivations, the uprisings continued. As important as taking up arms was, as we will see in the next chapters, the Cristero movement was more than a mere military campaign. It was a cause—shared, supported, and organized—by hundreds of thousands.

Newlyweds.
Cristero Manuel Moreno Aldrete and his young bride were one of many couples married during the Cristiada.

3.

The Life of
The Cristeros

THE CRISTEROS: A HUMBLE BAND

A young student who joined the Cristero army wrote of his initial encounter: "The first group of Cristero soldiers made a very poor impression on me. Poorly dressed, even more poorly groomed . . . they gave me [the] impression of rural pilgrims, each one accidentally armed with a rifle."

The poor attire described was evocative of the deeper divisions in Mexico. There was a visible Mexico and an invisible Mexico. Visible Mexico included the political, cultural, and intellectual elite, which dominated Mexico's domestic and foreign affairs. Invisible Mexico was comprised of the country people who constituted the nation's majority, and yet were seldom taken into consideration. They had very little influence in government, but that is not to say that they were powerless.

Indeed, it was "invisible Mexico," the country people, who rose up, filling the ranks of the Cristero combatants and their civilian supporters. They formed a rural, multi-class coalition that lacked only the involvement of the wealthy and the agraristas.

For example, in the Quintanar Brigade (comprised of 2,000 men), most of the soldiers were small landholders, sharecroppers, and cowboys. Many were young—about one in five were under twenty years old, and the average recruit in Colima was between seventeen and twenty-seven years old. Additionally, many had families: three in five were married; and of those, 90 percent were fathers.

Here an important point should be noted. Many historiographers believe that logically the peasants would have backed the government, since it supported agrarian reform—even though it is now known that land reforms

AGICA

An elderly volunteer.
Age was one area in which the Cristeros—as a band of volunteers—could differ greatly from the Federal army, which paid for its soldiers. The elderly Captain Rito López appears in this photograph.

Cristeros in training.
These soldiers of all ages were among
General Jesús Degollado's south Jalisco division.

Cristeros of the Huichol Tribe.
These Cristeros from the town of San Sebastian recognized the authority of General Pedro Quintanar. Like other areas of Mexico, the war was divisive among the Huichol community. The soldiers pictured here lost their leader, Juan Bautista, in an ambush by pro-Federal Huichol.

were rarely made by and for the peasants. But this was largely not the case. For some historiographers, this "aberrant" behavior displayed by these people was attributed to their class, their lack of awareness, their petit-bourgeois mentality, or their plain ignorance. But there is, however, another explanatory factor: religion.

While some variation in motivation is to be expected among any such varied group of people, such unity of purpose among the Cristeros and their supporters reveals the seriousness of the religious crisis that moved all segments of the rural society to action.

Additionally, it is worth emphasizing the exceptional degree of social participation in the Cristiada. People took up the cause regardless of differences in age and gender, convenience and prudence. Those who generally did not take part in warfare—the elderly, children, women, and the indigenous groups—each participated in the Cristiada. At times, they were even the ones most responsible for triggering the rebellion. Knowing that they were often spared from punishment and jail, these often marginalized groups were vocal and at times reckless. Thus, in the beginning, Calles did not see anything but "sacristy rats and frail old men."

With the exception of 1810—the beginning of the Mexican War of Independence—it would be difficult to find a moment like this in Mexican history. The Cristiada signified a national moment in time, characterized by groups that were defined by their refusal to participate in a history that was not theirs, and that seemed to be unfolding against them (against the rural population in general and the indigenous communities in particular). They were nationalists and patriots in their own way, acting out of love for Mexico and their Catholic faith.

LIMITED RESOURCES

This grassroots element contributed to the distinctiveness of Cristero culture—from their clothing to their weaponry to their resources. In photographs it is easy to distinguish Cristero soldiers from the trained Federal troops. The Federals were outfitted in official military uniforms, complete with high boots. The Cristeros, on the other hand, had no consistent uniform. In fact, at first, the only identification the Cristeros had was a black armband, the sign of mourning. Later, this became a red and white armband, which represented Christ.

With home ties so strong, it was also easy to distinguish the rural Cristeros from the city-dwelling ones. Cristeros of the rural group wore sandals and often had long hair and long beards. The city dwellers were better outfitted, with shorter haircuts, moustaches, khaki clothing, and boots.

Always far behind the Federals in terms of resources, Cristero soldiers often had to fend for themselves for clothing and supplies. What little they had came from their own homes or from the *Cristeros mansos*, the homes of non-combatant Cristero supporters. In a time of trouble, General Manuel Michel of the 3rd (Cristero) Regiment from south Jalisco had to appeal to his sister for supplies: "I've got a lot of men without clothing, and I need blankets . . . there are also some without shoes. I want more cigarettes, salt, five kilos of the best quality wool, two dozen batteries for reflectors, 100 aspirin tablets, oxygenated water, and salve."

Cristero supporters from the country and the cities aided the Cristero cause in different ways as well. The people of the countryside provided food and provisions directly to the soldiers who lived in remote areas, whereas people from the towns worked to improve organization, propaganda, and supply lines. Town and country were in continuous communication with each other, and the flow of refugees reinforced this continuity.

Arms and ammunition were highly sought by the Cristeros. Initially, like clothing and food, weapons, ammunition, and horses were supplied by the soldiers themselves. Those who did not own good weapons often had to make do with slings, sticks, machetes, and poor quality firearms.

AGICA

A Cristero distinction.
This Cristero wears a black armband, which was worn by many Cristeros as a sign of mourning.

Four young officers.
Note the difference in the uniforms of these Cristero officers, who are (from left to right) 1st Lieutenant Lupe Camarena, Major Heriberto Navarrete, 1st Lieutenant Jesús Jiménez, and 2nd Lieutenant Salvador Camarena.

Additionally, it was nearly impossible to get ammunition from the United States. The arms embargo allowed the U.S. government to provide the Mexican Federal army with supplies, but it strictly prohibited the sale of weaponry to the rebel forces.

As the war continued, arms were sought from beyond personal resources. Since trains and railway stations were under government surveillance, ammunition had to be cleverly concealed for transportation, often labeled as nails or some other inconspicuous heavy cargo. (More on this topic later.)

Troops of the Sahuayo zone, Michoacán.
General Ignacio Sánchez, an educated man from an affluent family, sits in the middle of this photograph. He is easily distinguished from the rest of the troop by his uniform-like attire and city-fashion grooming.

Eventually, as the Cristeros gained skill and organization, they learned to acquire most of their arms and ammunition from Federal sources through covert dealings, raids, and confiscation after victorious battles. Thus, by the end of the war, Federico Vázquez (an important Cristero leader in Durango) could say, "All the arms and ammunition with which we are fighting the government, we took from the government itself; and a proof of this is that all the horses which we handed over when we laid down our arms [at the end of the war] were government property."

Food was another major need. Besides obtaining food through acquisitions and generous donations, the Cristero military organization proved efficient in organizing agricultural activities. Sometimes regiments were transformed into units of plowmen, sowers, harvesters, and muleteers. (This will be discussed more in Chapter 5.) As one Cristero wrote, "We do our best to take in the harvest in the cooperative of lands of Valparaíso, as well as the land of the agrarians and part of the municipality's haciendas." The Cristeros had to carry out the harvest very quickly, since it had to be done before the Federals came. The Federals were always eager to keep the corn to meet their own needs. And when this could not be achieved, they would burn the crops before they were harvested.

AGICA

Military supplies.
This soldier with the Cristero cavalry is well equipped with ammunition and even binoculars, which were likely stolen from the Federales.

AGICA

Cristero cavalrymen.
Under the words "*Viva Cristo Rey!*," José Martínez and Rafael Aguilar of Encarnación de Díaz, Jalisco, pose with rope, ammunition belts, and riding clothes.

In Focus

Cristeros and Federales
A Striking Contrast

At the onset of the Cristiada, Federal authorities had high expectations about defeating the Cristeros, and the reasons were obvious. Their troops had a distinct advantage over the Cristeros when it came to pay, resources, camps, training, organization, weapons, and even their uniforms.

In these photographs, one can see the makeshift nature of the Cristero army. The Cristero soldiers were volunteers—passionate, but untrained, unconventional, and far from ideal. Weapons and resources varied in quantity and quality. They were attained from a variety of sources—their homes, their families, and their neighbors—and included stolen goods from the Federal regiments. On the other hand, the passion for their cause was arguably their greatest motivator, giving them the strength to grow and persevere against their enemy.

As the war progressed, the Cristeros were also able to claim one thing the Federal army could not: an increase in troops joining the cause. By 1929, Cristero soldiers, who had numbered 20,000 in June of 1927, had grown to an army of 50,000. Although the Federal (non-auxiliary) troops still outnumbered the Cristeros, there was a decrease from about 80,000 to 70,000 by the end of the war. Federal officials had to continually work to replace the tens of thousands of soldiers who deserted each year that the rebellion continued.

If Mexican history had one thing to teach the Cristeros and the Federal army, it was this: one should never underestimate the power of a grass-roots revolution.

Camp accommodations.
This typical outdoor Cristero camp in Colima, supplied and staffed by volunteers, shows a unique level of informality and dependency.

AGICA

In contrast . . .
Staffed by paid personnel, Federal garrisons were often located in areas near train stations, enabling easier transportation of troops and supplies.

Armed and ready.
This Cristero poses with his automatic pistol—
a broomhandle Mauser.

Federal infantry and their weapons.
While at times short of men, the Federales rarely suffered
from arms shortages like the Cristeros did. Even the Federal
daily "minimum" allocation of ammunition—250 rounds per
soldier—significantly surpassed the Cristeros' daily allocation
of 20 rounds per soldier.

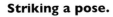

Striking a pose.
This group of Cristeros (above) stands in sharp
contrast to the Federal officers in military pose
(at right). The Federales are representative of several
military ranks, including a colonel, two lieutenants,
and a second lieutenant.

STRENGTHS AND WEAKNESSES IN THE CRISTERO ARMY

In many ways, the strengths and weaknesses of the Cristero army stemmed from its very nature as a popular, multi-class uprising, wherein peasants and other volunteers formed a makeshift army to fight the defects of a society they ultimately sought to restore. Thus, as the Cristero army battled the government and the laws, it had to navigate challenges within its own ranks as well.

Often, the best soldiers were part-time, entwining family life and Cristero service with frequent visits home. Sometimes an entire squad returned home to eat, feed their horses, or work before the rains came; and their wives or mothers would delouse them and wash their clothes. Their reasons for returning home were diverse: one left after not receiving word from his parents; another, to see his ill children. One soldier asked permission to leave so he could work the land in place of his sick parents; another, to earn a little money to save his family from destitution. Many soldiers simply felt overcome by homesickness and wanted to see their hometowns. These country men, both officers and soldiers alike, had to work the land and see their families.

Strong family ties also meant that the strength of units fluctuated as soldiers made visits home. Some organization—whether official or unofficial—helped lessen dramatic fluctuation in troop numbers through scheduled leaves. As one recalled, "Many took turns. I knew families where once the father would go, then the next time a son, and the next time another." One can also see this principle at work in the Valparaíso regiment:

Family ties. Cristeros pose with their family in an encampment of General Lauro Rocha's soldiers.

AGICA

AGICA

At the Hacienda de Tetapán.
As an example of the evolving and sometimes democratic military hierarchy, General Carlos Bouquet, whose troop appears here, was elected by his soldiers.

The discipline could not be rigorous, not because of the quality of the volunteers, but because of the fact that everyone had to attend to the sustenance of their families . . . With time, we were fixing these problems. The Valparaíso Regiment was organized so that each squadron . . . had its residence or families nearby, and they had weekly passes to visit their families, change clothes, etc. . . . each corporal went . . . accompanied by his seven soldiers. [This brought] more vigilance, more protection, more cleanliness, and much more peace of mind through the corps.

Another military inconvenience was that the combatants did not like moving too far from their home territory. And when ordered to do so, some even refused to follow their commanders. This regionalism pervaded the officers as well. Rare was the officer like Anatolio Partida, who had what General Aurelio Acevedo regarded as a special skill: the ability to leave his own territory. Similarly, at first the Cristeros of Michoacán refused to recognize the authority of General Jesús Degollado because they preferred their own leaders from Tingüindín and Los Reyes.

Extreme democracy and extreme individualism facilitated the beginnings of anarchy within the ranks, with many soldiers operating in accordance with personal desires, and fighting their own war for their own reasons. In the spirit of absolute egalitarianism, even differences of rank were not as enforced; it was difficult for some to accept that commanding officers had the right to a horse and binoculars, even when there were not enough for everybody.

Unpredictable leadership.
Felipe Sánchez (left), who operated in northeast Jalisco, was accused of abandoning another general's offensive.

AGICA

At times, soldiers even took the liberty of choosing—or refusing—to follow their leaders. During one expedition, Captain Pedro Cordero was entrusted with some men, and together they were placed under the command of Colonel Langarrica in Nayarit, near Huajimic. After a few weeks, Captain Cordero wished to return with his men to Zacatecas and place them under the command of General Justo Ávila. Colonel Langarrica, rather than forcing his authority over these troops, left it to a general consensus, saying, "Well, if all of your men are in agreement, then there's no problem, but if the majority want to stay with me, then either all or none must go." As it happened, only four of Cordero's soldiers wanted to leave with Cordero, and thus, the entire troop stayed with Langarrica. Cordero, for his part, fled in the dark one night, fearing a mutiny after his men showed such a display of loyalty to Langarrica.

Poverty and lack of communication deteriorated the chain of command, and conflicts between officers—especially lower officers—were numerous both on and off the battlefield. General Acevedo found his command seriously hindered at one critical moment by insubordination and a lack of cooperation among soldiers:

I reiterate my complaint and request the superior officers to investigate in order to define responsibilities. I say "responsibilities" because Major Anguiano retreated without orders, bringing with him in his desertion 200 men who were not under his command. . . . That he was supposed to be part of the advance on Santa María is clear, and this means he had even less reason to retreat as he had not even fired a shot, his cavalry had not suffered and his soldiers were not defeated by the weariness of combat. The desertion of Anguiano . . . meant that other forces were left in danger and other operations were left unfinished—operations that would have resulted in a victory heard far beyond our movement.

In another incident, Cristero officer Pedro Sandoval was abandoned in mid-attack by officers Felipe Sánchez and Mayor Chema Gutiérrez. A year later, Sandoval paid them back with the same treatment when he abandoned them both in the midst of battle.

Conflict off the battlefield damaged units as much as conflict on the battlefield, creating division and exacerbating disorganization. A number of areas were especially precarious: the division of recruitment responsibilities, requisitions, collection of war taxes, and the distribution of plunder after battle. Unfettered criticism and personal insults fed individualism, leading to heightened tensions and even duels. Some captains spread ill will against colonels for withholding spoils. As one soldier said bluntly, "If they give us orders, well . . . they should also give us something else, and they give us nothing . . . so what right do they have to give us orders?" Within the units, partisan spirit arose, pitting one faction against another. Conflict was only further exacerbated by the poverty facing the troops. After going two days without food, Major Refugio Luca-

AGICA

Cristeros kill a steer for food.
Activity like this one earned the Cristeros derogatory nicknames such as "cow-eating, starved, shirtless, sandal-wearing thieves."

tero and his men killed two cows to eat. Their superior disapproved and accused the men of robbery, giving them an ultimatum: either they leave or he would, since "he had already washed his hands of [them]."

In the end, the nature of the guerrilla war allowed the rise of banditry and excesses of all kinds. It was easy to respond to anarchy and lack of discipline with a hasty resort to executions of the guilty. Although unable to suppress it completely, the Cristeros were aware of these weaknesses and—as we will see in later chapters—did what they could to lessen the dangers of internal division, bad behavior, and excessive punishment.

WOMEN IN THE WAR EFFORT

Although the history of the Cristiada oftentimes seems to be a history about men and their actions, the fact is that an undeniably decisive role was played by women.

Even before the warfare started, the active role of women was a noticeable and sought-after support in the civic struggle. In 1925 and 1926, the women were among the first to participate. This led Unión Popular leader Anacleto González Flores to mobilize women in his civic campaign. He later praised them as the staunchest supporters of the boycott and considered them the Unión Popular's driving force.

In 1926, after the implementation of the Calles Law and the closure of churches, it was the women who were the most determined to stand guard over churches. The most famous case of this occurred on July 31, 1926, the day before the church ceremonies were officially suspended. At the Church of the Virgin of Guadalupe, in the important city of Guadalajara, women stayed on and occupied the church—and with good reason. A few days later, on the night of August 3, the army arrived at the church. Again, the bells of the church rang out, summoning the people of the neighborhood, and a violent battle lasting hours ensued. The army was held off from entering the church, but the next morning, an armistice had to be negotiated so that the more than 400 women and children were allowed to leave the church, while 390 men were conducted to the Federal barracks for further questioning.

Perhaps unexpectedly, it was a mix of faith and pride that also helped trigger the explosive rebellion. Many men took more secondary roles, standing up to the government and its soldiers only to defend their women companions. And yet, we also heard of women requesting more. A woman would tell a man that he was not a man if he accepted such atrocities committed against the faith without retaliating. A sister would goad her fifteen-year-old brother by telling him that he lacked the worth possessed by the defenders of "God's Cause." Prodded by their wives, mothers, girlfriends, and sisters, the men left for combat until many townships were left practically without men, while women worked the land to feed combatants or followed them into the mountains.

As the war progressed, the Cristero soldiers would not have been able to hold up without the constant help of women spies, suppliers, and organizers, who bore full responsibility for logistics and propaganda. This exceptional participation by women took the form of a role redefinition. As was

Motivating resistors.
After the government closed her convent, Sister Concepción de la Llata Acevedo ("Madre Conchita") drew a following with her zeal, charity, and resistance. She was imprisoned when one of her followers, José de León Toral, assassinated president-elect Obregón.

the case in many other places, in Mexico, women were closely dedicated to the home, the kitchen, and the Church. During the Cristiada, we find many examples of their dedication to family and faith opening up into new expression and new roles, especially among the working class. Considering the women's strong involvement in the parish, the restrictions on religious practice was an issue close to their hearts. In some ways, the same conditions that normally excluded women from leadership positions in economic and political issues situated them in a prime position to pave the way for an immediate, unanimous rebellion.

Women's involvement soon became formalized into an organization. After Unión Popular leader Anacleto González Flores was killed unexpectedly early in 1927 with his plan for organizing Cristero support unfinished, Luis Flores executed his plan and created a special outlet for female involvement. A young Cristero general in Jalisco described this new plan:

> Don Luis Flores was the name of a very ingenious gentleman . . . [who] with much diligence and good work, risked his skin to organize brigades and regiments with a group of good young women. After giving them good training and advice, he sent them to cities, haciendas, and towns with the detail troops to buy cartridges. Upon obtaining the ammunition in baskets, sacks, or better yet, in their vests, they were ordered to carry it themselves to our camps.

On June 21, 1927, just as the Cristero military was maturing, women's involvement in the Cristiada underwent its own vital turn when the first Joan of Arc Women's Brigade was established by Refugio Ramírez and sixteen young women. Purposed to support the war effort, the Brigade was a military group organized in regiments of 650 women, complete with the usual military ranks of generals, colonels, majors, captains, etc. The groups were designed to procure funds and provide supplies, ammunition, intelligence reports, and shelter to the combatants, in addition to hiding them and providing them with medical care.

The Brigade was named after Saint Joan of Arc—"the good girl from Lorraine"— who was canonized just a few years earlier in 1920. In the fifteenth century, she had led a popular French resistance against the British, thus epitomizing the union between religion and patriotism. Beginning in Zapopan, Jalisco, the organization soon extended throughout the country, even establishing itself in the Federal District in January 1928. According to tradition, those 17 young founders became 17,000—although in reality, their ranks swelled to 25,000 by the end of the war.

Execution of General Manuel Reyes.
A former Zapatist general, Manuel Reyes was one of Madre Conchita's followers. She persuaded him to take up arms during the Cristiada, and he was executed as a result.

Secrecy for the Brigade was important due to the sensitive nature of its work. Operating clandestinely, its members took an oath of obedience and secrecy. Additionally, once a woman achieved a certain degree of responsibility, she would never be left for long working in the same place and in the same branch of activity. Senior officers continually changed their identity and residence.

The Brigade proved to be very effective. From 1927 to 1929, it mobilized thousands of women who, by night and day, came and went from the cities to the battlefields. The Brigade women were mostly young and unmarried, between the ages of fifteen and twenty-five, and supervised by leaders no older than thirty. Auxiliary groups were comprised of older women, married

Leading women into the war.
María Goyaz (also known as "Celia Gómez" and "Celia Ortiz") was one of the four generals of the Joan of Arc Women's Brigade, and eventually became the head of the entire organization. She personally founded a brigade in the Federal District—Mexico's capital region. This was a remarkable feat eclipsed only by the fact that the government did not become aware of the Brigade's existence until the spring of 1929, almost two years after it was established.

women, and even children. Recruits hailed from all social classes, with the majority coming from the lower-middle class, especially from the densely populated city neighborhoods and the rural countryside. In the beginning, the Brigade's leadership was comprised of young women from the lower middle-class and those who had attended Catholic schools, but as the war progressed small-town girls quickly comprised the rank and file in a proportion of 90 percent. Even among the generals, the social and occupational backgrounds were humble; they were typists like María de la Luz Laraza, or junior employees like María Goyaz.

This suddenly conscious feminism even led the Women's Brigade to try to lead the war effort. They made each Cristero regiment the responsibility of one leader of the Brigade, who worked closely with its Cristero general to help provide the regiment with supplies and provisions. Later on, Cristero Commander-in-Chief Gorostieta reined in the Brigade's zeal by limiting it to the essential activities of administration, finance, medical care, propaganda, and provisioning. As we will see, some women went even further.

The most important duty of the Brigade was to deliver ammunition to the Cristeros. The essential supplies came from the manufacturing plant in Mexico, thanks to Catholic laborers and the support (or corruption) of certain authorities. Supplies were also obtained from military factories. In one instance in Coalcomán, the women were able to obtain ammunition directly from the Federal troops, who secretly traded the ammunition for food. As Federal General Cristóbal Rodríguez explained:

> There were civil servants, small town authorities, and even unscrupulous military men who forgot their duties and fell into the traps of these Loreleis of Saint Joan of Arc, providing them with cartridges from our factories. So the Cristeros fired ammunition made in the years 1927, 1928, and 1929, when our own troops still used those made in 1925 and 1926.

Stored in numerous small hiding places around the city, the ammunition passed with utmost secrecy to the young women from the provinces. None of the women knew their contacts, and they were always taken across the city blindfolded and at night. La Merced Market was an important center for the Brigade's activities. It helped camouflage their missions under the façade of commercial operations, often hiding the ammunition in coal, cement, or corn lorries. In the later days of the war, the Brigade even worked extensively with the complicity of some railroad workers, sending packages with false labels from Mexico City.

When the Cristeros could not get into the villages to pick up the ammunition, the women would bring it to them by transporting it in special vests worn underneath their dresses. Resembling shirts with many hollow pockets, the vests could carry between 500 and 700 cartridges of ammunition, which was triple the military allotment granted a soldier during the war.

AGICA

Amparo Mireles.
A leader of the Joan of Arc Women's Brigade in Zapopan, Jalisco.

AGICA

Catalina de la Peña.
A member of the Joan of Arc Women's Brigade in Xochimilco.

With these heavy loads of ammunition, the women rode the trains to Guanajuato, Oaxaca, Morelia, Guadalajara, Colima, and Tepic, while having to dodge the multiple control posts that surveyed stations and railways since the start of the war. Ammunition carriers would make at least one trip every three weeks.

In 1929, in a different example of dedication and international sympathy for the Cristero cause, Carmen Macías was sent to San Francisco through Mazatlán and Nogales by following one of the organization's "channels." There, she collected $7,000 among the Mexican residents in California to purchase ammunition. Fortunately, the war ended shortly thereafter; and upon learning of the suspension of hostilities, Macías cancelled her order.

Some women who possessed considerably more scientific knowledge than the Cristeros worked as crafters and instructors. They taught the Cristeros how to manufacture explosives, blow up trains, and handle batteries and detonators. There were risks: three, Sara Flores, María Gutiérrez, and Faustina Almeida, even died while preparing explosives.

Overall, women's support was critical and undeniable: Cristero Governor Miguel Gómez Loza of Jalisco even insisted upon the essential role of women in combat areas, where they had a decisive and often fundamental role, not as fighters, but as technicians and nurses in charge of the wounded.

Indeed, the care of the wounded hidden in the villages or towns was an important responsibility of the Brigade under the direction of Dr. Rigoberto Rincón Fregoso. While coordinating and assisting the efforts of the peasants to amass food supplies, members of the Brigade established rudimentary field hospitals in Los Altos, Colima, and south Jalisco, and an underground hospital in Guadalajara.

Still others in the Brigade took their military mission extremely seriously. In Guadalajara at the end of the war, they did not hesitate to resort to violence, carrying out kidnappings and executions to obtain ransoms, protect combatants, and deal with spies. Using every means at their disposal, they even organized dances in the villages so as to win the confidence of the Federal officers and obtain information. With the help of Andres Nuño and led by Josefina de Alba, these women organized a Direct Action group within the Women's Brigade, members of which killed a schismatic priest, Felipe Peréz, who was a government spy.

The combination of secrecy, skill, and absolute loyalty helped ensure that the Brigade remained stable and resilient in its dangerous work. Among its 25,000 members, there was not a single recorded defection. And, despite the

Pat down for pedestrians.
The difficulty of smuggling arms to Cristeros—a job often accomplished by women of the Brigade—is obvious here, as police in Mexico City search a man for hidden arms.

crisis, the Brigade suffered no major mass arrests by the government—until the end of March 1929.

During the three years of this bloody war, women both inside and outside the Brigade risked their lives for the cause in numerous ways. Their courage was incredible, but often came with a price. Many of these heroic women were jailed or raped, while still others lost their young lives—a fate they accepted with an unbending spirit.

Consider, for instance, María del Carmen ("Carmelita") Robles, the heart of the resistance in Huejuquilla, whose martyrdom earned her the reputation of being a saint. Carmelita founded the Daughters of Mary, a small community of about fifteen women, the youngest only fifteen years old and the oldest a widow of sixty-five years. Together, they lived a religious life, similar to that of the "beguines" of Europe's Renaissance. Carmelita herself was a young and brilliant woman. Courageous and a good speaker, she defeated Federal General Juan Bautista Vargas, who was in charge of the zone, in a public debate on religion, the revolution, and the State. Her determination proved fatal, however. It is unclear whether the general was romantically interested in her, or simply wanted to seduce her. But what is clear is that one day he took the whole community as his prisoners and left Huejuquilla with the women. During the night, Carmelita disappeared, and later, some of the women were raped and met other horrible fates. The youngest, María, whom I interviewed years later, told me that she was forced to stay for years as the wife of one of the soldiers. Forty years later, the remains of Carmelita Robles were found in a house that was being demolished to make way for the opening of a new street. They were solemnly buried.

María del Carmen Robles.
Along with her companions in this rare newspaper photograph, María (seated in the center) was imprisoned on January 18, 1928.

AGICA

Toñita Castillo.
One of many heroic members of the Women's Brigade, Toñita Castillo carried ammunition, medicine, money, and information to the combatants. She appears on horseback (second from left) with her mother (far left).

Then there was Agrippina Montes, called *La Coronela* ("The Colonel"), who organized the uprising of Cristero General Manuel Frías in Colón, and spread the uprising throughout the region with the energy of a soldier, although she herself was not a military commander. (So great was her reputation that the Federals even imagined her commanding the troops in the Sierra Gorda region.)

One woman—Petra Cabral—even replaced a civilian leader after he died. Known affectionately as "Doña Petrita," Cabral served as a kind of superintendent of the Valparaíso Regiment commanded by General Aurelio Acevedo. In my interviews with Acevedo, he told me many times that without the women, they would have been lost. "The poor little ones—*las pobrecitas*—were so valiant and suffered so much!" he would say.

The secretive work of these women meant that many of these heroes were unknown, and many of their efforts were poorly documented. This is especially true for those women whose husbands supported the government. Even the wife of Secretary of War General Joaquín Amaro, Elisa, was strongly opposed to the government's religious restrictions, attending secret church services and taking care of Cristero orphans. There was also a woman in President Calles's family who lent her house to serve as a warehouse for ammunition in Mexico City.

Whether known or unknown, what can be said with certainty is that the efforts of these heroic women were indispensable to the Cristero struggle.

Cristiada Timeline 1926

THE STATE AND THE CHURCH	DIPLOMACY AND U.S. RELATIONS	CATHOLIC IDENTITY, PROTESTS, AND THE WAR

THE STATE AND THE CHURCH

February 23
Government agents occupy La Sagrada Familia Church, inciting a riot. Seven Catholic protesters are killed.

June 3
Calles tells Archbishop Mora y del Río that no agitation "will be capable of changing the firm purpose of the government" to enforce the law.

June 14
Calles Law is signed.

July 24
Episcopal Committee of Mexican bishops votes to suspend Church liturgies.

August 1
Calles Law takes effect.

August 21
Mexican bishops meet with Calles in an effort to resolve the legal restrictions, but to no avail.

September
Mexican congress rejects petition with 2 million signatures to reform the constitution.

December
Mexican government finishes the year having spent one-fourth of its national budget on military expenses.

DIPLOMACY AND U.S. RELATIONS

May 10
Mexico expels the Vatican's Apostolic Delegate to Mexico, Monsignor Caruana.

June 12
U.S. Secretary of State Frank Kellogg warns that Mexico is "on trial before the world" for violating the Bucareli oil agreement.

August
U.S. receives more religious refugees.

August 3–5
The Knights of Columbus establishes the $1 million Mexican Fund.

September 1
Knights of Columbus delegation meets with President Coolidge regarding the Mexican situation.

October
The League's decision to pursue an armed struggle alienates U.S. support.

December 12
On this day—the feast of Our Lady of Guadalupe—U.S. bishops publish a pastoral letter on the Mexican situation.

CATHOLIC IDENTITY, PROTESTS, AND THE WAR

February 4
El Universal quotes as current some critical remarks of the constitution made many years in the past by Archbishop Mora y del Río, stirring agitation.

April 21
Mexican bishops declare "the moment has come to say *NON POSSUMUS* (WE CANNOT)," regarding the religious situation.

June 25
Mexican Bishops assert, "It would be criminal on our part to tolerate such a situation."

July 16
The League proclaims a national economic boycott.

August
Initial uprisings take place, marking the beginning of what is now called the Cristero rebellion.

September
The Cristeros celebrate their first victory over Federal forces.

18 November
Papal encyclical on Mexican persecution, *Iniquis Afflictisque*, is published.

December
The League names January 1, 1927, as the date for official insurrection.

Receiving Christ in Communion.
With hats removed but weapons still in hand, Cristeros pray as the priest distributes Communion during a Mass in Los Altos.

4.

Soldiers of Christ the King

RELIGIOUS FERVOR

Just as their Catholic faith played a vital role in their personal lives, so was religion a vital part in the life of the Cristeros. From the ever-present banners of Jesus, Mary, and the saints that were carried into battle, to the well-known cries of "Long live Christ the King" or "Long live Our Lady of Guadalupe," to the camps that were alive with Mass, prayer, and songs—the Cristeros kept faith alive in their lives.

Cristeros would meditate on biblical texts, which had been passed on to them through oral tradition and through the liturgy of the Mass. They were most inspired by those passages proclaiming events that involved the end of the world or the destiny of humanity, such as the announcement of the ruin of Jerusalem, the final judgment, the prophecies of persecution, and the Beatitudes.

AGICA

Carrying Christ.
Cristeros on horseback carry a banner with the words "*Viva Cristo Rey*." Other flags and banners often included pictures of Our Lady of Guadalupe.

The State's political program of the 1920s stirred up resentment among the people, and was even regarded as having religious significance. Seeking to stabilize the recovering country and secure its place in the changing world, the Mexican State underwent modernization by centralizing power under the State and by trying to unify Mexico's cultural diversity through the

Religious celebration.
Banners and indigenous dance are included in this celebration of Our Lady of Guadalupe in December of 1927.

formation of a new Mexican identity. Seeing their religious beliefs, institutions, and values ignored or even suppressed, the rural masses viewed the State as a tyrant—a King Herod, an antichrist, a devil whose kingdom was manifested in the chaos of lawlessness, torments, and massacres. Apocalyptic signs of doom were found in natural and political events—in the evil government, in the De la Huerta rebellion (1923–1924), in the drought, and in the deluge during the spring of 1926. Through this biblical lens, persecution was less of a surprise and more of a last sign indicating that the period of the "evil king" had begun.

In the Cristeros' testimonies, it is common to see the zeal of converts in their language and culture. After all, Christianity had been there for little more than four centuries. In 1926, its age in years was that of the Church at the time of Saint Augustine, who lived just a few centuries after Christ.

The government, in naming this band of rebels "Cristeros," gave important imagery to the uprising. Christ lent his name to this war—the Christ who was crowned with thorns and gave his life for humanity. And in the war, this sacrificial spirit was renewed as the Federal army hanged, burned, skinned, and executed the growing band bearing Christ's name.

Standing up for the freedom to practice their faith, Mexico's people transformed this historic moment of persecution into sacred days, thus elevating the lives of those touched by the tragedy into something glorious.

KNIGHTS OF COLUMBUS

As the government tried to refashion the practice of Catholicism into something purely "Mexican" by taking over churches and expelling any foreign hierarchy, another Catholic group—with members in both Mexico and the United States—caught its attention: the Knights of Columbus (K of C). In Mexico, this group was known by its Spanish name, the *Caballeros de Colón.* (More information on the background and mission of this organization appears on page 145.)

By the late 1920s, the Knights already had deep roots in Mexico as an organization connecting the Catholics of North and Latin America. The Order of the Knights of Columbus had established Guadalupe Council No. 1050 as its first council in Mexico in 1905. Then Supreme Knight Edward Hearn was given a most cordial welcome there by the leading Catholics in Mexico City and was received personally by President Profirio Díaz. The Archbishop of Mexico, Próspero Alarćon, was also glad to have the Knights active there to assist in the social activities of the Church, which had been invigorated by Pope Leo XIII's encyclical *Rerum Novarum.* The Knights expansion into Mexico, as well as into Canada, the Philippines, and Cuba, reflected the Order's increasingly international presence.

By 1923, there were forty-three councils in Mexico with some 6,000 "Caballeros." When the Mexican Revolution, which began in 1910, took an anti-clerical turn in 1914, that further stimulated the growth of the Caballeros, whose relations with their U.S. brothers proved to be very important to bringing information to the American public about the situation in Mexico from 1925 to 1938.

International brotherhood.
Active with the Knights as State Deputy, Luis Bustos (below) was also co-founder of the League in Mexico. Representing the Order in Mexico, a delegation of Knights (shown at the bottom of the page) is photographed at the organization's 1922 annual convention in Atlantic City, New Jersey. Despite increasing hostilities, the Order grew dramatically in Mexico until the Cristiada began.

Additionally, K of C councils built strong ties with the Catholic hierarchy by having both local and regional chaplains. In fact, over twenty of the ninety priests killed in the Cristiada were Knights of Columbus, and some were killed with the fellow Knights of their council, accentuating the ties. Some Cristeros were also Knights of Columbus, including General Luis Navarro Origel, who is famously called *El Primero Cristero* ("The First Cristero").

In the Mexican government's eyes, the Caballeros brought another challenge: internationality. While several purely Mexican organizations rose to combat the anticlerical actions of the State, the headquarters of the Knights of Columbus was outside Mexico. With hundreds of thousands of members in the United States—members who could be a potential source of resources—and with strong foreign ties built by the fraternal nature of the organization, the Knights had strengths that no other rising political Catholic organization in Mexico could claim. This connection also gave the Knights in the U.S. access to information about the situation in Mexico—something that will become important, as we will see in Chapter 7.

Although the Order of the Knights of Columbus did not provide support to the Cristeros' war effort, it remained a target for the Federal government. The Mexican Knights who had traveled to the United States for the 1926 convention were barred from returning to Mexico, forcing them to take up residence in Los Angeles—where many other Mexican refugees would also find a new home. In Mexico, the K of C headquarters was attacked, ransacked, and its records destroyed. Soon the Knights of Columbus in Mexico was forced underground.

And if the K of C was seen as a danger to the State's agenda, being a Knight had its own perils. To join, one had to be a practicing Catholic, so being a Knight was proof of one's allegiance to the Catholic Church. Thus, membership in the Caballeros brought its own dangers, as shown in the death of Yocundo Durán of Chihuahua, who was captured while walking home one day in January 1927. Federal General Valles, who had just come out of a tavern, spotted Durán. First, Valles had one of his soldiers ask Durán if he was a member of the Knights of Columbus. Durán confirmed, asking if there was any evil in it. Durán was declared a "subversive Catholic" and immediately shot. His body was carried home to his wife in a bricklayer's cart.

Relic of a raid. When Federal soldiers raided the Knights of Columbus offices in Mexico City, they were ordered to bayonet this painting of Our Lady of Guadalupe. But they refrained from damaging her image, and bayoneted the area around her instead.

THE CLERGY

A different, but no less vital source of spiritual support came from the clergy. Finding a priest, however, was difficult, as priests could no longer be public about their ministry and had to be exceptionally discreet in celebrating the sacraments. The suspension of religious ceremonies forced all the Catholic liturgies and rites—Mass, baptisms, marriages, etc.—to be performed in secret. Getting caught at a clandestine liturgy could be dangerous, both for the priest and for those attending.

Moreover, imprisonment and exile reduced the number of priests in Mexico. Shortly after issuing the Calles Law in 1926, the president expelled all foreign priests in Mexico—about 400 in number. Instantly, Mexican Catholics were deprived of 10 percent of their priests. Many Mexican-born priests and religious (including bishops) were imprisoned or expelled, further reducing the number of available priests. Additionally, by 1929, at least ninety priests were executed as the Federal forces sought to effectively sever the Cristeros from their clergy.

The vast majority of priests did not take up arms. To the State, their ministry was reason enough. Take, for example, several priests (and Knights of Columbus members) who were canonized by Pope John Paul II. Father Rodrigo Aguilar Alemán sacrificed his life to protect the identities of seminarians. Father Luis Batís Sáinz was put before a firing squad for refusing to submit to the anti-religious laws. Father Mateo Correa Magallanes was executed when he refused to break the seal of confession of his fellow inmates. While praying the rosary, Father Miguel de la Mora

Parish without borders.
Dressed in vestments, a priest is ready to celebrate Mass at the Cristero camp at Tetilla, in southern Jalisco. Beside him—also breaking the law with her religious attire—is a nun wearing a habit.

AGICA

Safety in secrecy.
Here, people attend Mass at a clandestine chapel in Zacatecas. As all religious ceremonies were forbidden by law, priests had to be very discreet when it came to celebrating the sacraments and continuing their priestly ministries. The performance of Catholic rites and liturgies, including Mass, baptisms, marriages, confessions, and last rites, were punishable by imprisonment and even death for both the clergy and those in attendance. These rites and ceremonies were performed with great discretion and often held in the homes of the faithful.

de la Mora (not to be confused with Archbishop Miguel de la Mora) was shot for signing a letter that spoke out against the anti-religious laws. Father Pedro de Jesús Maldonado Lucero, who was caught administering the sacraments, was beaten and later executed. While preparing to say Mass, Father José María Robles Hurtado was captured and killed the next morning.

Not all those executed were Knights. The most famous priest killed was Jesuit Miguel Pro. Falsely accused of the assassination attempt on former President Obregón, he was executed along with his brother and two of the actual culprits without a trial. (See "The Execution of Father Miguel Pro" on page 89.) Thousands came to honor him at his funeral, exclaiming, "Make way for the martyrs of Christ the King!" In 1988, Father Pro was beatified by Pope John Paul II.

Additionally, by the nature of their guerilla warfare on the outskirts of urban areas, the Cristeros' sacramental life depended on priests who were willing to endure the same conditions as the Cristeros themselves: living undercover, away from Federal centers of control. The Federal government was aware of this, and strategically withdrew almost all the priests from rural parishes and forced them into the larger towns and cities. This practice not only reduced the number of priests available to the Cristeros, but also allowed government officials to keep a closer watch on the priests, who were easier to monitor in the cities. As a result, there were about as many priests who were openly hostile to the Cristeros as there were priests sympathetic to them.

The priests who supported the Cristeros helped in roughly three areas: chaplain support, financial support, and military support. Their military involvement, however, was rather small; despite the fact that the government often targeted priests as "ringleaders" of rebellion, only five priests actually bore arms against the State. In fact, the majority of the priests who supported the Cristeros sought peace and refused to encourage violence. For example, during a mass uprising in Totatiche, Jalisco, that went against the will of Father Cristóbal Magallanes, the priest explained, "The Church does not need weapons for its defense. The Lord takes care of it."

The rest of the priests who were "sympathetic" to the Cristeros served as chaplains, administering sacraments secretly, or they would collect alms. In the Cristeros' camps, they offered Mass and heard confessions. With the

Martyred Knights.
Of the ninety priests killed during the Cristiada, twenty belonged to the Knights of Columbus. These six were among the first to be canonized as saints.

Rodrigo Aguilar
Alemán

Luis Batís
Sáinz

Mateo Correa
Magallanes

Miguel de la Mora
de la Mora

priest shortage and with soldiers living so close to their homes, families would sometimes attend Mass in the makeshift camps as well. As one person remarked, "Now that the priests had left, the only priest in the Valley of Jérez and Tepetongo was Father Félix de la Castañeda in Juanchorrey, and the faithful came from all over the region, coming by night in caravans."

As the Cristeros' revolutionary activities divided Catholics and incited Federal retaliation, it became even harder for the Cristero army to find priests. General Manuel Michel was lucky to have his cousin, Father Guadalupe Michel, as his company's chaplain. But in March 1929, when Father Guadalupe was shot in Manzanillo, Colima, the general had great difficulty finding a replacement for him. As Father B. Santiago, another priest, told him, "In all this region, there is not one of my profession who will accompany you in your adventures. Those whom I have approached do not want to even talk about it, because they do not want to have anything to do with you."

Father Miguel Pro.

Despite the laws forbidding the practice of religious rites and celebrations, the elusive Father Pro continued to tirelessly tend to the spiritual needs of the faithful. Among his many accomplishments, the thirty-six-year-old priest had arranged for a number of "safe houses" throughout the city in which Mass and the sacraments could be celebrated. He also visited prisoners to offer comfort and secretly hear their confessions, and catered to the poor— helping impoverished families pay their rent and feed their children. When President Calles became aware of the ceaseless apostolic activities of this underground cleric, a warrant was issued for his arrest. When Father Pro was eventually picked up for a crime he didn't commit, Calles was determined to have him executed in spite of his innocence. (See "The Execution of Father Miguel Pro" beginning on the next page.)

Pedro de Jesús
Maldonado Lucero

José María
Robles Hurtado

In Focus
The Execution of Father Miguel Pro

Perhaps some of the most iconic images of the Mexican persecution are the photographs of the execution of Father Miguel Pro, his brother Humberto Pro, Juan Antonio Tirado, and Luis Segura Vilchis. The men were charged with an assassination attempt against former President Álvaro Obregón, although only two—Tirado and Vilchis—were guilty. (The innocence of Miguel and Humberto Pro was declared prior to the execution; after the execution, they were exonerated.)

President Calles ordered the execution without a trial. He also expressly wished the presence of reporters and photographers to document the event, which took place on November 23, 1927. Calles believed that the official reports and photographs would discourage further Catholic resistance and activism. The plan backfired. In fact, the execution only fueled the religious conflict to reach new levels of resentment and hostility on both sides, while the publication of the photos in the United States and beyond helped to raise sympathy for Mexican Catholics.

Father Miguel Pro

Humberto Pro

Juan Antonio Tirado

Luis Segura Vilchis

The executioner.
In this photograph, Federal Chief of Police Roberto Cruz speaks with the father of Miguel and Humberto Pro. Cruz kept President Calles informed throughout the investigation and was personally given the order to carry out the execution.

The personal side of a priest's execution.
The father of Miguel and Humberto Pro attends their execution. He nearly lost a third son, Roberto, who was also taken in for questioning, but later released.

Incognito.
Father Miguel Pro walks to his execution in civilian clothes. He was known for using creative disguises to avoid capture while continuing his priestly ministry.

A last prayer.
The falsely accused priest kneels to pray before his execution. Bold in his underground ministry, Father Pro secretly continued saying Mass. Part of the "evidence" used against him was the discovery of his Mass kit at the home of Segura Vilchis.

Imitation of Christ.
Before he is executed, Father Pro stands with head held high as he faces the firing squad. In a gesture of obvious symbolism, he stretches out his arms to form a cross before the shots are fired.

Crowds of mourners.
Thousands lined the streets in Mexico City for the Pro brothers' funeral procession. Within days, miracles were attributed to Miguel Pro, who was canonized as a saint some decades later.

SAINTS OR DEVILS?

The Cristero rebellion attracted truly moral and religious men, as well as those with less reputable character. At the two behavioral extremes, we find two priest-generals—Father Aristeo Pedroza and Father José Reyes Vega. Father Pedroza, nicknamed "the pure one," motivated his troops and later the entire Los Altos Brigade with an iron discipline. Father Reyes Vega, commander of regiments in west Guanajuato, was nicknamed "Pancho Villa in a cassock." He was particularly censured for his love affairs and the ease with which he sent Federal prisoners to the firing squad. Nevertheless, he proved to be a natural-born strategist capable of defeating the Federal army in open battle.

AGICA

Father Pedroza, "The Pure One." One of only five combatant priests, Aristeo Pedroza (playing chess here, against Father Vega) earned the nickname for his impeccable morals.

In the wake of the Mexican Revolution from 1910 to 1920, some men who had followed the real Francisco "Pancho" Villa now saw the Cristero war as an opportunity to correct mistakes and atone for sins committed in the previous revolutions. General Aurelio Acevedo explained:

Our movement is in defense of the rights of the Apostolic Roman Catholic Church, and we treat our people as Catholics and citizens of this nation. Our leader is Christ the King and, therefore, this is an orderly movement that includes all those who never took part in previous revolutions and are now ready to take on the world. In our ranks are [also] soldiers of previous wars, but they obey the new order and set aside their old grudges and personal hatreds, like any soldier of Christ. General Ávila had accepted these conditions and had behaved well. The same could not be said of some who were friends of his in other times. Those who try to play the *Villistas* will be expelled immediately, by order or by force, like those who joined us in the beginning and did not submit to the regimen of order.

As General Acevedo mentioned, General Justo Ávila showed a great transformation. As a former officer under Francisco "Pancho" Villa from 1913 to 1920, Ávila and his troops had been terrible marauders, killers, and rapists. But during the Cristiada, he reformed his ways as commander of the Guadalupe Regiment of the Quintanar Brigade. He prohibited the slightest theft; banned women from living among his troops; and prohibited his soldiers from having any women other than their legitimate wives, so that, as he explained, "My troop is not sullied. I don't want people like that." In a similar way, another

Villa follower, the once infamous Colonel Sabino Salas, having grown tired of killing, reformed himself and even granted pardons to his enemies.

The nature of guerrilla warfare could not prevent all banditry and excesses, and this posed problems within the Cristero ranks. In 1928, General Esteban Caro, leader of the Western Sector of the Southern Division and eastern Nayarit, and famous for his superhuman valor, began to slide down the moral slope toward *bandolerismo* or banditry. When those from Atenguillo, Jalisco, made accusations of rape against Caro, General Jesús Degollado decided to intervene, circulating a message to all the officers who were anticipating the imposition of the death penalty for this crime. Then, although aware of the danger of chastising Caro in front of his own troops, Degollado went to him unaccompanied, reprimanded him severely, and ordered Caro's own escort to arrest him. Thereafter, Caro repented and asked permission to return to service as a simple soldier, on the condition that a chaplain accompany him. His request was accepted, and Caro returned to service with Father Lorenzo Plascencia, who witnessed and confirmed Caro's conversion of heart up to the moment of Caro's death in 1929, during a charge on the enemy.

Others, however, did not change their ways so readily. At the same time that Caro fought and died as a reformed man, one of his officers, Jesús "the Zarco" Zepeda, believed the time had come to return to the criminal ways of his superior. In April 1929, he was tried for insubordination and banditry in the Ayutla and Tenamaxtlán regions (in Jalisco). The Navarro brothers, from the Etzatlán region, also preyed on their own through banditry until General Degollado sent General José Gutiérrez to bring them under control. In other instances, the Cristero Nemesio López resorted to theft, and was later disarmed and discharged in December 1926 by General Pedro Quintanar, while J. Rosario Guillén, an officer assigned near Cocula, Jalisco, was executed for rape by General Gutiérrez. One Cristero told me about Martín Calderón, who "was the oldest revolutionary; his life full of crimes and immoralities . . . [who] joined the revolution thinking that it was like all the others"; but after fighting "well for several months . . . he realized that it was not like the previous ones and . . . left." Later, the Cristeros wanted Calderón executed for murdering a woman. "From then on, he was the greatest enemy of the Cristeros, becoming an agent of the Talpa government."

In the face of such anarchy and lack of discipline, it could be easy to

AGICA

Father Vega, "Pancho Villa in a Cassock."
In contrast to Father Pedroza, priest-general José Reyes Vega was known for his less-than-saintly character. He was also known for the infamous 1927 train raid (see pages 44–45).

hastily resort to executions of the guilty, just as the State did. Aware of this, Cristero authorities tried to lessen its use without suppressing it completely. Cristero military and civil authorities struggled to rule with peace and morality, as expressed in the following "Instructions to be followed by guerrilla officers":

1) First and foremost, observe strict morality among your soldiers . . . 2) Appear relentless with the enemy, taking all that belongs to them and distributing it equitably and with your own hands among your soldiers. 3) If you obtain merchandise on the road . . . demand bills . . . provide a duplicate receipt . . . to use to inform the command . . . 4) If you obtain cars or trucks, keep careful records of them . . . 5) If you confiscate merchandise and liquor of any kind is among it, throw it away immediately. 6) Upon taking merchandise from any establishment, demand that the owner give you a copy of its value . . . 7) For no reason should you allow your soldiers to take anything for themselves.

The moral dimension of the Cristero movement was more than an ideological stand; it served important practical and military purposes as well. For instance, the authorities worried greatly about alcohol trafficking, gambling, drinking, and public celebration, as these could all potentially lead to violence while increasing the army's vulnerability to ambush. Drinking and gambling were punished severely, and parties themselves were prohibited from the time the war was declared in August 1926. The presence of chaplains sometimes helped keep behavior in check, as in the case of Father Ramón Pérez, chaplain of the Southern Division, who halted a victory party by breaking bottles and a guitar. While the priest's actions initially provoked anger and protest from the men, eventually they "held themselves in check," for they respected the chaplain "as a friend and as a father." And though the Cristero leaders had nothing against music, they understood that "where there is music, there is wine, and the enemy can surprise us drunk."

AGICA

From Federal soldier to Cristero.
Federal army veteran Lorenzo Arreola eventually commanded a Cristero division in Nayarit. His experience as a Federal soldier might explain his mischievousness. In 1927, overjoyed (and somewhat drunk) after capturing the town of Ameca, he telephoned the Federal headquarters and invited the Federales to evacuate the place.

The stark contrast between the pious priest-general Father Aristeo Pedroza and the unprincipled priest-general Father José Reyes Vega mentioned earlier in this chapter shows the range of people fighting for the Cristeros. Yet, whatever an individual Cristero's moral disposition may have been, the determination and dedication of the Cristero army to morality was undeniable, leading one ranch boss to say, "I swore I would not return to take up arms because I believed it was not possible to bring morality to troops, but it is true that you have accomplished it, although I don't know how."

FROM MARTYRDOM TO GOLDEN LEGEND

Literature, song lyrics, and movies have popularized the image of the brave Mexican who is indifferent to life and death, while his killers weep out of admiration. In the Cristiada, the anecdotal repertoire is likewise full of heroic, proud, and amazing deaths that left witnesses and even the executioners filled with envy and esteem. But there was a significant difference: the countless examples of courage displayed by Cristeros when facing death grew from their religious fervor and the religious nature of their cause.

It was not indifference to life or resignation to fate that made these men and women face death so bravely. Most importantly, they saw themselves as becoming companions of Christ, and they understood their sacrifices in light of his cross. General Aurelio Acevedo, who saw his daughter Nieves being born in the shade of a nopal cactus, described how he viewed in "the person of the wretched Cristeros . . . a similarity with the birth of [God's] Sacred Son in Bethlehem."

Many Cristeros felt strongly that they were living during an extraordinary period in time and would later describe the war as a time of "great adventure, so saintly and noble." Some even went so far as to see the persecution against the Church in Mexico as a great favor, the proof of the love of the Virgin of Guadalupe and Christ the King for their country. For them, a life given for this cause would advance the salvation of Mexico and the world. Indeed, the Cristero veteran Ezequiel Mendoza Barragán even quoted Revelations 6:11—a reference to martyrs waiting in heaven for the end of times— saying of his fallen comrades, "Each of them was given a white robe, and

AGICA

Martyrs of León.
This postcard commemorates the death of three young Catholics, executed by the government in Guanajuato.

they were told to be patient a little while longer until the number was filled by their fellow servants and brothers who were going to be killed as they had been."

Just as in their lives, the tradition of remembering and reciting passages from the Bible was an important element in their expression of faith. For some, it continued even at the point of death. It was in these sacred texts where many discovered their lofty dignity. Echoing Matthew 10:28, Cosme Herrera Valencia, a civilian executed by Federal General Carrillo in Degollado, Jalisco, for refusing to serve in the army, said before dying, "I claim the life of my soul, not of my body."

Often, the Federals would give captured Cristero soldiers the opportunity, in lieu of death, to withdraw their allegiances and join the Federal side. Many, as in the case of Cosme Herrera Valencia, chose to die rather than give in. Pedro Muñoz, a Cristero from the Valparaíso Regiment, dictated a letter just before dying, recounting: "My mother came to see me at Fresnillo. She spoke to two lawyers. One said I should join the Callista ranks, but I did not give in." Likewise, Norberto López, executed by a firing squad in Encarnación de Díaz in 1928, refused the pardon offered to him, saying that "since I took up arms, I was determined to give up my life for Christ; I am not about to put my fast to waste at quarter to twelve."

To some extent, this willingness to confront violent death in defense of religious liberty seemed to go against basic human fear. But because of their belief in God and heaven, death was not entirely feared, and knowing that death might be very near was even welcomed. In peaceful times, the "faithful" valued preparing themselves for death spiritually, dreading the possibility of dying suddenly or in their sleep without being able to receive the sacraments. Additionally, being killed for their faith was believed to be one of the best expressions of one's love of Christ, for which one would be welcomed into heaven. Honorio Lamas, a young man who was executed with

Revered as a martyr.
The body of Colonel Cayetano Álvarez of the Guadalupe Regiment in Los Altos is laid out with the palm branch—a symbol of martyrdom.

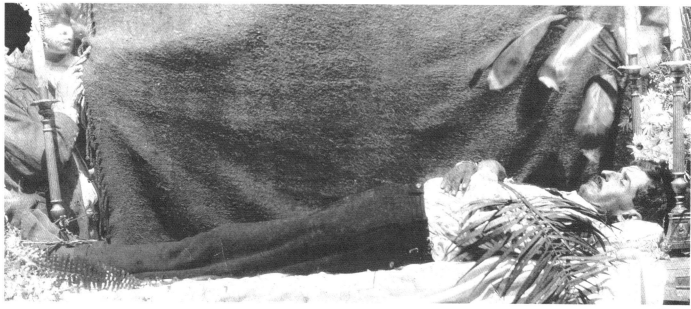

AGICA

his father, Manuel Lamas, offered these words of consolation to his mother: "How easy it is to get to heaven now, Mother!" One Cristero went so far as to say, even to the possible chagrin of the priest to whom he spoke, "If I am going to die for Christ, I don't need a confession . . . It is said that blood baptism is better than ordinary baptism."

Thus, it is understandable, if amusing, to hear also of Father José María Espinosa—a poorly educated parish priest who had great difficulty in entering the priesthood due to his lack of education. He thought that he could distribute "safe-conducts" to those who died with courage, guaranteeing them heaven.

Whether "theologically correct" or not, all of these examples show the belief in the purpose and worth of a martyr's death. As famously expressed by the early Christian theologian Tertullian, "the blood of the martyrs is the seed of the Church." Cristero colonel Ezequiel Mendoza Barragán explained:

> You and I regret in a heartfelt way the death of those men who by faith gave up their lives, families, and other earthly interests; and shed their blood for the sake of God and our beloved homeland as true Christian martyrs do. Their blood, together with that of our Lord Jesus Christ and that of all the martyrs of the Holy Spirit, will afford us from God the Father the blessings we hope for on earth and in heaven.

A heavy burden.
The body of Jesús Lopes is held up for one final portrait. The Cristero from Michoacán was killed in front of his wife and young son.

Confident about the righteousness of their cause, these martyrs believed that they were given a necessary part to play in God's providence.

Whether immediately witnessing the executions, making funeral arrangements afterwards, or collecting the blood of martyrs as a relic, the population always participated in these exemplary deaths—the deaths of family, friends, and fellow Catholics. Josefina Arellano, who witnessed the death of her very young brother-in-law, Silverio, described it this way:

> Silverio, who was younger than my husband, lifted the ridged tile that covered the door, and greeted the government with the sweet cry of "Long live Christ the King!" . . . And when the sound of his voice faded, he was already on his way to receive martyrdom's palm and his crown, because he would always say that he was a Catholic with no interest other than his love for Christ.

Continuing her narrative, she recalled what she did afterwards:

> Leaving the kids in the arms of Domingo [her brother], I lifted the ridged tile to go out, stepping on the dead. I stood at the door. Oh, my God! What did I see? Over the fence, a multitude of weapons pointed at me. My eyesight became foggy, my body shuddered, but I realized that this hour represented my victory, I imagined the crown and almost touched the palm.

Making an example.
The brutalized body of Father Gumersindo Sedano of Zapotlán el Grande, Jalisco, is propped up and tied to a tree. He is identified by the paper at his knees.

EJECUCION DE CRISTEROS POR SOLDADOS FEDERALES EN LAS AFUERAS DE SAN GABRIEL JAL. EL 8 DE OCT. DE 1927. EN EL MISMO SITIO LOS MILITARES FUERON EMBOSCADOS SUFRIENDO LA MISMA SUERTE.

Artistic memory.
This painting depicts the execution of five Cristeros in Jalisco, on October 8, 1927. The text notes that later, some Federal soldiers received the same treatment.

The memory of these martyrs, even decades after their death, still had the power to move people. In 1963, when the remains of Carmelita Robles—founder of the Daughters of Mary in Huejuquilla (and whose story is presented in Chapter 3)—was recovered, people again came together to mourn and celebrate a fallen daughter. A wake lasting eight days was held, and people came from all around Mexico.

Countless expressions of the longing for heaven have been recorded among the Cristero survivors. In several places, even the unarmed elderly were reported to have joined the uprising, exclaiming, "We need to earn our way to heaven now that it's cheaper," or "How much our grandparents would have appreciated earning thus the assurance of heaven, and now God provides it for us; I'm ready to leave." Some even expressed disappointment afterwards at not being chosen among the martyrs. Claudio Becerra, spared because of his young age, was the only survivor of the twenty-seven people who were shot in Sahuayo (Michoacán) on March 21, 1927. Years later, in 1965, he recalled the heroic deaths of his companions as he wept at their crypt, lamenting that "God didn't want me to be a martyr."

This talk about heavenly rewards and the hope that their trials and martyrdoms would be steps toward establishing a new age did not impair the Cristeros' ability to be open to peace. They felt that martyrs might please God with their faithfulness, but that the death of the enemy was not pleasing to God. This was shown by their obedience in accepting peace terms even when they had the upper hand in the war.

Many of these martyrs have since been officially recognized for their holiness and faithfulness to Christ. On May 21, 2000, the first twenty-five Mexican martyrs were canonized by Pope John Paul II. Of the twenty-five men, fifteen hailed from Jalisco; the rest were from Aguascalientes, Chihuahua, Durango, Guerrero, Michoacán, and Zacatecas. Twenty-two were priests and three were laymen.

Each of those canonized had been killed—martyred—during the Cristiada; and each of these martyrs was a civilian, not a combatant. They were often tortured before being hung or shot by a firing squad. Included among them were Father Cristóbal Magallanes, who served as the priest of Totatiche and was very much loved in the area of Huejuquilla el Alto in Jalisco; Father Agustín Caloca; Father Toribio Romo González of Los Altos of Jalisco; Father Luis Batís Sáinz from Chalchihuites, Zacatecas, whose assassination on August 15, 1926, caused the uprising of the famous General Pedro Quintanar; and Father David Uribe Velasco of Buenavista de Cuéllar, Guerrero, who was popularly known for his saintliness.

Along with those who have since been officially recognized, there are numerous others, fallen in secret, who bore witness to their deepest dignity through daily acts of faith. During that time, even claiming the body

Honoring the dead.
The body of Brigido González, shot by Federal soldiers in San Miguel el Alto, Jalisco, lies covered with flowers.

AGICA

Mourners at a tomb.
Makeshift graves like this one were not uncommon. Here, the body of a Cristero is covered with rocks and marked with a cross of sticks.

of a victim and holding a funeral were considered acts of insubordination and punishable under the law. Engaging in secret worship, hiding a priest, keeping the Blessed Sacrament, preserving images and relics, using forbidden badges, saying "Long live Christ the King!," pleading with authorities to stop an execution—all were punishable acts. And yet they were performed.

Over the years, I have compiled a list of 250 individuals whose previously untold sacrifices likewise merit the title of martyrdom. Today, their words, witnesses, and readiness to die may seem strange to us; but we cannot discount the fact that their suffering and death had meaning. Life and death had a place in God's plan—a plan filled with hope. When reflecting on his brother's death, Carlos Vargas described how, "In a way, I feel distressed, but bless his heart, at least he died on a good day; he passed away on Good Friday. As far as I'm told, he had a sweet death. Good for him!" As Doña Petra Cabral walked by civilians hanged by General Juan Bautista Vargas, she thought: "May God keep them in his sacred glory; the humble will inherit the Kingdom of Heaven."

As their deaths had more meaning, the grieving was different, perhaps more profound in light of God's providence. From being persecuted souls, these brave men and women became martyrs. Their deaths and losses were indeed cause for mourning and grief. But their faithfulness was cause to rejoice.

Cristiada Timeline 1927

| THE STATE AND THE CHURCH | DIPLOMACY AND U.S. RELATIONS | CATHOLIC IDENTITY, PROTESTS, AND THE WAR |

THE STATE AND THE CHURCH

January 18
U.S. military attaché estimates only 40,000 in Federal army (Federal army claims 70,000).

April 21
Mexican government exiles more Mexican bishops.

July–August
Meetings are held in San Antonio, Texas, between Mexican bishops and Mexican officials.

October
Serrano-Gómez rebellion against Obregón's presidential candidacy begins. It ends in November.

November 23
Father Miguel Pro and Humberto Pro are executed.

DIPLOMACY AND U.S. RELATIONS

January 1
Mexico's oil and land laws take effect, limiting foreign holdings.

July 18
James Sheffield resigns as U.S. Ambassador to Mexico.

September 20
Dwight D. Morrow is appointed U.S. Ambassador to Mexico.

December 13–14
Famed aviator Charles Lindbergh flies from Washington, DC to Mexico City as a gesture of goodwill.

CATHOLIC IDENTITY, PROTESTS, AND THE WAR

January 1
Rebellion officially begins, leading to insurrection in Mexico's entire central-west region.

April 1
Unión Popular founder, Anacleto González Flores, is executed.

April 19
Cristero General Vega and his troops raid a bank train, resulting in the deaths of Federal soldiers and civilians.

June
Cristeros total 20,000 in number.

June 21
Joan of Arc Women's Brigade is founded in Zapopan, Jalisco, to support the Cristeros.

July
The League hires former military leader Enrique Gorostieta as a Cristero commander.

Federal army pacifies the Yaqui rebellion, gaining more troops as a result.

August
U.S. and Mexico are at odds over the Nicaraguan Revolution.

November 5
Failed assassination attempt is made against president-elect Obregón.

December
Rebellion in the western region grows; Cristeros call themselves the "Army of National Liberation."

Christ at the center.
Posing with his officers under a banner of Christ the King, General Miguel Anguiano (seated) also served as a Cristero civilian leader. He later became a priest.

5.

The Cristero Government

THE DESIRE FOR GOVERNMENT

In the spring of 1927, in addition to the military revolution against the State, a new type of revolution began: the Cristeros started to organize themselves and the surrounding areas into a kind of parallel government. Before the Cristero conflict, they would not have even dreamed of such a thing, but the events of the war had changed this. The dramatic evolution of the conflict, the failure of legal recourse, and the spontaneous mobilization of the people all fed the hopes of the League's leaders. They soon desired not only to free the Church from the despised laws, but also to bring about the downfall of the regime and seize power for themselves.

From the first day of mass uprising in January 1927, the rebels expressed their determination to establish an essentially fair government, rooted in justice and popular democracy. In this regard, the uprising was more of a symbolic gesture of democracy than an effective force trying to attain it. It channeled the oldest concepts of democracy: the belief in a popular vote and in the virtues of the people's unanimous participation in government. One did not even need to bear arms to participate; rather, it was about demanding one's rights merely by being present.

The Cristeros' aspiration for a fair, organized government was strengthened as threats from the State continued and as their military needs increased. In many places, the unarmed masses instituted governmental changes by replacing town officials with new authorities who were elected by popular acclaim. Soon the Cristeros had created a government of their own—one that managed the "autonomous republics" from which the Federal army had been expelled. Eventually, Cristero governments were established in Jalisco, Guanajuato, Colima, Zacatecas, Coalcomán (Michoacán), and the Sierra Gorda.

THE UNIÓN POPULAR AND CRISTERO GOVERNMENT

The Cristero government succeeded only because of the zeal of many individuals. By utilizing the strength of other Catholic organizations, it kept alive the very sentiments that the Mexican Federal government sought to suppress.

One organization, the Unión Popular (UP), proved to be a remarkable instrument for the Cristero government, filling many high-level administrative and judicial positions. Founded before the outbreak of war by Anacleto González Flores (nicknamed "El Maestro"), the Unión Popular was created to advance the civil struggle against the government's anti-Catholic laws by spreading the teachings of the Church and helping Catholics organize the resistance. Inspired by the model of Mohandas Gandhi in India, González Flores was dedicated to nonviolent resistance. His Unión Popular became a civil and political organization composed of the masses.

The Unión Popular's popularity.
Open to everyone, the Unión Popular had broad influence throughout Jalisco and some of the surrounding states. This 1926 recruitment pamphlet draws attention to the League's ties with the Unión Popular in Aguascalientes.

"El Maestro."
Anacleto González Flores, founder of the Unión Popular, was known as "El Maestro" ("The Master"). While in hiding during the Cristiada, he was unwittingly betrayed by an ACJM member, who was tricked into disclosing his whereabouts. This led to his brutal murder.

Flores died just as the war began, and soon the Unión Popular proved a fertile recruiting ground for Cristero officials. Financed by dues that were minimal yet consistent, the UP elected its leaders democratically and recruited new members; soon its membership grew to 100,000. Members were absolutely loyal to their local organization leaders right down to the last village. In the vast zones of Jalisco and west Guanajuato, where the Unión Popular was most influential, the Cristeros sustained combat for three straight years—except for a brief respite in March and April of 1929, when they undisputedly controlled the regions.

One main responsibility of the clandestine government was to keep up the war effort by organizing people to provide logistical support and information. For this job, the Unión Popular was transformed into a military and administrative network. Under its direction, the towns and cities were organized in blocks that were grouped into distinct sections. The rules of underground life were soon assimilated. Civilian leaders filled many roles, as one document outlined their responsibilities:

> The local civilian leaders of the National Liberation Government in the State of Jalisco, who will nearly always be the same leaders of [the] Unión Popular, will have the following obligations and powers: 1) keeping the enthusiasm for the movement alive and strong; 2) assisting the civilian zone leader in the collection of taxes; 3) assisting our army as much as possible in duties such as recruitment, and the collection of provisions necessary for war and survival; 4) keeping close watch over our soldiers and defectors to avoid waste of weapons and ammunition; 5) investigating and keeping track of weapons and ammunition held by civilians; 6) keeping constant surveillance and reporting on enemy movements; 7) organizing and directing postal service to our government and army; 8) ensuring that, when in transit through your jurisdiction, our army has access to everything it needs to survive; 9) assisting our soldiers' families, as well as the widows and orphans; 10) ensuring that justice is done by bringing crimes before the authorities, whether military or judicial; 11) keeping close watch over the conduct of those who support the work of Calles.

As an organization in a volatile time and place, the Unión Popular also proved its durability by surviving the deaths of its leaders. First, in April 1927, Anacleto González Flores became a martyr for the cause when he was brutally murdered by Federal soldiers. He had refused to divulge the location of Cristero leaders, so the soldiers tortured him to death—they hung him by his thumbs and stabbed him repeatedly with a bayonet until a fatal thrust pierced his heart. After the execution, two others assumed leadership of the Unión Popular: Andrés Nuño, a fifty-year-old trade union member; and the organization's treasurer, Miguel Gómez Loza,

A blow to the Unión Popular.
UP secretary Luis Padilla Gómez is seen here at work. He was picked up by Federal agents the same night they captured González Flores.

AGICA

Two brothers, one funeral.
Pictured here is the funeral procession of Luis Padilla and brothers Ramón and Jorge Vargas. The brothers were caught hiding Anacleto González Flores in their home. All four men were executed together.

a thirty-five-year-old lawyer. Governor Gómez Loza had already proven his independent spirit and active involvement in the resistance. Even before the mass Cristero rebellion of January 1927, he had been jailed fifty-eight times. In March 1928, a year after Anacleto González Flores's martyrdom, Gómez Loza was also killed. In 2005, both were beatified by Pope Benedict XVI.

In 1927, Miguel Gómez Loza was named the Cristero governor of Jalisco. He established his base near Arandas and had a printing workshop hidden under a range of caves. Always busy, he incessantly organized and collaborated with local leaders, who provided him with weekly reports through a network of channels.

So sound was the organization in Jalisco under Gómez Loza that when General Enrique Gorostieta was put in charge there after Gómez Loza's death, he preserved the system of government as established, making only minor modifications. In 1928 and 1929, for instance, he stipulated that both civilian and military leaders would simultaneously control the region. This helped to increase collaboration between civilian and military leadership, while at the same time maintaining civilian independence. (Gorostieta's role in the Cristiada will be further detailed in Chapter 6.)

By September 1927, the Cristero administration was well established, and a special zone for the city of Guadalajara was created. Additionally, in order to establish civilian commands in the south and west of Jalisco, contacts were set up with General Jesús Degollado, the commander of nine Cristero regiments (with a total of 7,000 men) in south Jalisco.

In December 1927, there were fifty Cristero municipalities in Jalisco. By 1929, that number had reached ninety-two, along with the eleven in southwestern Guanajuato. Together, they constituted 90 percent of all the municipalities in those regions.

The Cristero government was divided into six main commissions: finance, war, propaganda, welfare, information (including espionage and the courier service), and justice. Each commission reached the local level. In every town, war department commissions operated. The justice commissions likewise had headquarters in all the towns, and popular juries were established in all but three municipalities. The propaganda service—with its printing press hidden in Culebra Hill—published the pamphlet *Gladium* and distributed its leaflets throughout the state.

Some of these government areas worked closely with the Joan of Arc Women's Brigade, which was discussed in Chapter 3. With the collaboration of the Brigade, the espionage and postal service network covered the entire zone, while the leaders of the smallest districts, the *ranchos*, provided the Brigade's security. The local commissions that assisted families, widows, orphans, and the wounded also worked together with the Brigade.

Not all regions experienced a dramatic overturn of Federal officials. For example, Coalcomán declared its independence from the Federal government in April of 1927, but both police and judicial responsibilities continued to be carried out by those who held the positions before the Cristiada. This included Ezequiel Mendoza Barragán, who held a Federal office since 1910 under the presidency of Porfirio Díaz. The region also continued to be guided by Father José María Martínez, who could even be considered the real governor of the entire region since before the Cristiada.

It can be said that until the summer of 1928, the Cristero civilian government acted autonomously. The Cristeros came to control the Los Altos region inside an area bounded by Guadalajara, Ocotlán, La Barca, Yurécuaro, Jalpa, San Diego, Lagos, Jalostotitlán, and Cañadas. The region was divided into nine sectors, each under a designated leader. A tenth sector, located in the western part of Guanajuato, was under the authority of Gómez Loza and collaborated militarily with Fathers José Reyes Vega and Aristeo Pedroza, important military leaders of regiments in the Altos Brigade of Jalisco and western Guanajuato. In turn, the sectors were divided into subsectors, municipalities, hamlets, and ranchos.

AGICA

Another dire replacement.
General Enrique Gorostieta is shown while on campaign in Los Altos. He assumed control there after the death of Governor Gómez Loza.

THE CREATION OF A BALANCED GOVERNMENT: THE CASE OF ZACATECAS

While many Cristero records were destroyed during and after the war, fortunately, the records of the Cristero government in the Zacatecas region were preserved. They provide us with invaluable insights into why and how the Cristeros sought to organize themselves and the regions brought under their control. Instrumental in this preservation was Aurelio Acevedo—mentioned in the Preface for being so helpful in my research on the Cristiada—who played an active role in developing the Cristero government and who eventually became the acting governor of Zacatecas himself.

I think Acevedo's words to those involved and his later recollections offer a good idea of why and how the task was achieved. "We were not just going to take part in a brawl, we were going to fight in defense of our liberty," he said as commander of the Valparaíso Regiment. "It was the opposite of a revolution, the opposite of the chaos of Carranza's movement [during the Mexican Revolution]. We had to organize ourselves properly."

To this end, Acevedo issued a new decree outlining some basic rules oriented toward preventing moral lapses. The decree, which was signed by his superior, General Pedro Quintanar, read in part:

> Since the National Liberation Army [i.e. the Cristeros] controls a significant part of the state's territory, and given the urgent need to maintain order and morality in the towns under the control of the Liberation Movement, the operation's head office decrees the following: 1) . . . The authorities constituted by the tyrant are not recognized any longer, and new authorities are established in all areas . . . 2) The constituents will continue to pay taxes . . . 3) The sale of alcoholic beverages is strictly prohibited . . . 4) Exports of cattle and cereals are categorically forbidden . . . 5) Equally forbidden, for the duration of the homeland mourning period, are all public entertainment activities.

While using General Quintanar's authority in issuing the decree, Acevedo also criticized the fact that military and civil authority were constantly confused. As a remedy, Acevedo organized a constituent congress, bringing together the acting administrative and judicial authorities. It was an idea that had occurred to him after summoning a meeting of priests for the purpose of obtaining chaplains for the soldiers. The only case of such a congress during the war, this meeting of the Regional Board of Administrative and Judicial Authorities was held in May 1928 by the Liberation army in Mezquitic, Jalisco. The members of the constituent congress then elected five members to form a committee for the purpose of drawing up a General Ordinance.

Of particular importance to General Acevedo was that the Cristeros avoid repeating the disastrous mistakes made by the military in Mexico's history of revolutions by working to establish and safeguard civil order. In a speech

A voice for order.
General Aurelio Acevedo, an ACJM leader and governor of Zacatecas, was one of the few Cristero generals to survive the years of religious persecution.

AGICA

AGICA

Double mission.
Like many Cristero leaders, Ildefonso Loza Márquez served both in the Cristero military and as a civil authority in Los Altos. After the war, Federal General Saturnino Cedillo helped him relocate to San Luis Potosí for his own protection.

that set the tone for the General Ordinance, he said, "This would be what educating our people is all about—separating everything that is twisted and evil brought about by the revolution, and imparting a more orderly character to our liberation movement." He continued:

> After eighteen years of fratricidal struggle, the military has grown used to living like savages, guided solely by brute force. None of the previous revolutions resulted in the establishment of any kind of government, and this is why many of those who are now militants under the Liberation Army's banner share the same habit of viewing the civilian government as an enemy . . . A revolutionary never wants to be tied to anyone or anything; oftentimes not even to his own superiors, and always recognizes only sheer force. The law . . . who cares about the law? This is viewed as a strange thing, a strange animal. Mexico needs reconstruction, and it needs it quickly. So it is necessary to rebuild as soon as possible while simultaneously controlling the homeland territory. Yes, waging war and organizing; waging war and moralizing; waging war and governing . . . How are we to work? It already has

been said: by exerting control and organizing. The military advances a little bit, it controls a town, and the organizers will go there to fulfill their mission: set up a government, create guarantees, and impart these to all. A town was taken; the enemy retreats without the likelihood of returning. The population, hungry for freedom and justice, receives us with great displays of joy. . . . We must provide the people with all of the necessary guarantees. We ought to do the opposite of what the enemy does.

Acevedo also spoke of the importance of establishing civilian structures necessary for post-war reconstruction:

> It is true that when towns become theaters of combat, military authority rules over everything. . . . [B]ut . . . when the din of war is not heard any longer, everything ought to return to normalcy.

To achieve this, however, the civilian authorities needed a means whereby they could enforce these laws. Thus, under Article 37 of the General Ordinance, regional militias were given a dual function. During a military campaign, they were under the charge of military commanders; but at other times, they acted as police, taking their orders from civilian authorities. By safeguarding civilian power, military authorities and soldiers in particular could not evade civilian justice.

Whenever Cristeros of the Zacatecas region captured a town, they would organize it efficiently. For instance, the five regiments of the Quintanar Brigade quickly came to control an extensive region extending over nine municipalities: Chalchihuites, Fresnillo, Monte Escobedo, Susticacán, Tepetongo, and Valparaíso in Zacatecas; and Huejúcar, Huejuquilla el Alto, and Mezquitic in Jalisco. The region included 100,000 inhabitants and was spread over an area that was about 50 percent larger than the state of New York. This "liberated territory" boasted both a civilian and a military government, justice and police departments, tax and school systems, postal service, and an organization of agricultural work. Cristero control over the zone was such that General Acevedo could travel by himself safely from Laguna Grande to Huejuquilla, since the Federals never dared to go there with fewer than 800 men. The Cristeros lived in the towns, except at nighttime. They left in order to avoid surprises and to let their horses graze. When Federal army invasions took place, the people would hide in the San Juan ravines.

The administrative capital of the Cristero government was established in Huejuquilla el Alto, a town with a population of 15,000 that was favorably located at the entrance to a mountain range and close to a ravine. The Federal army could never keep a garrison there, so, with the exception of a few days, the town square remained in Cristero control throughout the war.

Thus it was that the Cristero government spread through Zacatecas and beyond.

For the Cristero military leadership, winning battles and defending territory was only part of the focus. Another crucial element was the effort to organize and govern the regions that fell under Cristero control.

This map of west-central Mexico highlights the places of particular significance to the strength and organization of the Cristero cause. These pages also provide information on these locations (which are numbered 1 through 9 below and correspond to the numbers on the map), as well as the states or regions where they are located. The information includes the importance of these areas and offers a brief glimpse into the unique initiatives pursued and accomplishments made by the Cristero government and the military leaders throughout the war.

STATE OF JALISCO

The heart of the Cristiada, this region included the Cristero capital as well as some of the Cristeros' most organized examples of self-governance. It was governed collaboratively by civilian and military leaders, including Governor Gómez Loza and Generals Vega and Pedroza.

★ Huejuquilla el Alto

The Cristero capital with 15,000 inhabitants, this city was strategically located at the entrance of a mountain range near a ravine. It included the region's judicial center and thirty-six schools, which were dispersed on remote ranches.

1 Mezquitic

This was home to the 1928 Mezquitic Congress, which created guidelines for Cristero government.

2 Cerro Grande

This mountainous area was a refuge for families uprooted by the war and seeking safe haven from persecution. Throughout the war, the area never fell under Federal control and came to have nine schools serving over 500 children.

3 Los Altos Region

This region was under complete Cristero control. For administrative purposes, it was divided into nine sectors, and came to have over 2,000 civilian leaders and 300 schools by May 1929.

4 Arandas

Just outside this city, Governor Gómez Loza established his base on a nearby ranch.

SOUTHERN JALISCO

Run by General Manuel Michel, this region extended from Zapotitlán to the foot of the Colima Volcano. Michel was known for swift justice and policies of large-scale economic mobilization to help alleviate the suffering of the poverty-stricken population.

5 Zapotitlán

As home to General Michel's ranch, Zapotitlán saw Michel take on his most personal involvement in repairing the region's devastated economy. Here, the General himself worked the land alongside twenty-five agricultural laborers.

STATE OF ZACATECAS

This vast region with 100,000 inhabitants quickly fell under control of the Quintanar Brigade. Here, the Cristeros lived in the villages by day, and moved out only at night to avoid ambush. Thanks to its governor, Aurelio Acevedo, Zacatecas was one of the few regions whose Cristero civilian and military archives were almost completely preserved, making it an important contributor to historical study on the Cristero government.

6 Valparaíso

By 1928, Valparaíso included nineteen schools for 600 children. By the war's end, these numbers doubled.

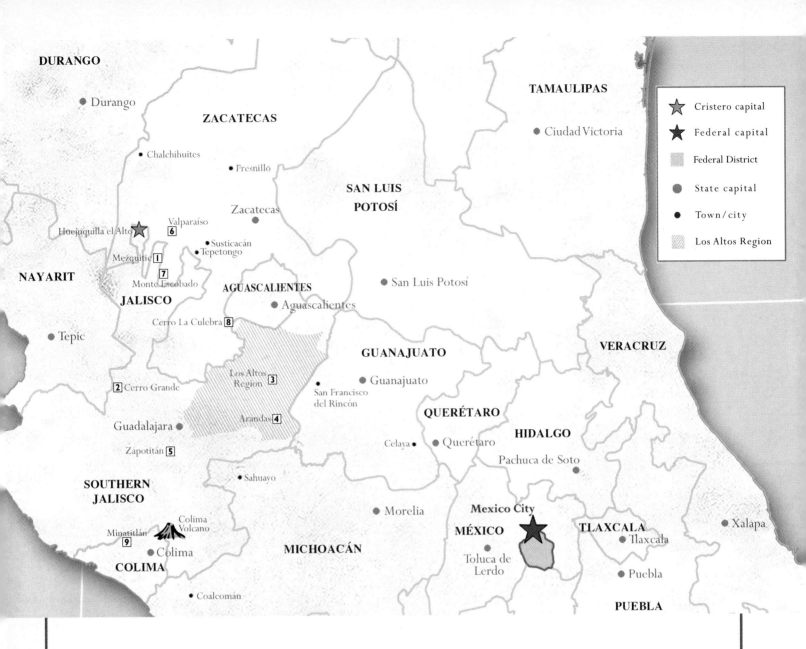

Los Altos Region 3

7 Monte Escobedo

At the Mezquitic Congress, the mayor of this city sought increased civilian authority to ensure that no crime, even those committed by soldiers, would go unpunished.

8 Cerro La Culebra

Strategically located, Cerro La Culebra was home to the Cristero printing press, which put out the resistance newspaper *Gladium*.

COALCOMÁN REGION

Unlike other areas, Coalcomán resembled an autonomous republic, where civilian life continued normally, functioning around the agricultural calendar. The region remained under the unofficial authority of a priest, Father José María Martínez.

STATE OF COLIMA

Supervised by military leaders Andrés Salazar, Dionisio Ochoa, and Miguel Anguiano, Colima lacked a real civil government. Its leaders were fully occupied with the war, and the state's cities and towns remained unsafe for Cristeros and their families, who were forced to live in the volcanic region and assume a nomadic existence, hunting and picking wild foods to survive.

9 Minatitlán

Unlike the purely military government focus throughout the rest of Colima, in Minatitlán, Cristero civil authorities functioned normally.

CIVIL AND MILITARY JUSTICE

Justice was administered by several officials: the *Juez menor* ("minor judge"); the justices of the peace named in each municipality; and the military commander, with the right of appeal to the *Juez de letras* ("judge of studies"), who was installed in the Cristeros' capital city of Huejuquilla in September 1928.

The organizer of the judicial system, Colonel Viramontes, arranged for an experienced lawyer from Valparaíso to assume the post of *Juez de letras*. To work alongside this main judge as a secretary, Viramontes assigned a former parish secretary, Bonafacio Ibarra, a man who would prove adept at managing the Cristero justice system. Ibarra knew how to resist the pressures from the military and demanded that officers proceed systematically—by investigating alleged crimes, turning in those responsible, and ensuring the application of penalties. He himself scrupulously maintained the files of criminal and civil actions. Crimes included theft of livestock and corn, rape, man-slaughter, and homicide.

During the war, it was difficult to imprison the guilty, so prison sentences were typically changed to fines, which, in the case of homicide, were sometimes accompanied by lashes. For instance, Jesús de la Torre, sentenced to ten years in prison for murder, had to compensate the mother of his victim by paying her 500 pesos.

Conversely, military justice handed out severe penalties: a soldier who killed a fellow soldier was tried, convicted, and executed; the rare desertion, treason, or rape was punished with death. For "defaming priests," two Federal supporters, Jesús Franco and José Nava, were executed by a firing squad on October 17, 1927, and March 7, 1928, respectively. In general, slanderers were punished with a series of fines, while the fourth offence raised the possibility of the death penalty. In lieu of an execution, however, offenders were often given a fixed

Internal conflict.
General Pedroza was involved in a famous case of Cristero military justice. He sentenced to death fellow Cristero Victoriano Ramírez ("El Catorce"), who was accused of insubordination. The controversial sentence led some Cristeros to defect in protest.

Disillusioned by a verdict.
Once a Federal official, Miguel Hernández (at left) led the San Julián Regiment of Cristeros. He later left in protest over the killing of "El Catorce."

amount of time to leave the region. As a result, more than one offender went free, thinking that he owed his life to military justice.

The severity of the military authorities and the judges' unconditional support for the sentences encouraged many civilians to come forward with complaints of criminal behavior, such as, "We (the residents of Lagos) can no longer put up with Fernández, who goes around boisterously with women and fires his guns while drunk." In another instance, after an investigation, Cristero commander Victoriano "El Catorce" Ramírez ordered the execution of a soldier who had been accused of stealing corn from two farmers. General Aristeo Pedroza punished some of his soldiers who were caught charging a toll to mule drivers on the highway from Arandas to Atotonilco. He also began proceedings against Cristero soldiers who had abused civilians in Lavaderos.

SCHOOLS AND EDUCATION

The Cristero government promoted education as well—an area needing special attention due to the restrictions in education imposed by the Calles Law. In the countryside, the majority of the schools had been Catholic parochial schools, which the government had closed down. At the same time, Mexico's own public schools were being forced into inactivity due to the resignation of teachers (the majority of primary school teachers were Catholic women) and the boycotting by parents of school-age children.

With the schools in crisis, the Unión Popular's role in promoting and providing education was vital. Cristero municipalities sought to keep all schools functioning—even small village schools, such as the one at Tanques de Santa Teresita (Valparaíso, Zacatecas), where fifteen families enrolled sixty children. The school consisted of nothing more than a couple teachers who wrote on a blackboard that was set up under the trees. Functioning in semi-underground conditions, schools relied upon the financial support of parents, who were expected to send their children to school. Those who did not do so received a warning; they were then penalized for subsequent violations.

Beginning in March 1928, General Acevedo named an inspector general to establish new schools, collect dues to pay the teachers, and visit the schools that were financed by heads of families. The main obstacle was not the resistance of the parents; they were easily persuaded by their own passion for education, as many had to learn to read on their own and regretted their missed opportunities for childhood schooling. Rather, the main opposition came from the administrators of the haciendas, who had been putting the children to work according to the agricultural schedule.

Still, the results were good. For example, at the end of 1927, the municipality of Valparaíso had nineteen schools with 600 students; in two years, those numbers doubled. Similarly, by June of 1929, the municipality of Huejuquilla had thirty-six schools, even in the most remote ranchos. The same was true in Jalisco; and in 1929, 300 schools were functioning in Los Altos.

Traitor, agitator, and spy.
Mario Guadalupe Valdéz (at left) worked the Cristero justice system detrimentally against El Catorce. Spurred by his personal enmity for the ranchero, Valdéz forged incriminating letters and claimed El Catorce plotted against his life. Valdéz later defected and became a Federal informant.

Bonds from the League.
Bonds with a value of 10 pesos helped raise money for the League's administration, and by extension, the administration of the Cristero government.

FUNDING AND FINANCES

Every month, Cristero Governor Miguel Gómez Loza of Jalisco required his subordinates to fill out a questionnaire providing information on a list of active and passive enemies, taxpayers, and "Catholics assassinated by the tyranny." Among such matters, financial issues took up a good part of the administrators' efforts, as finances were of utmost importance in the continuation of a war with seemingly no end in sight.

In September 1927, Governor Gómez Loza issued a decree imposing a tax of 2 percent every six months on the real value of all capital held. In each municipal district, a committee was responsible for determining that value. Based on the committee's work, by November of 1927, Gómez Loza established a land registry and set the assessment of taxes for the Los Altos region at 300,000 pesos. But that winter, when the great concentration of Federal troops under General Amaro took place, Gómez Loza observed that the "money issue started looking pretty grim. Hardly anything was collected, even for essentials. We will soon issue a decree lowering taxes, taking into account how poor people have become as a result of the concentration. May the Lord help us!" Out of the projection of the 300,000 pesos sought from twenty-five municipalities, only 25,000 pesos were collected from six municipalities.

In light of such failures to meet funding projections, the Cristeros had to confront the stark reality that only the poor were actually paying their taxes. When submitting their collections, Cristero tax collectors would say things like, "I am pleased to send you another 1,000 pesos . . . this is only from the good-willed poor. . . . I haven't stopped pestering the rich, with little to show for it." "As is the case everywhere, when it comes to tax collections, the poor are the ones who are actually kind. Don Juan brought you 1,500 pesos."

While the poor suffered, the very affluent Braniff family, for example, sheltered by the government, evidently refused to pay taxes. Retaliation became a consideration; in fact, the only factor that prevented the Cristero Víctor López from blowing up the Braniff family's dam, as he had earlier threatened, was the hardship it would have brought to the residents of Jalpa de Cánovas.

The funds that were raised were scrupulously counted and apportioned between the civilian and military governments, with the largest portion of the civilian government's money set aside for purchasing ammunition. Such careful attention and prioritization of funds was important not only to the war effort but also to keep the trust of those who sacrificed to contribute to the cause. In some cases, funds were siphoned off to other areas or even personal activities—for good or for ill. Reputations suffered in such cases. Governor Gómez Loza realized keenly the importance of financial transparency and was known to cut off working with those less reliable. Midway through the war, in January of 1928, Gómez Loza sent 25,000 pesos to a representative of the League in San Antonio. When he was informed that "nothing has been received here," he bitterly remarked:

> That money belongs to this region; it is intended for supplies, and not to help other localities. I need to know if we can expect to receive something, because if this fails, the consequences would not be good: the taxpayers would think their efforts have been worthless and would accuse us of fraud.

After this disastrous experience, Gómez Loza and the Cristeros of Jalisco were even more judicious about who transported their tax revenue.

LNDL Stamps.
Ranging in value from 50 centavos to 1 peso, these stamps helped raise money for the Cristero cause through the National League for the Defense of Religious Freedom.

Lottery—for liberty.
Promoted by the League, these lottery tickets sold for 25 centavos each. A picture of José de León Toral, Obregón's assassin, appeared on the back.

ECONOMIC MOBILIZATION

At the height of the war, food and supplies were diminishing. With the Federal army's scorched earth policy, workable land and excess crops were destroyed to prevent them from falling into Cristero hands. At the same time, the Federal reconcentration policy relocated civilians from their country dwellings to the city. Along with their property, the government seized abandoned produce, supplies, and other goods. This caused untold civilian suffering and also hindered Cristero troops, who were accustomed to receiving food and supplies from generous civilians. In a letter to General Acevedo, Father Adolpho Arroyo—a priest with the Valparaíso Regiment—further outlined the situation:

> The economic situation has increasingly worsened and the threat of hunger looms. The infinitesimal sources of wealth that used to exist are now depleted, with no more grains left. Agriculture has been reduced to nearly one-quarter of its original size due to the defenders' often excessive spending, the enemy's burning of all grain supplies, the theft of cattle, the ban on cattle sales by their owners, the veto on commerce (even on essential merchandise in places where liberators wage war), the departure of the affluent . . . government loans and our own loans.

Governor in overalls.
Governor Miguel Gómez Loza rests in Los Altos—part of his vast jurisdiction.

This production shortage—particularly of corn, a staple of daily life—was a fundamental problem. In Zacatecas, the 1929 harvest was the second worst of the century (behind that of 1907) with production down 75 percent. In the Bajío, the loss was 35 percent, and in the Altos, 60 percent.

As requests for assistance filtered up the hierarchical channels, authorities were compelled to take over the reins of the entire economic life of the Los Altos region. In response to such difficulties in production, the authorities, with military support, utilized resources like land and water in order to help produce corn. As requested, General Acevedo had the reservoir at San Juan Capistrano's hacienda regulated. Water was requisitioned, as was the unused plowable land on the haciendas. The military commanders also seized (in a friendly way, if possible) all of the unworked land that was left by agrarians and the Cristeros' rich enemies—the proprietors and merchants of Mezquitic who had taken refuge in Jeréz.

With the Cristero appropriation of land and water, agricultural laborers were in steady demand. Agricultural work was accomplished by mobilizing both the military and civilian labor force. The military organization proved efficient in coordinating agricultural activities, with regiments transformed into units of plowmen, sowers, harvesters, and muleteers. Work orders were issued and strictly enforced:

> Taking into account that the majority of our territory lacks laborers dedicated to sowing . . . we believe it is prudent and necessary to rule

that, during the current agricultural year, every twelve-year-old male takes up the yoke to sow. This will make it possible to have a greater number of yokes—enough to at least produce the necessary corn to feed the population. All those who are of the stipulated age and have not become farm workers during the next rainy season will be subjected to a fine of 100 pesos.

A similar labor arrangement took place during the harvest, with physically capable persons ordered to work on certain days. They were also instructed to supply draft animals and "everything necessary to do the job, so

The army comes to town.
Federal troops march alongside civilians in this Mexican town. The government's reconcentration policy moved people (including priests) from the rural areas into large towns, which often had greater military presence.

A moment of rest.
Cristeros relax at a seemingly peaceful
hacienda in La Escoba, Jalisco. Many haciendas
and farms were devastated by the war, which
left them fallow, burned out, or abandoned;
still others were appropriated.

that there is no need to go back" to get more tools. The men had to work quickly in order to finish before Federal troops could take the crop or burn it. When the harvest was not finished in time, the Cristeros would burn it themselves. Eventually, under the supervision of the authorities, the harvested corn was distributed among the soldiers, their families, the agricultural workers, and the refugees.

Although pleasing to the men of the Catholic trade union, who in 1923 and 1924 had dreamed of implementing their own land reform, the Cristeros' mobilization policy angered the seriously affected hacienda owners, who derogatorily referred to the Cristeros as "cattle-eaters" and *huarachudos* ("dirty sandal-wearers"). During the economic mobilization, the hacienda owners lost their land, water resources, seeds, and animals each time the Cristeros discovered them unused, which was often the case. The haciendas of the region, which had not recovered from the great crisis caused by *Villista* banditry that had occurred during the Mexican Revolution (1910–1920), were often unused or abandoned. In addition, the uncertainty of the Federal government's agrarian policy, which involved redistribution of vast tracts of land, dissuaded many of the owners from returning to farming, thus making absenteeism the norm. Confident in the validity of their cause, the Cristeros felt justified in appropriating this abandoned land—an action that was later reproached as theft.

While combating production shortage, the authorities also had to work to eliminate unfair pricing, which happened frequently, to the extreme disadvantage of the poor. In one incident, after learning that the Ameca hacienda owners had reaped a good harvest, but were still selling their corn for six pesos per 100 liters (a high price for a surplus harvest), the authorities stepped in; they prohibited prices higher than five pesos and deterred noncompliance with punishment, including confiscation of corn or its equivalent value. From June 1928 onwards, the Cristero government exercised strict control over the trade of corn, justifying its decision in this way:

> [T]he main obligation of any government is to procure the happiness of its people by providing the necessary guarantees to all, without class distinctions, whether they are poor, rich, wise, or ignorant. . . . The corn owners will not be able to complain about unfairness or lack of guarantees. Instead, they should blame their insatiable ambition and sordid greed, which [lies in wait for] the moment the needy suffer the most from the rigors of hunger, in order to exploit them as they please.

Owners were ordered to sell their surplus. Violators were punished with confiscation of their crops and administrative fines of 50 to 100 pesos.

Though scandalous to the rich, the Cristeros viewed these economic measures as indispensable to their cause: "There is an implicit contract between the people and us, and it is that they expect that we . . . set them free. And

A harvest during the Cristiada.
This group of mostly women and children carry garlands of harvested crops. There was a marked decrease in many crops during the Cristiada, especially in the active war areas, such as Zacatecas, which produced only one-quarter of its usual harvest.

this is why they take food out of their own mouths and give it to us. Therefore, this is the reason propelling us to fight for them in every way we possibly can."

With their seizure of haciendas, the Cristeros had economic crimes of their own to punish, particularly when it came to the management of resources found on the abandoned farms. Violations were reported, even as late as January 29, 1929, when General Acevedo received word that:

> There is a grave situation going on at the San Juan Capistrano Hacienda [where 120 soldiers lived with their families] that is detrimental to the liberation movement, and that is the irresponsible waste of the few assets that were left at the hacienda. . . . [The soldiers] take heads of cattle to butcher without permission . . . when the cowboys come to examine the hide, they are even dismissed with insolence. . . . The soldiers of Alejandro Martínez and Vázquez alone slaughtered 200 animals . . . take into account that the defenders actually waste the greater part of the beef, hide, and the rest.

In many ways, such excesses were understandable. Hunger was ever-present and constituted a bad counselor. With the Cristero ban on the exportation of cattle and the Federal blockade on products from the region, cattle appeared to be in surplus. And with the landowners absent, and their administrators not daring to fight armed peasants, cattle were a target for hungry soldiers, who had eaten very little meat in their lives. Moreover, it was difficult to resist the temptation to carouse and squander, especially if the men thought that the enemy would be coming the next day to burn the produce that had been carefully saved. Vengeance, too, was a motivator, as the wasteful consumption primarily affected the possessions of the wealthy landowners. Although squandering and theft received harsh chastisement and punishment, it remained a problem. In June 1929, General Pedro Quintanar severely reprimanded Florencio Estrada and his men for taking horses from a hacienda. The slaughter of cattle was forbidden unless it was taken from the enemy.

The Federal reconcentration policy, in which rural civilian populations were relocated to city centers, posed its own strategic and economic problem for the Cristeros. Not only did the Federal troops gain easy access to abandoned property and goods, but at the same time, the Cristeros were deprived of a customary source of food and supplies. In an effort to lessen the consequences of reconcentration, civilian authorities took charge of the security and protection of abandoned goods. Township and ranch leaders worked incessantly to store food and supplies. The hiding places that served as provision depots were required to have the capacity to feed the Cristero regiments for a period of three months. Other hiding places were also used to keep the largest possible amounts of food and supplies from falling into Federal hands. The depots helped offset the effect of the reconcentrations by ensuring provisions for combatants and civilians, even in highly dangerous and highly guarded areas. By hiding food and supplies that would have otherwise been seized for the Federal army's use, the Cristeros even prevented the reconcentration of certain towns in January 1929, and blocked the food supply of some garrisoned town squares.

It is important to note that while many regions suffered greatly from the economic fluctuations imposed by the war, some areas, such as the Coalcomán territory, remained largely unaffected. Though having to resist two Federal attempts for recapture, the people of the Coalcomán region—except for those of the upper-classes, who quickly fled the region and were not expected to return until peace was restored—carried on with life as usual. Accustomed to living off local resources, they were largely self-sufficient; only once or twice a year did they depart from the region to sell cheese or animal hides at the Peribán Festivals.

An invaluable leader.
After months of military defeats, the League hired Enrique Gorostieta Velarde—a man of great military skill and experience—to serve as commander-in-chief. Gorostieta would eventually gain the control and allegiance of about half the Cristeros and lead them to numerous victories against the larger and more experienced Federal troops.

6.

The War Changes

GENERAL GOROSTIETA: AN ENIGMATIC LEADER

The organization of civil life highlighted the need for order in the Cristero army. After several months of military defeat, the League abandoned the idea of directing the movement itself, and searched for a leader with military skill and knowledge to direct the Cristero war effort. It found these qualities in General Enrique Gorostieta.

Gorostieta's background and experience immediately set him apart. He hailed from a respectable Monterrey family and was a descendent of a hero in the war that the Spanish fought against French occupation. As a military school cadet, he possessed a talent for artillery, and in 1914, during the Mexican Revolution, he became the youngest general at age twenty-seven. During the war, Gorostieta gained military experience in President Francisco Madero's army, first fighting with General Victoriano Huerta's campaign against rebel leader Pascual Orozco, and later working with General Felipe Ángeles against Emiliano Zapata.

After Madero was assassinated by Huerta, Gorostieta also fought against the American invasion of the Port of Veracruz during Huerta's reign, but his brilliant military career was ruined when he ultimately ended up on the losing side of the war; Huerta was challenged and overthrown by the "Constitutionalists," who were led by Venustiano Carranza and his supporters, including Obregón

A military man.
Enrique Gorostieta Velarde (seated second from right) with fellow soldiers during a 1914 campaign of the Mexican Revolution. That same year, he became the youngest general at age twenty-seven.

and "Pancho" Villa. Because of Gorostieta's ties to Huerta (including the fact that his father was one of Huerta's ministers), he was unable to join the Constitutionalists, and so he exiled himself to Cuba until 1920. That same year, Carranza was assassinated and Obregón became president.

When the League sought Gorostieta in July 1927, he was working in a soap factory—a job he detested, but one that allowed him to use the scientific knowledge he had gained as an artillery officer. Unlike the legendary belief that Gorostieta was an atheist and a freemason, he was, in fact, a devout Catholic who had much in common with the Cristeros and was sympathetic to their resistance. He, too, detested the political regimes of Obrégon and Calles. Poorly paid and tired of civilian life, Gorostieta hired himself out to the League as a mercenary, grabbing the opportunity for revenge and a favorable adventure.

For the first time in the war, the Cristeros finally had a commander-in-chief—one who would eventually gain the control and allegiance of about half the Cristeros. The fit was perfect. As both a theorist and an outstanding soldier, General Gorostieta, at age forty, understood the guerrilla war like no one else. He also held an irresistible allure over the Cristeros, just as the country folk held an irresistible allure over him. A rather mysterious character, Gorostieta

Military excellence. When he accepted the League's offer to join the Cristeros, Gorostieta (right) joined another astute strategist, General José Reyes Vega (center).

AGICA

adopted the Cristeros' cause on his own idealistic terms. A brilliant artillery officer and a man of discipline and classical formation, he relished the prospect of leading the underdog Cristero forces, whom he learned to admire and love. And with these humble fighters, he engaged in guerilla warfare, using every advantage of terrain and surprise against the larger and more experienced Federal forces.

Gorostieta also appreciated and protected the work of the Women's Brigade, harnessing their zeal for essential activities in administration, medical care, finance, propaganda, and provisioning. At one point, the League sought to bring the Brigade under its patronage and grew hostile when its proposal was turned down. General Gorostieta, along with General Manuel Michel, was quick to praise the Brigade and reprimand the League for disrupting the vital work of these women with such internal politics.

Gorostieta could also see beyond the battles to appreciate the greater goals of the Cristeros. Beyond the abolition of persecutory laws, he could see that the destruction of the Calles regime was being proposed. This made some people wonder if he himself would seek the presidency, leading one American military attaché to attest in 1929 that all political media started to become interested in this "formidable combatant." Indeed, Gorostieta had the necessary military background and ambition to reach the presidency, and—considering the Mexican Revolution—he would not have been the first victorious general to occupy the presidential chair. Nevertheless, these speculations would never be proven one way or another, because the bitter war would take its toll on this proud soldier.

THE TIDE TURNS

After the defeats suffered during the spring of 1927, the Cristeros learned how to fight and became difficult to vanquish. And by July of that year, the Cristero movement solidified and strengthened.

This new momentum was already noticeable when General Gorostieta joined the cause. He came into closer contact with the movement, gained a better understanding of the war, and tested his methods in a small region from September 1927 to February 1928. After this maturation period, he was quickly able to extend his sphere of influence to the six states of Jalisco, Nayarit, Aguascalientes, Zacatecas, Querétaro, and Guanajuato in June of 1928, and soon became the national leader of the insurrection. Eventually, about half of the Cristeros—25,000—would recognize Gorostieta's authority and operate under his command, while another 25,000 would continue to operate autonomously as bands of varying sizes without any order in their territories.

In October and November 1927, the Cristeros were so well entrenched in Jalisco that the government could no longer protect the haciendas and foreign-owned mines. (This was helped by the fact that Generals Francisco Serrano and Arnulfo Gómez, angered by Obregón's decision to run for re-election, declared themselves in open rebellion against Calles and Obregón. This caused the Federal army to concentrate its efforts on Mexico City.) In late January 1928, upon returning from a campaign in Colima, Secretary of War Amaro again requested more troops, planes, and funds to fight off the Cristero uprising that now stretched over thirteen states of central Mexico, from Tehuantepec to Durango. A second wave of army regrouping brought about a second string of uprisings, and by March 1928, the rebels numbered 35,000. Thus, even while lamenting the lack of ammunition, Gorostieta could write: "Our struggle continues to go well. In fact, it's going so well that the *Callistas* are losing their sleep . . . and rightfully so, because they are flying too low."

The government, however, still had many strategic advantages over the Cristeros. It ruled over cities, railways, and borders. It also continued to have something the rebels would never have: support from the United States.

The power of U.S. support was felt strongly in Mexico's recent revolutionary history. During President Obregón's presidency, the Coolidge administration aided his defense against the Huerta rebellion (1923–1924) by agreeing to sell war material, including rifles, machine guns, ammunition, aircraft bombs, and airplanes, totaling over $1 million. Obregón was even granted permission to transport Federal troops through Texas. In 1929, newly elected U.S. President Herbert Hoover followed his predecessor's example. He maintained

Cristero victories publicized.
This bulletin describes recent Cristero victories, which are attributed to those who gave their lives for the cause. One such person was Unión Popular founder, Anacleto González Flores (pictured).

Beyond colleagues.
Pictured with fellow Cristeros, General Degollado (kneeling) and General Carlos Bouquet (far left) shared not only the war, but also family—Degollado was married to Bouquet's sister, Soledad.

the 1924 arms embargo, which allowed the exportation of arms and ammunition only to the Mexican government and effectively prevented arms from reaching Cristero hands. With this agreement, the Mexican government was able to purchase directly from the U.S. War Department. On one occasion, the purchase was for 10,000 rifles and innumerable rounds of ammunition, a sale for which U.S. Ambassador to Mexico Dwight Morrow received a rare phone call from Emilio Portes Gil (Mexico's interim President after Calles), expressing the government's extreme gratitude. Similarly, the sale of U.S. commercial airplanes was embargoed for all but the military—a great commodity since these were easily converted into fighter planes. Although such support of the Mexican government provoked heated debate in Washington and created political factions, the policy continued throughout the war.

The intensity of the Cristero rebellion was not uniform throughout Mexico. The isolated centers of resistance declined, were extinguished, or were rekindled intermittently in Coahuila, San Luis, and Veracruz. The rebellion set the pace in Guerrero, smoldered in Puebla, and spread in Oaxaca, Mexico City, and Morelos. In the three large regions where the Cristeros were already firmly established, the Federal army was weakening, while Cristero control began to span the entire west-central region from San Juan del Río to the Pacific Ocean.

The Federal military planned a big offensive for the winter of 1928. It gathered the maximum number of troops, artillery, and aircraft in Jalisco—thirty line regiments, six regiments of mountain artillery, and three squadrons of aircraft. It recruited intensely, bringing troops from faraway regions to guard the railways, freeing up units for battle.

But when the army launched its first attack, it found the enemy area empty of opposition forces. Apparently, the Cristeros had been prepared for the government offensive. They had even stored away the harvests of the resettled peasants and issued them receipts for their goods. Even though Federal officials could enrich themselves through the pillage of civilian populations—and these people endured untold suffering, tested by hunger, exposure to the elements, and smallpox—nevertheless, the actual effect of the Federal military's actions was contrary to its intentions. The people's spirit of resistance, far from faltering, was made even stronger.

From monument to memorial.
In 1928, the Mexican government bombed this famous monument of Christ the King, which was located on Cubilete Hill and had been dedicated just five years earlier. After the Cristiada, the monument was rebuilt, and remains a significant reminder of the Cristeros.

"Table of Honor."
The Secretary of War himself, General Joaquín Amaro (back row, third from right), is honored by an evening of religious ridicule and desecration in San Joaquín's Church. The evening included a parody that mocked the Divine Office (daily prayers), a sermon delivered from the pulpit that derided Catholic clergy, and champagne that was drunk from chalices.

PRESIDENTIAL UPHEAVAL

In the middle of negotiations with the Church and the ever-more-deadly conflict with the Cristeros, Mexico City itself faced difficulty. In 1928, as Calles's presidency neared an end, Obregón was handpicked to return to the presidency. Of course, it was difficult for Calles to ensure an Obregón victory in free and "democratic" elections, but the task was made easier when both of Obregón's opponents, Generals Serrano and Gómez—who had led the previously-mentioned rebellion in Mexico City—were executed. Obregón's expected return to the presidency promised some ray of hope for reaching an agreement; in fact, U.S. Ambassador Morrow and Obregón had set a date, July 17, 1928, to meet and confirm a definitive settlement of the religious conflict.

However, on that day, violence again broke out. While attending a victory party at Mexico City's La Bombilla restaurant, President-elect Obregón was shot and killed. A Catholic radical, José de León Toral, had been mingling at the party and began sketching Obregón. Seeing the sketch, Obregón let the young man sit at his table to finish the drawing; but instead, Toral drew a gun and shot him. In just a few minutes, the hopes for the agreement that was to be reached that very afternoon were dashed.

While many details surrounding Obregón's assassination remain unclear, what is obvious is that his death resulted in an unanticipated halt to the diplomatic bids for peace to which he was deeply committed, and prolonged the war another eleven months. José de León Toral was executed, causing some to consider him a martyr (although his case certainly did not qualify as "martyrdom" according to the Catholic Church's guidelines for sainthood).

Obregón's assassination stalled the negotiations, and by October of 1928, the situation looked dismal indeed. The *Economists' Report for International Bankers* confirmed Ambassador Morrow's analysis that without religious peace, no solution to the economic crisis in Mexico could be expected:

The once and future president. This photograph, one of the last of General Álvaro Obregón, was taken on July 8, 1928, just nine days before his assassination.

> One of the most disturbing factors in Mexico's economic situation is the conflict between the Government and the Catholic Church. . . . The deadlock is deplorable, for a solution would perhaps do more than

The assassination of President-elect Obregón on July 17, 1928 was, at least on the surface, a victory for the Cristeros. When Obregón was shot at a party celebrating his electoral win, President Calles and the Mexican government lost a former president and the future head of state. Moreover, the timing of the assassination—just days following Obregón's election—cast distrust on Calles himself, with many people suspecting his hand in the murder. But Obregón's assassination also brought some sympathy to the State, much like the Cristeros had experienced with Father Miguel Pro's execution several months earlier.

The assassin, José de León Toral—a Catholic, an artist, and a father of three—was dubbed a fanatic, and his action was vigorously condemned by many individuals and groups, including the National Catholic Welfare Council in the United States.

Toral was tried and executed by firing squad on February 9, 1929. His last words were *"¡Viva Cristo Rey!"* Interestingly, Toral had a personal connection to the previous assassination attempt against Obregón; one of those accused of the crime was his friend Humberto Pro—whom the State executed, despite his innocence.

Humberto's death caused Toral to take a more active role in the religious cause and to see the desperate situation firsthand. Tragically, the day Toral chose for the assassination was the day his victim was scheduled to meet U.S. Ambassador Morrow to try to resolve the religious issue.

Moments before the assassination.
At the banquet table, Obregón looks at a sketch made by José León de Toral, who stands directly behind him. Seconds later, Toral emptied his automatic revolver into Obregón's side. Toral later reflected on the moment, saying that Obregón's smile almost stayed his trigger finger.

Upturned chairs, peace talks tabled.
At the time of the assassination, the live music prevented many from hearing the five gunshots; yet the unfolding drama was sign enough that something had happened to President-elect Obregón. Here, a soldier stands guard at the crime scene.

Courtroom theater.
Toral sits before the judge who will decide his fate. Months earlier, the same courtroom was dissolved into chaos when a band of *Obregónistas* stormed the courtroom, demanding that Toral be handed over for execution. The district's procurator general had to reprimand the rioters while standing atop a table before order was restored in the court.

A father with his son.
The day before Toral's execution, his family was allowed to see him for the last time—and for the first time, Toral saw his newborn son. Here, Toral stands with his own father in one of their final photographs together.

AGICA

Oh, Muerte, ¿dónde está tu aguijón? Job.

...He terminado mi carrera. He conservado la fe. Ahora, me será donada la corona de justicia por el justo Juez. S. Pablo.

El Señor
José de León Toral,
de 28 años de edad, falleció hoy a las 12 horas 30 minutos, en el seno de Nuestra Madre la Santa Iglesia Católica, Apostólica, Romana, confortado con todos los auxilios espirituales.

Sus afligidos padres, esposa, hijos, hermanos, hermanos políticos y demás parientes, lo participan a Ud. con el más profundo dolor, suplicándole rue. gue a Dios Nuestro Señor por el descanso eterno del alma del finado.

México, 9 de Febrero de 1929.

El duelo se recibe mañana a las 16 horas en la casa número 214 de la 6a. calle del Sabino y se despide en el Panteón Español.

In memoriam.
On the day of Toral's funeral (announced here), over 100,000 people lined the streets. To control the crowds, police and the military used high-powered hoses and fired a number of warning shots, which resulted in one reported death and multiple injuries.

An early exit.
This political cartoon depicts the difficult position Calles found himself in after Obregón's assassination. In fact, many feared full-scale collapse. (Artist: Alfonso de la Torre)

anything else to bring about revival of confidence, economic recovery, and advance. Neither party is ready to give way on the major principles involved. But in considerable measure, the conflict appears to rest upon misunderstandings, and there are some grounds for hope that a solution may be found within a reasonable time.

But political unrest and elections could not be put off forever. Because of Calles's political ambition and position, rumors arose that President Calles himself had planned Obregón's assassination. Between August 1928 and February 1929, a schism grew between the *Callistas* and the *Obregónistas*, who had just lost their preferred candidate. The growing bitterness between the two factions ultimately benefited the Cristeros by drawing Federal troops away from the Cristeros in order to pacify these other conflicts. In an attempt to silence such rumors, President Calles appointed his friend Emilio Portes Gil as interim president. (But as we shall see, this in no way meant an end to Calles's political control over the country.)

By January 1929, military actions were so numerous that it became difficult to track the war on a day-to-day basis. In some areas, there was not a single town square that was spared from being attacked each week. Within a period of thirty days in Los Altos alone, over 100 battles took place. The government was forced to cut the salaries of its officials by 30 percent; and for the first time, politicians began to express misgivings about the future. In the legislature on February 13, 1929, Senator Lauro Caloca warned:

Passing on the presidency.
President-elect Emilio Portes Gil (right) is pictured here with President Calles.

A new president.
Newly inaugurated President Emilio Portes Gil (center) sits with his cabinet on December 6, 1928. Included in the photograph is Secretary of War and Navy General Joaquín Amaro (seated with sash).

We have spent two years fighting the insurgents and we are still not finished with them. Are our soldiers incapable of fighting peasants, or is it that we do not want to finish the rebellion? Then let us say so at once, and not keep throwing more fuel on the flames. Don't forget that if three more states really rise in rebellion, with the three that are already in revolt, then the Public Power is in danger of collapsing!

Caloca's colleague, Juan de Dios Robledo, asked what solution could be found when the only absolutely sure measures of quelling rebellion were too awful to consider: "We are not going to kill 30,000 people in Jalisco!" Meanwhile, Ambassador Morrow, whose efforts for peace will be considered in the next chapter, likewise grasped the severity of the situation with the following observation: "Despite all of the efforts undertaken by the president and the military, it seems unlikely that peace will be restored, as long as the religious matter remains unsolved." And soon enough, the situation would deteriorate to such an extent that even General Amaro himself would be brought to the same realization.

FALSE HOPES—
THE VASCONCELOS CAMPAIGN
AND THE ESCOBAR REBELLION

Leading a war that was becoming more and more an impasse of forces, Gorostieta considered the upcoming presidential elections in November of 1929 as a possible hope. José Vasconcelos—a man sympathetic to the Cristero cause—was running as an independent candidate against Pascual Ortiz Rubio (Calles's choice). In January of that year, while Vasconcelos toured various cities, Gorostieta contacted the candidate in an effort to get him to publicly join the Cristero cause during the campaign season. But Vasconcelos sent word with a different proposal: he and Gorostieta would meet the day *after* the election, effectively postponing any alliance. Like Madero (who deposed President Díaz after a rigged election in 1910), Vasconcelos—through the elections—wanted to first express his indignation toward the government's hostility, demonstrate the government's deceitfulness, and make an appeal to the people. Then, after the election, the Cristeros would provide Vasconcelos with the necessary military force.

An unwilling ally.
On July 9, 1929 in Mexico City, José Vasconcelos takes the oath as the presidential candidate under the banner of the National Re-Electionist political party.

Gorostieta was disappointed that Vasconcelos did not join the movement immediately, and he feared that the government would find a solution of its own before autumn. His projections proved correct. As far as Calles and the State were concerned, to some degree it did not matter if there was any official alliance between Vasconcelos and the Cristeros. The Cristeros' presence made the elections difficult, and Vasconcelos's popularity among the urban middle classes filled a gap in the Cristero opposition. Realizing the seriousness of the situation, the government saw the need to make peace with the Church and disarm the Cristeros. The next month, in February, President Portes Gil even sent an emissary to Gorostieta to discuss possible peace terms. But Gorostieta, for his part, tried to dissuade the bishops from being too hasty in their negotiations and warned them to be on their guard.

Shortly after Gorostieta's disappointing exchange with Vasconcelos, another promising alliance from a different movement came on the horizon for the Cristeros. In early March 1929, the ambitious Generals José Gonzalo Escobar and Francis Manzo led a rebellion in Mexico's northwest region, calling for the overthrow of the Portes Gil administration as a mere instrument of Calles. On March 3, these *Obregónista* rebels issued the "Plan of Hermosillo" in which they severely criticized the Portes Gil-Calles administration, accused Calles of betraying the revolution, and named General Escobar as the leader of a new resistance movement.

Having at their disposal 25,000 men (which came to approximately one-third of the Federal army at the time), and aware that they had little political support and were denounced by the United States, the Escobar insurgents sought support from the Cristeros. To this end, they promised General Gorostieta that they would supply his men with desperately needed ammunition, and abolish Calles's legislation in areas that were brought under their control. For the Cristeros, this was a compelling and seemingly hopeful prospect. Their need for ammunition was great, and Escobar could easily equip them with entire trainloads of amunition. Moreover, the relaxation of religious restrictions was an end prompting many to take up arms in the first place.

The government responded to Escobar very quickly. With General Amaro recovering from injury, Calles had himself named to Amaro's former position as Secretary of War and set about compiling a force of 35,000 men to quash the rebellion. Calles conscripted unconventional recruits—the agraristas, regional militias, veterans from General Cedillo's private peasant army, prisoners, the unemployed, and trade union workers. Moreover, he pulled troops from the west to meet Escobar's forces in the north. He also had help from the United States, with American pilots flying "Mexican" planes (as recounted in the U.S. press). Within three months, Calles's army quelled this last rebellion, which was hindered by poor leadership and an unclear political agenda. Escobar abandoned his troops and found safe haven in the United States and eventually Canada.

Although Calles quickly extinguished the coup, it showed him how the Cristeros' discontent could be used for political goals other than those the Cristeros themselves desired. Thus, after the victory was won, President Portes Gil told Ambassador Morrow that in order to avoid a new civil war, it would be necessary to reach an accord before the presidential elections in the fall.

For the Cristeros, although the advantages of the rebellion were not the ones initially anticipated—in fact, Escobar never delivered a single shotgun cartridge—there were other benefits. For two months, the rebellion engaged a third of the Federal army and forced the government to lessen its presence

A friendly "enemy."
Deep in conversation several years before the Escobar rebellion, José Gonzalo Escobar (right) and Joaquín Amaro (left) were fellow officers in the Federal army.

War along the border.
Here, Federal soldiers are entrenched in combat against the Escobar rebels. Many images of the Escobar rebellion made it into the U.S. press, as the uprising took place in the regions bordering the United States.

against the Cristeros during that time. General Gorostieta, however, was not convinced by the supposed "benefits" of the Escobar outcome, and observed the situation with pessimism:

> With the military uprisings, our situation has worsened instead of improving. It might not seem that way, but if the matter is considered calmly, it will become evident that it is indeed the case. The movements taking place in the North will have the same outcome as those of Veracruz due to the lack of prudence on the part of leaders and officers, who are lost in the ocean of betrayal and ambition. After their defeat, Calles the Turk will turn on us. He will come with a great number of troops, with high morale and pride in their victory, against our men, who lack supplies as usual.

To avoid this gloomy future, Gorostieta took preemptive measures and ordered an immediate offensive, targetting road links first. Between March 3 and May 15, 1929, he conducted a series of significant operations, taking advantage of the thinning Federal troops in the west by crushing the remaining, unsupported auxiliary troops in the area. With these attacks, nearly the entire western zone, except for the major cities secured by entrenched Federal garrisons, fell under Cristero control. Durango also fell after the great battles from Puente Grande to Ocotlán against General Cárdenas's division that was advancing to Sonora. Gorostieta prudently resisted the temptation to take certain cities, which could have been "worse for us than Capua was to Hannibal." (In this way, he avoided the fate of past revolutionary Miguel Hidalgo, who captured Guadalajara in 1810, but later watched as his 60,000-man army was crushed by Felix Calleja's small army at the nearby Calderón Bridge—an event that was a damning precursor to Hidalgo's capture and execution a month later.)

After Gorostieta's successful attacks, even General Amaro lost his composure for the first time. He told President Portes Gil that the west was up in arms and that it would be vital to come to an agreement with the Church.

Disillusioned officer.
Infamous for carrying out Calles's command to execute Father Miguel Pro, Chief of Police Roberto Cruz (center, with left hand in his pocket) later fell from Calles's grace and joined the Escobar rebellion.

After a victory.
Federal troops board trains out of Mazatlan after defeating the Escobar rebels, who had attempted to take control there.

THE NEED FOR RESOLUTION

In the months leading up to June 1929, the Cristeros had come into their own in terms of strength and numbers, and the Federal government was suffering because of it. Militarily, the Cristeros had won many victories that devastated the Federal army and swept whole regions under Cristero control. The Cristeros' cause had infused itself into civilian life, too, and as the civilians spread the cause through every dimension of Mexican life, military action became only one expression of unrest. And civically, the Cristero government had grown and adapted to the needs of the people in each area. As General Gorostieta observed on May 20, 1929: "Our movement is supported by the people. We have over 2,000 civilian authorities, 300 schools."

Indeed, the popularity of the Cristeros' cause created serious problems for the government in seventeen states of the Federation, especially in the central western part of Mexico, the country's most populated area.

The impact was tremendous. The Federal army saw massive desertions, and the economy fell even further from its already dire straits. As an American report dated May 3, 1929, stated: "The commercial and financial situation currently is poor. There is practically a moratorium on debt . . . the general opinion . . . is that if the government is incapable of eliminating the Cristero bands that infest the country, or if an agreement is not reached with the Church to resume worship services, the possibility of a return to normalcy is now unlikely."

The Cristeros' success, however, could go only so far. They were the force of unrest that provoked a great and urgent desire in the Church and State to restore peace; but negotiations were a different matter. Consequently, it was not the Cristeros but rather a handful of Mexican bishops who pursued private discussions with Presidents Obregón, Calles, and later Portes Gil on many occasions throughout the war from 1926 to 1929. These bishops keenly felt the damage wrought by persecution and war upon the people, especially as experienced in their own dioceses. As we shall see in the next chapter, this growing pressure within Mexico would soon be joined with diplomatic finesse from the United States.

Sending a message that backfires.
This photograph created such negative worldwide press that President Calles ordered all future hangings to be carried out away from the train tracks.

CATÓLICOS AHORCADOS JALISCO

Cristiada Timeline 1928

THE STATE AND THE CHURCH

January
Vatican officials meet with Mexican bishops and Ambassador Morrow in Cuba.

April 15
Government's "apology" at Celaya lays ground for positive negotiations.

July 1
Obregón is re-elected president.

July 17
President-elect Obregón is assassinated by José de León Toral.

November 30
Emilio Portes Gil is appointed interim president.

DIPLOMACY AND U.S. RELATIONS

February 9
Calles cancels a planned meeting with Father Burke. His cancellation increases Cristero support.

March 27
Oil agreement is reached between U.S. and Mexico.

April 4
Calles and Father Burke meet at San Juan de Ulúa to discuss the religious laws.

May 17
Calles meets with Archbishop Ruiz y Flores, Ambassador Morrow, and Father Burke. Together they iron out details for a future agreement.

May 31
The League writes to the pope, criticizing the Mexican bishops' involvement with the U.S.

June–November
The compatibility of Catholicism and faithful citizenship comes under question in the U.S. as severe anti-Catholic prejudice undercuts the campaign of Al Smith—the first Catholic presidential candidate.

November 6
Herbert Hoover wins the U.S. presidential election.

CATHOLIC IDENTITY, PROTESTS, AND THE WAR

January
Federal General Amaro requests more troops, planes, and funds.

Cristero forces reach 35,000.

March
Governor Gómez Loza, leader of the Cristero government, is executed.

Cristero government names General Aurelio Acevedo inspector general of schools to further the educational system.

May
Guidelines for the Cristero government are drawn up during a meeting of the Regional Board of Administrative and Judicial Authorities.

June
General Gorostieta extends his leadership over Cristeros in six states.

July
After Obregón's death, hostilities are suspended for a month.

September
Cristero government installs a justice system in Huejuquilla.

December
Massive Federal offensive begins.

Border control.
During the Cristiada, this immigration office was located on the border between Calexico, California and Mexicali, Mexico. Interestingly, in 1926, Mexico's legislature passed a law restricting Mexican emigration. The law required emigrants to obtain permission from the local government.

7.

American Confreres

OBSTACLES TO U.S. INVOLVEMENT

We began this book with the crisis that provoked the war: the conflict of the State and the Church *within* Mexico. Now, as the book approaches its conclusion, this theme returns in a new and perhaps unexpected light. We will uncover how the war provoked a resolution for reconciliation—a resolution facilitated and supported through Church and State officials *outside* Mexico.

The invitation for U.S. involvement began a few weeks after the Calles Law took effect. On August 20, 1926, just before the annual meeting of the U.S. bishops, Father John J. Burke, executive secretary of the National Catholic Welfare Conference (NCWC), asked Bishop Díaz, who at the time was serving as secretary of the Mexican Episcopal Committee, what he believed the United States could accomplish in Mexico. The exiled Bishop Díaz answered, "We believe that Washington . . . would be able, through diplomatic channels and with fullest reserve, to use its good offices with the government of Mexico to make it see that the anti-religious laws cannot be approved." Three years later in 1929, Bishop Díaz's hope that America would successfully use its "good offices" in obtaining an agreement with the State would be fulfilled. But prior to that achievement, many difficulties had to be overcome.

A full agenda.
As U.S. ambassador, James Sheffield faced many volatile diplomatic issues.

Exhibition in Washington DC.
This KKK parade down Pennsylvania Avenue took place in the summer of 1925 and extends as far as the eye can see. The U.S. Capitol is barely visible in the distance. That year, the KKK boasted 4 million members.

The first obstacle was the very man with the most responsibility for Mexican-American affairs—U.S. Ambassador to Mexico, James Sheffield. In many ways, Ambassador Sheffield proved unwilling and unsuited for such a delicate and controversial challenge. He was known at times to be duped by the press on Mexican affairs. He also irritated Mexican officials by over-estimating international influences upon Mexican government officials. In a final show of weakness, in the summer of 1926—just as Mexico's Church-State conflict was heating up—Ambassador Sheffield told President Calvin Coolidge that he did not want to remain in Mexico.

Shortly after, in September of that year, Sheffield seemed to give up on any prospects for peace, stating, "None of us is able intelligently to diagnose the condition between the Church and State in Mexico. . . . No foreigner can understand the Mexican nature. Even men who have lived for twenty-five years in the nation do not understand the mental processes of the people."

Granted, being ambassador to Mexico was no easy task in the 1920s. Although the United States took a significant step when it recognized Obregón's and subsequently Calles's presidencies, relations between the two countries remained precarious, to say the least. Tension was escalated when the Mexican government pushed to nationalize its property by repossessing all land owned by foreigners (many of whom were Americans), including oil lands and even land acquired before 1917. Thus, it is not surprising to learn that only a year after the Cristiada began, Ambassador Sheffield resigned suddenly when he left Mexico to go on a "vacation"—bringing twenty-seven crates of possessions with him.

Another major obstacle to the U.S. involvement was a social one: bigotry in various forms. This was still the period of the rise and development of anti-immigrant nativism, as well as anti-Catholic, anti-Black, and anti-Jewish societies. The most infamous were the Ku Klux Klan (KKK) and the Sons and Daughters of Washington. To the Klan, the Mexican was seen as a combination of black and Catholic—even worse in its eyes than a Catholic Irishman!

At the time, the Ku Klux Klan was still a growing organization, boasting 4 million members in 1925—about 3.5 percent of the total U.S. population. In September of 1926, the Klan presented U.S. Secretary of State Frank Kellogg with a resolution formally requesting that the United States *not* intervene in the Mexican situation. A few days before, the Klan's "Imperial Wizard" announced that he had delayed his re-election because he wanted "a united Klan" behind him for his plan: if the League of Nations or a European country interfered in Mexico, then "thank God there are enough Klansmen in America to repel them" if the United States did not do the job first.

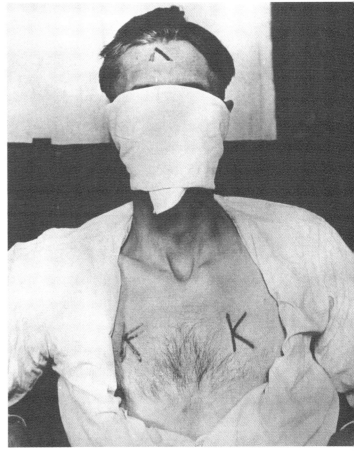

Anti-Catholicism in America.
In an effort to make him renounce his Catholic faith, the Klan kidnapped Nelson Burroughs and held him captive for seventeen days. They branded the initials KKK into his chest and forehead.

Klan members also continued to play important roles in politics. By 1923, the KKK celebrated the election of the first Klansman to reach the U.S. Senate, Earle Bradford Mayfield, while in 1928, during the midst of the Cristiada, Klansman John Porter was elected mayor of Los Angeles. During the presidential election of 1928 between Herbert Hoover and Catholic Democrat Al Smith, the Klan constantly attacked Smith, even lining the road of his campaign trail with burning crosses.

Against such a backdrop, the U.S. government moved slowly regarding the Mexican situation. Indeed, considering the volatile relationship with Mexico, and the fact that the persecution was "safely" quarantined within Mexico's borders, it is not surprising that correcting Mexico's government for persecuting Catholics was hardly considered a priority.

Showing their strength. Ku Klux Klan members hold a rally around a burning cross on August 10, 1925. Such public displays highlighted the Klan's power in the United States at that time.

THE KNIGHTS OF COLUMBUS
IN A PUBLIC EDUCATION CAMPAIGN

In many ways, the people and government of the United States needed to be awakened to the Mexican situation. From the beginning of the Cristiada, the Knights of Columbus (K of C) took on this role. Working with the Catholic hierarchy, the K of C played an important part in defining the issues and mobilizing U.S. public opinion on behalf of the Catholics in Mexico.

Founded in 1882 in New Haven, Connecticut, the Order of the Knights of Columbus is a fraternal benefit society that was created to provide Catholic men and their families with social and religious activities and initiatives, and to care for Catholic widows and orphans. It was created during a time when the majority of such societies were non-Catholic, and life was characterized by hard labor and early death for immigrants. The Knights of Columbus offered its members a system of life insurance that provided death benefits to their families. This allowed widows to escape the "poor house" and keep their children out of public institutions. As such, the K of C was from the start an organization with Catholicity and charity at the core of its mission.

In 1905, the Knights of Columbus established its first council in Mexico. Through its councils and yearly convention, this fraternal organization continued to build ties between the Mexican Knights and the U.S. Knights. Therefore, when Mexican Catholics (including fellow Knights) were persecuted, and when strong anti-Catholic sentiment prevented the United States from responding, the Knights of Columbus had much at stake and immediately took a stand.

On the international stage.
An actor in his early career, Supreme Knight James Flaherty received international recognition for the work he did caring for soldiers during World War I, and for his efforts in fighting racial and religious bigotry in the 1920s.

By coincidence, the Knights of Columbus held its annual Supreme Convention in Philadelphia just three days after the Mexican bishops suspended public religious services in Mexico. At the convention, in front of 25,000 Knights, including Knights from Mexico and some members of the Mexican clergy, Supreme Knight James A. Flaherty denounced the Mexican government's persecution of Catholics and criticized the U.S. government's silence on the issue. Copies of the resolutions were then sent to President Coolidge and Secretary of State Frank Kellogg.

The religious question, the Knights argued, must be included in any official dealings between Washington and Mexico. On September 1, 1926, Presi-

Shifting priorities in Washington. The Knights' delegation, received here by President Coolidge on September 1, 1926, urged U.S. involvement in the Mexican crisis.

dent Coolidge received the Knights' delegation and promised his commitment to bring about a solution to the troubles that beset the Mexican people. The Knights were quite satisfied by this change of position. From then on, it would be on the agenda of the U.S. government, a government that would leave behind its previous policy of non-involvement in what was once deemed a purely "domestic" problem.

In addition to its efforts in putting the Mexican crisis on Washington's agenda, the K of C resolution created the Mexican Fund, a pledge of $1 million collected from members that was to be used for two broad causes: to provide direct aid to refugees, and to educate the U.S. populace about the true situation in Mexico, including the brutality, the despotic politics, and the anti-Catholic ideology that was rampant in Mexico's government and labor unions.

In this, the K of C's first big success was internationalizing news of the conflict. Trusting that Americans would want to do something if only they knew of the atrocities in Mexico, the Knights spent a little more than half of the Mexican Fund on publicizing the facts. The Order published and distributed pamphlets, ranging from single-page fact sheets to longer booklets on the Mexican situation. In all, over seventeen different titles were published, with 5 million copies distributed to the public. One pamphlet contained an article written by David Goldstein, a leading figure in the trade-union movement at the time.

Additionally, the K of C provided funding to other Catholic media projects and news outlets, including the Jesuit journal *America*, a major Catholic news contributor. In fact, the work of Jesuit Father William Parsons, editor-in-chief of *America* and an authoritative voice on the Mexican situation, was largely enabled by money received from the Mexican Fund. Also, the Knights of Columbus funded the publication of a few major works, including the *Pastoral Letter of the Catholic Episcopate of the United States on the Religious Situation in Mexico*, which had over 2 million copies printed and four editions published. The K of C also utilized the pages of its own magazine, *Columbia*. In 1926 and 1927, nearly every issue of *Columbia* included at least one article (and usually more) concerning the Mexican situation. (At the time, the magazine's circulation hovered around 750,000 per issue, and of that number, almost 7,000 copies were in public libraries.)

Along with funding writers to research and publish on the Mexican crisis, the Knights also employed public speakers to give informational lectures to diverse—and often very large—audiences across the country. In one instance, an estimated 7,000 were in attendance.

While the majority of money from the Mexican Fund was spent on educational and related expenditures, still almost half the Fund was dedicated to direct outreach for Mexican refugees. This was not an entirely new task for the Knights. The Texas Knights were particularly familiar with the destitution suffered by the refugees. The borders between countries became increasingly obscured when an estimated 1.8 million Mexicans crossed to the United States between 1926 and 1929. As one of the intermediaries between the Order's funds and the recipients, Cardinal Patrick Hayes of New York worked closely with the Order to aid refugees, including those in Oklahoma, San Antonio, Los Angeles, and San Francisco.

Part of the Knights of Columbus campaign.
Distributed by the Order, these informational pamphlets on the Mexican situation pointed out some of the constitutional and ideological problems behind the treatment of Catholics in Mexico.

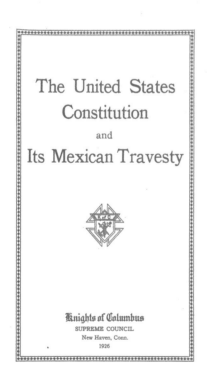

During the middle of the Cristiada, contentious relations between the United States and Mexico received help from a unique "ambassador": the renowned pilot, Charles Lindbergh. Famous for making the first nonstop solo transatlantic flight from New York City to Paris in May 1927, Lindbergh completed another historic trip later that year. At the invitation of President Calles himself, Lindbergh flew from Washington, DC to Mexico City on December 14. This time, rather than a feat of aviation, the flight was a dramatic diplomatic gesture—a show of U.S. goodwill toward Mexico. Dubbed the "Ambassador without a portfolio," Lindbergh described his goals for the flight in *The New York Times,* suggesting that through such endeavors "fundamental emotions, common to all people, are stirred and result in expressions of friendliness." Although Lindbergh landed in Mexico City hours later than his expected arrival, he was greeted by large and exuberant crowds, which included President Calles.

Although the significance attributed to this diplomatic gesture may seem unusual today, the need for it only further highlights the serious tensions between the two countries at the time.

Interestingly, another bond was made through this event: while he was in Mexico City, Lindbergh was introduced to Ambassador Morrow's daughter, Anne, whom he would later marry.

Overnight fame.
After an over thirty-three hour flight, "Lucky Lindy" arrives in France and is swarmed by a crowd of 100,000. *The New York Times* wrote that "not since the armistice of 1918 has Paris witnessed a downright demonstration of popular enthusiasm." The night before Lindbergh's arrival in Mexico, thousands of eager Mexicans slept outside at the airbase. They didn't want to risk missing a glimpse of the famed plane and its pilot.

Cause for celebration.
President Calles declared the day of Lindbergh's arrival a national holiday; all government offices and businesses were closed. Here, Lindbergh is taken through the streets of Mexico City as thousands greet him from the sidewalks.

Unconventional diplomacy.
Calles characterized Lindbergh's flight as a "priceless embassy of goodwill." Later, Mexico's president was left beaming after the famed aviator treated him to a plane ride over his palace at Chapultepec. Upon exiting the plane, Calles remarked that it was "smoother than a train ride." Here, Lindbergh and Calles appear with Morrow at Mexico's National Stadium.

A "hero" for Anne.
Ambassador Morrow's daughter Anne, who once wrote that her life's ambition was "to marry a hero," first met Lindbergh during his goodwill tour to Mexico. The couple is shown here while back in the United States, where they married in 1929.

This cartoon portrays one public opinion of the U.S. involvement in the Mexican situation.

President Portes Gil appears as an obedient dog faithful to Calles's commands in this take on who really ran the presidency.

ENVISIONING U.S. SUPPORT: DIFFERENT PERSPECTIVES

Having a presence in both Mexico and the United States, the Knights of Columbus was able to facilitate a flow of information between the two countries. Gathered in reports, the information made it from Mexico into the hands of influential U.S. leaders in the Church, State, and a number of other organizations. Soon, many of these organizations became active in helping to raise awareness. For example, William F. Montavon, legal counsel for the National Catholic Welfare Conference, wrote a fifty-page brief of well-authenticated facts documenting the Mexican situation, including a list of atrocities committed against the Catholics there. The National Council of Catholic Women addressed President Coolidge, also urging him to respond. The pressures exerted on congress by U.S. Catholics never stopped.

The American Federation of Labor (AFL) also added its voice to the movement, even though its previous leader, Samuel Gompers, sympathized with President Calles's policies. In August 1926, the Associated Building Trades Council of Philadelphia and Vicinity (of the AFL) denounced the violations of the rights, liberties, and conscience of Mexicans and called upon its AFL members "to give their earnest support to the people of Mexico in their masterful struggle against great odds." The statement issued a further request to the President: "We call upon the Honorable Calvin Coolidge, President of the United States, and urge him to use every righteous power at his command" to help the Mexican people. On August 3, 1926, President William Green of the AFL wrote a long letter to Luis

Killing "the chicken that lays the golden eggs" refers to the U.S. oil concessions and how Mexico benefitted the U.S.

This image shows "Uncle Sam" offering Ambassador Morrow to Lady Mexico, who shows coy interest.

The U.S. presidential seat, occupied by Hoover, is shown to be an uncomfortable place, thanks to Mexico's revolution.

Morones, CROM leader and Mexican Secretary of Commerce, Industry, and Labor, in which he condemned the Catholic persecution. Some months later, Green even met with Bishop Pascual Díaz, who would become one of the major proponents of the moderate Mexican line and a leader in the Mexican Church.

Heightened awareness of the religious persecution and new calls for U.S. involvement ushered in different—and often clashing—perspectives on the various forms such involvement should take. On November 25, 1926, the Mexican legislature deliberated at length about the Knights of Columbus and the Mexican Fund. They even perused and read from the pages of *Columbia,* the K of C's magazine, which was later barred from being mailed in Mexico.

At the same time, leaders of the National League for the Defense of Religious Liberty anticipated essential financial support for the rebellion from its U.S. contacts. Before the outbreak of war, Cardinal Hayes and other U.S. bishops wrote letters of recommendation for League emissaries and even gave them money; but in October of 1926, as soon as the League's decision to pursue an armed struggle was made public, support was withdrawn, and the bishops requested that the letters from Cardinal Hayes and others be returned.

This diplomatic line infuriated League emissary Father Mariano Cuevas, a Mexican Jesuit and historian. At a meeting of U.S. bishops, Father Cuevas requested funds, proposed a U.S. boycott against Mexico, and asked that arms be made available to the rebels. The bishops' apparent lack of enthusiasm for the proposal aroused Cuevas's anger, and soon he burst into a tirade

LOVERS OF LIBERTY·· STAY OUT OF MEXICO!

Order in quantities at cost price from
THE QUEEN'S WORK
3742 West Pine Boulevard
ST. LOUIS, MO.

PRINTED IN U. S. A.

"Lovers of Liberty, Stay Out of Mexico!"
This pamphlet, distributed through the Catholic magazine *The Queen's Work*, calls on American tourists ("one of Mexico's largest 'industries'") to refrain from vacationing in Mexico.

LOVERS OF LIBERTY... STAY OUT OF MEXICO!

THE present corrupt, tyrannous, bloodthirsty government of Mexico is trying to draw American tourists into Mexico.

Why?

Because American tourists are one of Mexico's largest "industries."

American tourists bring millions of American dollars to enrich the party in power.

But do American tourists know that the government and party in control of Mexico violates all that America loves and reveres?

1. A small minority of ruthless tyrants keeps the great majority of Mexicans in subjection by armed force, injustice, trickery.

2. They permit only one political party in Mexico. Hence there are no free elections. The voter must vote for the tyrants in power or not vote at all. That party controls nationwide graft that has made its leaders multimillionaires.

3. They have adopted the worst principles of Soviet Russia.

4. They flagrantly disregard human rights. Parents are forced to send their children to communistic, atheistic schools. Property is ruthlessly confiscated. Only the party in power has any rights.

5. They have time and again flouted and disregarded American rights.

6. They make war on all religion, Catholic, Protestant, Jewish; have driven God from the land, and make the practice and preaching of religion a crime punishable by death, exile or confiscation.

7. They have shot and still shoot down all opponents. They have martyred hundreds of priests and nuns and thousands of peasants.

8. They have frequently endangered the lives of tourists by widespread terrorism which included armed attacks on places which tourists were visiting.

9. The country seethes with discontent and rebellion against this tyranny.

LOVERS OF LIBERTY... STAY OUT OF MEXICO!

against Yankee selfishness and imperialism, effectively erasing any lingering doubts the bishops may have had regarding their diplomatic course. Indeed, while the Mexican bishops were divided in their judgment of the armed rebellion, the U.S. bishops were unwavering in their decision to no longer support the League.

The Knights of Columbus followed suit; though prior to its declaration of war, the League received vital support from the K of C in the United States, afterward the Order absolutely refused to assist the war effort. Nevertheless, the Knights' Mexican Fund continued to cause a stir, both at home and abroad. Both political figures and journalists criticized the Knights for attempting or desiring to "interfere" with Mexican politics. Unfounded rumors soon arose that the Knights' money was going to the League to support the war effort. Incredibly, some even went so far as to declare that the Knights were rounding up an army to march down to Mexico.

Attacks upon the Knights' Mexican Fund came especially from the Ku Klux Klan and its supporters. In fact, the Klan was quick to denounce the Knights' plan and to offer $10 million to the Mexican government in its fight against Papism. The KKK also sent telegrams of congratulations to President Calles, asking him repeatedly for the full annihilation of the Church south of the Rio Grande. Moreover, even the U.S. Senate took notice as it hotly debated the Knights' fund for three hours in January 1927. The debate was led by Senator James Thomas Heflin, who contributed to KKK magazines and lectured around the country to audiences made up largely of KKK members.

In response, the Knights of Columbus stressed unequivocally that the money was being used only in the United States and only for peaceful purposes. And indeed, as the historian Christopher J. Kauffman explained in his definitive history of the Order: "Though rumors have persisted to circulate that a part of the Order's Mexican Fund went to the purchase of arms for the Cristeros, there is no evidence of such direct support." Eventually, the authors of the outlandish accusations were exposed as frauds, although these types of attacks continued for years. This necessitated on certain occasions the intervention of the K of C Catholic Affairs Committee to curb the spread of such untrue and malicious statements and pursue appropriate legal avenues to ensure that satisfactory retraction was made.

While rival opinions clamored for the last word, and new figures and organizations entered the fray, the U.S. State Department's analysis of the situation evolved in favor of helping Mexico reach a resolution. Through the advocacy of organizations like the National Catholic Welfare Conference and the Knights of Columbus, and the support of the U.S. bishops, resolving the religious issue became a priority for the U.S. in its affairs with Mexico. Gradually, it became an issue upon which other issues between the two countries depended. So as Ambassador Sheffield officially stepped down on July 18, 1927, and the undesirable post fell to Dwight Morrow, the Mexican papers ran bold headlines, declaring: "After Morrow, the Marines . . ."

THE RED PERIL OF MEXICO

Banned reading.
As part of its campaign to raise American awareness of the Mexican situation, the Knights of Columbus included at least one article in nearly every issue of *Columbia* published in 1926 and 1927. The November 1926 issue shown here was reviewed and debated by the Mexican legislature, which later decided to ban the magazine from being mailed to Mexico.

THE PATH OF U.S. DIPLOMACY

On September 20, 1927, the hope for reconciliation gained a new ally when Dwight W. Morrow replaced James Sheffield as the U.S. ambassador to Mexico. In contrast to Sheffield, Ambassador Morrow showed a better grasp of the situation—and even a desire to get involved, as a friend of his reflected:

> When Morrow told me he wanted to concern himself over the religious issue to see if he could fix it, my admiration for his marvelous boldness and self-confidence went up a notch; however, the high opinion that his good sense deserved in my eyes momentarily waned. I told him this was an explosive issue . . . and I would not deal with it, not even by mistake.
>
>   Mr. Morrow replied to me, "The country is utterly disrupted; the poor possess only the consolation that the Church provides, and there will be no true progress or peace if an accord is not reached. I don't think their difference is as ample as they believe it is. Their life experience is the same; they just approach it from different perspectives. If I can bring them a little closer, I believe they will see things from the same point of view, and will realize that they differ less than it seems."

Cordial introductions. U.S. Ambassador Dwight Morrow greets President Calles in this 1927 photograph. In his address of introduction (shown here), Morrow emphasized hopes for friendliness—which he received. This led Sheffield, Morrow's predecessor, to defend his own poor record as the result of unwillingness on the part of Calles.

Mr. President:
    I have the honor formally to make known to you that the President of the United States of America has appointed me Ambassador Extraordinary and Plenipotentiary to your Government. I hereby present to Your Excellency the letter of recall of my distinguished predecessor, the Honorable James Rockwell Sheffield, and tender at the same time my letters of credence.
    I enter upon my duties with full consciousness of the honor which my Government has conferred upon me in entrusting to my hands the representation of its interests in this great neighboribg State.
    I welcome the opportunity of cooperating with Your Excellency in finding a mutually satisfactory solution of the problems with which our two countries are now faced. It is my earnest hope that, animated by a common desire to promote the welfare of the United Mexican States and the United States of America, we shall not fail to adjust outstanding questions with that dignity and mutual respect which should mark the international relationship of two sovereign and independent states.

American Embassy in Mexico.
Morrow (front row, center) and the embassy staff.

However, after studying all the documents related to the matter, Morrow fine-tuned his analysis of the situation, recognizing the existence of genuine differences that only persistence and patient compromise could resolve. He said:

> Only a madman would try to fix the existing differences in matters of principle between the Church and Mexico. These differences are very well underscored in the document the bishops sent to President Calles on August 16, 1926, as well as in the President's reply, dated August 20. . . . If I understand it correctly, the bishops' letter seeks a degree of mutual tolerance that would allow for public peace and afford the Church relative freedom to exist and to act. Apparently, the only laws being criticized in specific terms are those that place conditions on the ministry and set a fixed number of priests. . . . The President's letter is extensively devoted to theory and philosophy, which are not his strong suit by any means . . . it insists on paragraph 50 of Article 130, which denies legal status to churches, and seems to say that religious ministers will be merely considered as professionals. Naturally, I believe the Church will never accept such a principle, and all other churches will agree with it on this position.

In October, before leaving Washington for Mexico, Morrow met with Father John J. Burke of the National Catholic Welfare Conference along with Under Secretary of State Robert Olds to discuss the religious question in Mexico. Despite their very different backgrounds (one a former partner at J.P. Morgan & Company and the other a Catholic Paulist priest), both Morrow and Burke quickly developed a sense of mutual trust that ultimately led to a

Although the "religious question" was considered by some to be a national problem, negotiating a compromise was an international endeavor that included statesmen and clergy from Mexico and the United States, and even input from the Vatican. Presented here are some of the individuals who played a significant role in the diplomatic conversations that led to the peace Accords of 1929.

President Plutarco Elías Calles.
As both president and later as chief advisor to his successor, Calles personally would be involved throughout the negotiations process.

Secretary of Education
Dr. José Manuel Puig Casauranc.
Puig Casauranc played an important role in delivering the famed "Apology of Celaya." In it, he publicly announced the administration's openness to reconciliation. He later became the Mexican Ambassador to the U.S.

Bishop Pascual Díaz.
A principle negotiator, Díaz was one of the many bishops exiled by the Calles administration. Although the administration exiled many clergy for being foreign-born, Bishop Díaz was Mexican.

President Emilio Portes Gil.
The negotiations, and eventually the Accords, would all happen on his watch as president.

William F. Montavon.
As director of the National Catholic Welfare Conference's legal department, Montavon worked behind the scenes with Father Burke. He met with Calles in preliminary meetings, and helped Morrow stay informed and connected to the Mexican bishops. For his work, he was made a Knight of Saint Gregory at the request of Pope Pius XII.

Bishop Leopoldo Ruiz y Flores.
Together with Bishop Díaz, Bishop Ruiz y Flores would lead the conversations and personal meetings with Calles.

Father John J. Burke.
Serving as executive secretary of the National Catholic Welfare Conference, Father Burke was also the first to initiate contact between the Mexican bishops and the U.S. State Department. He forwarded a message he had received from the bishops to the State Department.

Ambassador Dwight W. Morrow.
Dialoging as an ambassador, Morrow had to keep in mind not only the religious question, but also its impact on many other issues at home and abroad.

Oct. 3rd, 1927.

Hon. Dwight W. Morrow,
    4 East 66th Street,
        New York City.

My dear Dwight:

        Unless I hear from you to the contrary, I will come
to your apartment tomorrow morning at 10 o'clock as suggested
by you.   I may bring a few papers which we can look over, if
agreeable to you, on the Mexican situation and the policy or
lack of policy on the part of the State Department.

        I am still of the opinion that I would not be in
too much haste to get away, as it is much easier to make your
preparations here before you go than to attempt to complete
them after you have arrived.   Besides, according to the Evening Sun of today, I notice that a part of the Mexico City
Garrison has apparently revolted, and if things are to be much
disturbed, it is just as well to know what the situation is
likely to be and how you will be expected to meet it before you
have to actually face the situation on the ground.

        I hold very strong views that if the present Government
is overthrown and another Government installed, the United States
should refuse recognition of the new Government until we had
entered into some binding arrangement with reference to the

SHEFFIELD & BETTS   PAGE 2.

protection of American rights.   President Coolidge agreed
with me when I talked this over last year and promised that
no recognition would be accorded a new Government without
some such positive arrangement first arrived at.   I hope
he has not changed his views, and when in Washington I would
be glad to discuss this question with you and with him, if
agreeable to you both.   I may add that this same view is
strongly held by Mr. Schoenfeld and my Staff in Mexico.

        I have from time to time alluded to my conviction
that the only way to achieve results with the Mexican Government is to be firm and to make them understand that you mean
what you say.   Any attempt at modification or even conciliation where a principle of International Law is involved is
looked upon by them as weakness.   They are extremely keen at
reading your mind, clever in argument and, in the long run,
have seldom failed to get the better of us in note writing.
This was my reason for criticizing the position of the State
Department and Mr. Warren in having the interminable note writing
controversy over the oil and land laws.   It practically got
us nowhere and led Mexico to feel that we were content with
wordy protests and would not follow it up with any positive
action.   At any rate, I shall have opportunity, I hope, to go
into this matter more fully with you before you leave.

        Anticipating seeing you tomorrow, believe me

                        Very sincerely yours,

JRS:O

---

real cooperation in resolving the problem. For three years, both worked tirelessly in their communication with President Calles, meeting in private with him and arranging meetings with the bishops.

Morrow's arrival in Mexico City in late October 1927 could not have been at a more ominous time. The next month, an assassination attempt was made against former President Álvaro Obregón. Ten days later, President Calles ordered (without a trial) the execution of the Jesuit priest Father Miguel Pro and his brother Humberto Pro, who had been falsely accused of participation in the unsuccessful assassination.

While Morrow navigated a volatile Mexico, Father Burke visited President Coolidge in the United States on November 26, 1927. Burke spoke with him about the difficult balance of treating the situation as a domestic Mexican problem (requiring some autonomy) and a problem with international interest and consequences. Describing the meeting afterward, Burke recalled how, though "The President expressed his abhorrence of Calles's methods," ultimately President Coolidge concluded that the "matter . . . internationally would be looked upon as . . . Mexico's concern." Like many at the time, President Coolidge feared that any direct interference in the religious crisis might lead to escalation of tensions and possibly even war with Mexico. Cautious involvement and much discretion on the part of Ambassador Morrow were further necessitated.

On January 17, 1928, Ambassador Morrow and Father Burke met again in Havana, Cuba, for two days to discuss the situation. Both decided that the time had arrived to take the initiative in pushing for negotiations. They began planning a letter to President Calles, proposing a meeting between him and Father Burke.

But the plan was quickly foiled. After Morrow had set a date for the proposed meeting with President Calles for the following month, news of the meeting was leaked by members of the League. On February 9, just one day

In case of government overthrow . . .
In this letter, former Ambassador Sheffield brings up to Ambassador Morrow the possibility of the Calles government being overthrown. He then lays out the policies that he and Coolidge had agreed on—that no recognition would be given to the next Mexican government until American interests were adequately protected.

before the meeting was to take place, the *New York Herald Tribune* and other papers ran the story, which so annoyed Calles that he canceled the meeting.

This unfortunate turn of events had the additional effect of mobilizing pro-militants within the Mexican episcopate, including Bishop Leopoldo Lara y Torres of Tacambaro, who was especially critical of the diplomatic line being pursued. On February 27, Bishop Lara y Torres wrote a letter to Bishop Miguel de la Mora, who at the time was the secretary of the Episcopal Subcommittee, warning of how the "honorable" Father Burke "might . . . be charmed by our enemies and trust their promises and words." For his part, Bishop de la Mora put great faith in the war, even saying that "the armed defense provides lots of hope and now presents concrete possibilities of a not very distant triumph."

Posing a far greater hindrance to any proposed negotiations on the religious issue, however, was Mexico's controversial oil and land legislation. While many petitioned Washington to intervene—diplomatically or otherwise—delicate negotiations between Ambassador Morrow and President Calles managed to quell the storm. On March 27, 1928, after years of tension, dispute, and tactful diplomacy, amendments to the controversial legislation went into effect.

Seeking to preserve this fragile diplomatic achievement, Ambassador Morrow quickly turned his attention back to the religious situation. He was more aware than ever of how important it was to advocate a compatible approach that was amenable to U.S. interests, "pacifying" its neighbor to the south rather than causing disorder between the countries.

Morrow proved an astute negotiator. Unlike his predecessor, who was often derided for a deadly combination of narrow-mindedness, prejudice, and gullibility, Morrow was sensitive to the complex motives of both the Church and the State in Mexico that hindered bids for reconciliation. Aware that many of the Mexican bishops were in disagreement with the League and the Cristeros, and that Rome did not support armed resistance, he saw an opening for diplomacy.

Ambassador Morrow consulted a wide range of interested parties. With the help of Father Burke and NCWC lawyer William Montavon, he maintained contacts with

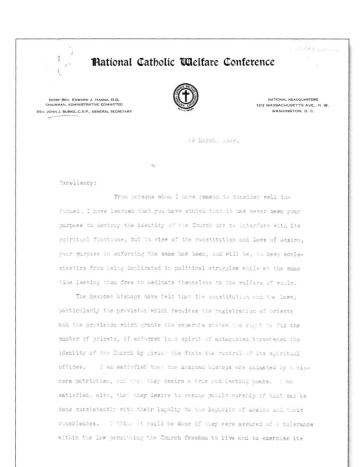

Planning a diplomatic date.
Scheduling a day to discuss religious issues is the subject of this letter sent to Calles from Father Burke.

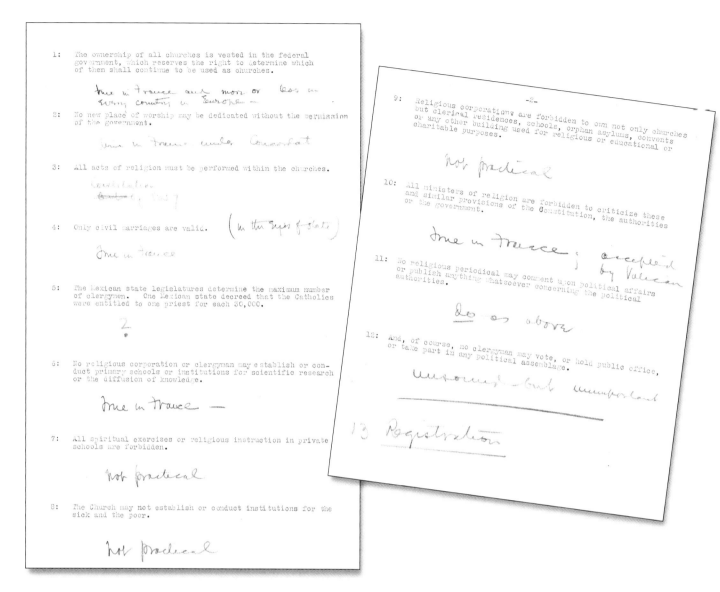

Morrow's notes.
Listed here are the major points of contention between the Church and State, with Morrow's handwritten notes below each item—some of which are deemed "not practical."

the two exiled Mexican bishops, Bishop Pascual Díaz (in New York) and Archbishop Leopoldo Ruiz y Flores of Morelia (in Washington). In fact, for several months, Father Burke had been hosting Archbishop Ruiz y Flores. Morrow also stayed in communication with the Vatican through the Vatican's Apostolic Delegate to the United States, Archbishop Pietro Fumasoni-Biondi, as well as some foreign embassies, including those of France and Chile.

Shortly after the resolution of the oil crisis, Burke and Morrow again planned a meeting with President Calles. Beforehand, Father Burke had tactfully requested and received authority from Apostolic Delegate Fumasoni-Biondi in the United States to meet with Calles, and the Mexican bishops were informed later. On March 29, 1928, Father Burke sent his letter to President Calles, and received a quick reply on April 4; that same day, Father Burke, Ambassador Morrow, and President Calles met in the old fort of San Juan de Ulúa in Veracruz. Calles was impressed by Burke, and said in parting, "I hope your visit marks the beginning of a new era for the life and people of Mexico." Importantly, the meeting concluded with a mutual feeling that there was an urgent need for a peaceful agreement, and that unreasonable demands should be left aside.

It was a good beginning, but more needed to be done. Ambassador Morrow requested another show of good will from President Calles. This was delivered on April 15 in what is known as the famous "Apology of Celaya." At an official ceremony, Mexican Secretary of Education Puig Casauranc, in the presence of President Calles and former President Obregón, affirmed that it was not the intention of the government to eradicate veneration of "the Virgin of Guadalupe, that divine image that is so dear to the hearts of all good Mexicans among other things." Soon after, when Bishop Pascual Díaz was informed of Casauranc's address, he understood it as a real sign that President Calles wanted to finally return to Catholics in Mexico their "hope and their right" to freely practice their religion.

On April 22, Archbishop of Mexico Mora y del Río died, and was replaced by Archbishop Leopoldo Ruiz y Flores as the new leader of the Church in Mexico. Consequently, for the second meeting with President Calles, Ambassador Morrow suggested that Archbishop Ruiz y Flores, who was also the president of the Episcopal Committee at the time, accompany Father Burke. On May 17, Calles received them in Mexico City for a positive meeting with results that the archbishop was pleased to report directly to the pope. In fact, after the meeting, Archbishop Ruiz y Flores left almost immediately for the Vatican.

However, not all parties trusted these overtures for negotiation. Just as many in the United States disliked increased contact with Catholic Mexico (fearing that the "Protestant" U.S. would become "Catholicized"), so some in Mexico feared that U.S. intervention would de-Catholicize Mexico with Protestant, secular, and Masonic values. This included some Mexican bishops who expressed their feelings to the League, which, in turn, sent a long letter to Pope Pius XI on May 31, 1928. The letter denounced the diplomatic work of Archbishop Ruiz y Flores and Bishop Díaz as participating in the United State's disastrous role in the de-Catholicization of Mexico. Many like-minded Catholics from outside the League, sharing the same fears, also signed this letter.

Despite such criticisms, everything appeared to be progressing smoothly and suddenly very quickly. But the tumultuous events at the end of 1928 (detailed in the previous chapter) would demand further patience from all—and a great amount of finesse from Ambassador Morrow. The assassination of President-elect Obregón abruptly halted the peace negotiations and even put a temporary damper on the war. Morrow found himself suddenly having to work with a new negotiator—President Portes Gil; and with the election of President Hoover, he had to answer to a new "boss." Along with continued disputes over the Mexican oil fields, Morrow also had to deal with requests from the Mexican government for military weapons to help suppress the Escobar rebellion, which had begun early in 1929. But now, there was hope as well.

A last day in office.
Calles attends an event marking his final act as president: the inauguration of the agricultural rural school in Tenería, on November 30, 1928.

Putting down arms.
The San Gaspar Regiment enters Jalostotitlán, Jalisco, in perfect military formation to surrender their weapons.

8.

The Closing of the War

AT THE ZENITH

In June 1929, after the Federal soldiers returned from quelling other rebellions in the North, the Cristero movement reached its zenith. Having beaten Federal General Cedillo in a pitched battle, the Cristeros were proving that they could maneuver above the regimental level. Earlier, on April 19, at Tepatitlán, three regiments commanded by Father Vega added to the recent string of victories by defeating six Federal units. Generals Gorostieta and Jesús Degollado (commander of the southern Jalisco division) had 25,000 armed and organized men, with another 25,000 Cristero soldiers, more or less organized, in the rest of the country. Although "seriously lacking in ammunition, which forced them into guerilla warfare," as Gorostieta observed, the Cristeros were "[d]isciplined and moral men that . . . formed troops of a caliber never seen before and never to be seen again in Mexico."

Everything was going extremely well at a time when the Army of the Federation was struggling. Yet General Gorostieta knew the difficulties still facing the Cristero cause—without money or ammunition, they could not counterbalance the financial, military, and political support for the government from the United States. The Cristeros had reached an impasse, as Gorostieta confided to fellow Cristero Heriberto Navarrete: "I don't know how this will end. The government will never be able to defeat us as long as all worship remains suspended, and we can't overpower it: there's an equilibrium of sorts."

Of particular concern to General Gorostieta at the time was his fear that the bishops would accept a poor solution simply to end the impasse. On June 1, 1929, just twenty days before the State and Church reached their accords,

Words of comfort
from Pope Pius XI.

On June 21, 1928, the pope sent this consoling message to the clergy and Catholic faithful of Mexico. In it, he asks that there be trust in him and the bishops, and trust in the negotiations that were currently underway.

June 1928

CONSOLATORY MESSAGE FROM HIS HOLINESS PIUS XI
TO HIS CLERGY AND TO THE MEXICAN PUBLIC.

His Holiness Pius XI, having heard of the anxiety and alarm which have been spread among the Clergy and Mexican public, due to rumors, fortunately unfounded, that have been circulated in these days in regard to an incomplete solution of the religious conflict, that loving Father desired to comfort and console his beloved people of Mexico with the following message, which arrived in the United States and from there was sent to Mexico:

HAVE CONFIDENCE IN THE HOLY FATHER AND IN THE EPISCOPACY, NEVER CEASING TO PRAY TO GOD AND TO THE VIRGIN OF GUADALUPE. CARD. GASPARRI. (His Excellency Cardinal Gasparri is the Secretary of State, who carries out the orders of the Holy Father).

Find here, venerable priests and beloved faithful, a wise plan for the regulation of your conduct in the present difficult circumstances. PRAYER AND CONFIDENCE, (together with action, since the true zeal of the glory of God is anxious to work for love of him and does all possible to procure the establishment of the reign of Christ in the world).

Pray, because all should be hoped for from God, the fount of all good, who with such tender love and great pity has supported us, in spite of our wretchedness, in the profession of our holy faith, during this terrible crisis, to the admiration of the Catholic world. And we should hope for all from God, through the mediation of the powerful prayers of our loving Mother, the Immaculate Virgin of Guadalupe

-2-

Guadalupe, who chose us as her preferred people and came to Mexico to be our help and our refuge and to HEAR OUR TEARS AND PRAYERS and to give us consolation and assistance.

Pray, yes pray to God and the Immaculate Virgin of Guadalupe! Prayer is omnipotent and passes beyond the clouds and binds the hands of God that he may not punish, and extinguishes in his hand the thunderbolt of anger, and opens the divine treasures that they may be shed upon the earth.

Do not cease praying, venerable priests and beloved faithful, to God and to the Virgin of Guadalupe, and the day of mercy for which we hope will not be delayed.

BELIEVE in the Holy Father, because he is the Vicar of Jesus Christ on earth; because as the visible head of the Church he is granted special assistance by the Holy Spirit in governing the flock of the Savior; because the Holy See, with experience of 20 centuries, and accustomed to handling the gravest problems of humanity, works always with prudence and deliberation, consulting the ecclesiastical heads, studying and scrutinizing the problems and exhausting all precautions that it may not err, and this, although in questions of faith and customs the Pope, interpreting officially, is infallible; because, in addition to all this, which is more than sufficient upon which to base our confidence, the present Pope has for us a tender interest and has shown himself in all this time a loving and compassionate Father of the Mexican Nation; and we, therefore, may be assured that he will do all that he can for our good.

WE SHOULD HAVE FAITH IN THE EPISCOPACY because the Bishops are the shepherds of the flock, placed by the Holy Spirit to govern the Church of God, and our Bishops are shepherds full of love for their dioceses and the laws of Christ

Christ, and for this reason have faced with great abnegation, dignity and impregnable fortitude all kinds of suffering and sorrow, in order not to harm the Church whose honor is in their keeping.

WE MUST HAVE FAITH IN THE POPE AND THE BISHOPS, because it is our duty, and is the wish of Jesus Christ, from whom came those solemn words pronounced to the Apostles and their successors: "Those who listen to you, listen to me, and those who scorn you, scorn me"; this is required of us as Catholics, because a glorious characteristic of the Catholics is to be disciplined, with that discipline whose motive power is faith, which makes us see our leaders as the representatives of Christ; with this discipline whose strength is the noble virtue of obedience, without which no government is possible; with that discipline whose principal stimulus is love of Christ and of those who show in their countenance the august brilliancy of an authority which proceeds from Christ.

Console yourselves, venerable priests and beloved faithful; do not fear, there is nothing to fear; and follow the stanch plan that has been outlined for you by the most high and the most beloved authority of the earth. Petition, unceasingly, of God and of the Virgin of Guadalupe, and rest confident in the prudence and wiseness of the Holy See, and, above all, in the Holy Spirit which assists it in governing the Christian world. Have hope in our God and we will not become confused.

Mexico, June 21, 1928.

THE EPISCOPAL SUB-COMMITTEE.

Gorostieta confided to a friend, sadly saying of the bishops, "They are selling us out, Manuelito, they are selling us out." The following day, Gorostieta was killed when Federal soldiers ambushed the group of Cristeros he was with. He had been crossing the plain between the highlands of Jalisco and the highlands of Michoacán with no more than fifteen men. Since it was dangerous to take this trip during the day with nowhere to hide, the group stopped in a small building of the "hacienda del Valle" to wait for nightfall. Suddenly, Federal troops arrived and surprised them. Gorostieta was able to jump on his horse, but the animal was killed—and soon, Gorostieta

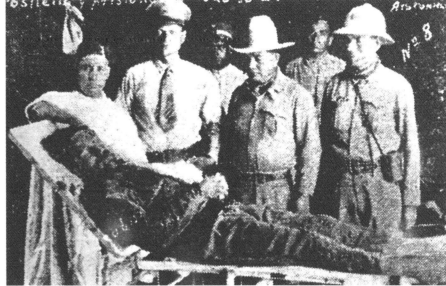

AGICA

Proof of death.
Federales pose with the body of General Gorostieta. It was sometimes customary for the government to photograph the corpse of an enemy leader to convince the public of its victory.

was dead as well. Some of his soldiers escaped, and the others were taken as prisoners.

The circumstances of Gorostieta's death were so improbable that some people speculated his death was not the result of mere chance; rather, some have suspected it was caused by a traitor, who must have alerted the Federales to Gorostieta's whereabouts. However, this is unlikely, because at the time of the ambush, the Federal soldiers seemed oblivious to the fact that they had killed the commander-in-chief of the Cristeros, realizing it only later on.

Nevertheless, in many ways Gorostieta was the greatest obstacle to the Accords of 1929, which finally ended the Cristiada. In retrospect, we can well wonder whether the Accords would have been impeded had Gorostieta lived long enough. While his military leadership catapulted the Cristeros from being a futile and disorganized group to an effective army, he had also demonstrated his political acumen by ac-

AGICA

Military succession.
After Gorostieta's death, the League appointed General Degollado as supreme commander. Noting others better suited for the post, Degollado (whose troops are shown here) initially declined the appointment, but eventually accepted it.

cepting talks with President Portes Gil in February. Moreover, he had tried to dissuade the bishops from settling with the government. Ultimately, he knew that if negotiations between the State and Church were reached, he could expect nothing, as obedience would follow: "Once the churches reopen, all of them will leave me; I know them well."

ACCORDS FINALLY REACHED

Facing the rapid degradation of the country's military, economic, and political situations, the government was forced to revisit the religious issue in May 1929. That month, Pope Pius XI named Archbishop Ruiz y Flores as the apostolic delegate to negotiate with the Mexican government. The pope had also gained a personal view of the situation from the American perspective when he met with Bishop Emmanuel B. Ledvina of Corpus Christi, Texas, who had helped the exiled Mexican religious for years.

June 21, 1929

I have had conversations with Archbishop Ruíz y Flores and Bishop Pascual Díaz. These conversations took place as a result of the public statement made by Archbishop Ruíz y Flores on May 2nd and the statement made by me on May 8th.

Archbishop Ruíz y Flores and Bishop Díaz informed me that the Mexican Bishops have felt that the Constitution and the laws, particularly the provision which requires the registration of ministers and the provision which grants the separate States the right to determine the maximum number of ministers, threaten the identity of the Church by giving the State the control of its spiritual offices.

They assure me that the Mexican Bishops are animated by a sincere patriotism and that they desire to resume public worship if this can be done consistently with their loyalty to the Mexican Republic and their consciences. They stated that it could be done if the Church could enjoy freedom within the law to live and exercise its spiritual offices.

I am glad to take advantage of this opportunity to declare publicly and very clearly that it is not the purpose of the Constitution, nor of the laws, nor of the Government of the Republic to destroy the identity of the Catholic Church or of any other, or to interfere in any way with its spiritual functions. In accordance with the oath of office which I took when I assumed the Provisional Government of Mexico to observe and cause to be observed the Constitution of the Republic and the laws derived therefrom, my purpose has been at all times to fulfill honestly that oath and to see that the laws are applied without favor to any sect and without any bias whatever, my Administration being

-2-

being disposed to hear from any person, be he a dignitary of some church or merely a private individual, any complaints in regard to injustices arising from undue application of the laws.

With reference to certain provisions of the Law which have been misunderstood, I also take advantage of this opportunity to declare:

(1) That the provision of the Law which requires the registration of ministers does not mean that the Government can register those who have not been named by the hierarchical superior of the religious creed in question or in accordance with its regulations.

(2) With regard to religious instruction, the Constitution and the laws in force definitely prohibit it in primary or higher schools, whether public or private, but this does not prevent ministers of any religion from imparting its doctrines, within church confines, to adults or their children who may attend for that purpose.

(3) That the Constitution as well as the laws of the country guarantee to all residents of the Republic the right of petition and, therefore, the members of any Church may apply to the appropriate authorities for the amendment, repeal or passage of any law.

National Palace, June 21, 1929.

The President of the Republic.

E. Portes Gil (Signed)

A presidential announcement. The Accords were read and signed by President Portes Gil on June 21, 1929 in the National Palace. This is Morrow's translated copy.

From that point on, everything moved very quickly, with Ambassador Morrow providing both intelligence and a willingness to use his "good offices." On June 5—just three days after Gorostieta's death—Archbishop Ruiz y Flores and Bishop Pascual Díaz returned to Mexico, where they met with Calles as part of a negotiating team. On the train ride there, Ambassador Morrow joined them in St. Louis, Missouri. Together, the three men ironed out the last details on their way to Mexico.

The negotiations between the bishops, President Portes Gil, and the mediators took place from June 12 to 21. Based on previous negotiations between Calles and Archbishop Ruiz y Flores through Ambassador Morrow and Father Burke, an agreement was reached. Morrow had composed a memorandum that both sides agreed to. The result was that anticlerical articles of the constitution would remain, but the Calles Law was suspended; the government promised not to register priests independent of those the Church recognized as priests; the churches were returned to the care of the Church; and amnesty was promised to the rebels. In exchange, the Church would recommence Mass and other services in the churches.

The Accords were announced on June 21, and published in the press on June 22, 1929. To relay the good news, Archbishop Ruiz y Flores sent a telegraph to Father Burke, saying, "Dear Father Burke, the work of reconciliation between the Church and the government of Mexico started by you and the National Catholic Welfare Conference in March of last year, has been crowned with the official documents signed today as the first step toward the final settlement. May God bless all the bishops, clergy, and people of the United States who are sympathizers in the days of trial."

Religious peace was restored in Mexico on June 24, 1929—at last! That same day, Bishop Pascual Díaz was elevated to Archbishop of Mexico, while Archbishop Ruiz y Flores continued to serve as apostolic delegate in Mexico. Both men paid a visit to the Basilica of Our Lady of Guadalupe in Mexico City to offer thanks to the Blessed Virgin.

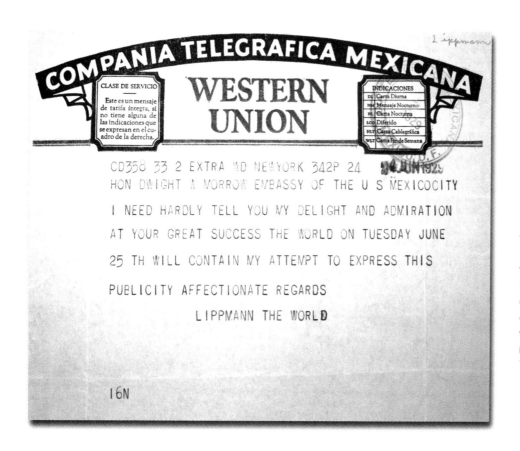

Congratulations from an influential journalist. Among the many congratulatory messages Ambassador Morrow received after the signing of the peace Accords was this telegram from noted journalist Walter Lippmann. In it, Lippmann—who was greatly concerned over the Mexican situation and maintained correspondence with Morrow during the negotiations—indicates that he will be announcing the news in his widely read column in *The World* newspaper the next day.

Celebrating his return.
A crowd greets Apostolic Delegate Ruiz y Flores at the Basilica of Our Lady of Guadalupe.

And in a little expression of how both countries were tied together, the Accords immediately resulted in Mexico's stocks increasing on the New York Stock Exchange.

Rome, trusting the guidance of the Church in Mexico to the negotiators, confirmed its resolve to remain prudent and committed to the matter. In dealing with the bishops, the Mexican government had, in fact, recognized the existence of the Church. While the Church waited for the laws to be modified (a final step that was not achieved until 1992), the government made a commitment to ensure that the laws would be enforced with a lenient interpretation. Later—as we will see in the next chapter—it would cost Rome time and effort to enforce this compliance among many Mexican Catholics, especially between 1932 and 1938, when the government failed to comply with the 1929 Accords. This would lead some to feel deceived and even betrayed by the famous *modus vivendi* (peaceful agreement). The arrangements (*arreglos*) that were made in 1929 were, however, in effect between 1929 and 1931, and again after 1938.

Church services resumed.
Archbishop Díaz presides at the inaugural Mass at the Basilica of Our Lady of Guadalupe in Mexico City. A glimpse of the famed image of Our Lady of Guadalupe is visible above the altar.

In Focus

Celebrated Homecomings

In addition to granting safe passage to combatant Cristeros, the peace Accords of 1929 saw the safe return of many others who had been forced out of society by the persecution. These photographs depict some of the small joys experienced at the war's end, as prisoners and exiles returned to their homes. Some of these deportees had been kept as prisoners on Islas Marías, an island chain seventy miles off Mexico's western coast in the Pacific Ocean.

Also returning to their local parishes were priests. And, of course, with the priests came the return of the sacraments and liturgies. But perhaps one of the most telling homecomings was the return of the famed image of Our Lady of Guadalupe, which had been hidden for protection and replaced with a copy during the war.

Pilgrims to the Virgin's shrine.
Officials estimated that 100,000 Mexican Catholics made the pilgrimage to pray at the Guadalupe Basilica on the day the Accords were announced.

A town greets its priest.
The parish priest from Soyatlán, in Jalisco, arrives atop a much-decorated horse. Interestingly, such celebratory displays even accompanied President Portes Gil, who, on the day of the Accords, was met outside his office by cheering Catholics.

Islas Marías prisoners return.
The freed prisoners shown here were all non-combatants. Fortunately, during their incarceration they received better treatment than expected thanks to the appointment of Federal General Francisco Múgica—a critic of the penal colony system—as head of the prison in 1928.

THE AFTERMATH OF WAR

In June 1929, there were 50,000 Cristeros fighting when the Mexican government and the Church made peace. The Mexican authorities offered safe passage to all Cristeros who came and surrendered their arms. However, when church bells rang out indicating that an agreement had been reached, most Cristeros spontaneously disbanded without bothering to appear before the authorities to receive safe passage. (In fact, only 14,000 presented themselves.) The war ended as it had begun. The Cristeros had started their uprising without permission, and they went back to their homes (if their homes were still standing) in the same way. They were just as poor as they had been before, if not more so. Their cause—which, as they said, was that of Christ and the Virgin Mary—was seemingly finished. Now, Christ had returned to the altars, and once again they were allowed to kneel before the Virgin in their churches.

The peacefulness with which the Cristeros complied exceeded the expectations of some, leading the U.S. military attaché to Mexico to write on October 15, 1929: "It was expected that after the religious warfare was ended, a number of the 'Cristeros' would turn bandits. This has not resulted."

Never had an insurgent movement in Mexico faced such a strong army, despite its defects, as the one formed by General Joaquín Amaro. Never was

A peace celebration.
A Cristero officer celebrates the hour of peace with his men.

Ready to return home.
Cristero troops in Jacona, Michoacán, are discharged on August 15, 1929—nearly two months after the Accords.

there a government backed so strongly by the United States. Never was there an insurgent movement with so few resources and such motivated supporters with such great perseverance. The war—well-fought though destined to go on because no decisive battle could be won—had a political solution. But the cost was high. In three years, around 90,000 combatants died, including 12 generals, 70 colonels, 1,800 officers, and 40,000 soldiers on the Federal side, and about as many on the Cristero side. These figures do not account for the losses suffered among the civilian population, for it was impossible to calculate the effects of the disruptions, hunger, and epidemics that had occurred during the war. There were an estimated 200,000 deaths, both civilian and military.

For the historian, calculating the cost of any war is difficult. The Cristiada is no different. In addition to casualties and military expenses, one must also consider the value of destroyed property, lost opportunities, economic turmoil and recession, and the massive exodus of Mexican citizens who sought refuge in the United States. Although the fall in the prices of nonferrous metals on the world market and the drop in petroleum production were both independent of the war, a drop in the value of other resources did stem from the Cristiada, and the agricultural heartland of Mexico suffered as a result. Between 1926 and 1929, the country's agricultural production dropped 38 percent (before the war, between 1921 and 1926, it had increased 60 percent). Corn production dropped 25 percent and bean production dropped by 50 percent. Little by little, the economic paralysis reached the small towns and all parts of the countryside.

During this time, emigration reached proportions that only exacerbated the serious economic problems in Mexico. For the first time in Mexican history, emigration affected not only the ranching areas, but also the cities and small towns. The incredible growth of provincial capitals like León and Guadalajara dates back to these war years, as does the growth of Mexican barrios in Los Angeles and Chicago. And many who took refuge in these places never left.

For the bishops returning to Mexico, there were many fond and grateful memories of the American clergy, who had been so helpful during their exile. Going forward, many would continue to preserve these new ties as they began the difficult process of rebuilding the Church in Mexico. Newly appointed Archbishop of Mexico Pascual Díaz would maintain friendly correspondence with the U.S. bishops and other American friends until his death in 1936. He even sent individual thank-you notes,

Urban disrepair.
Federal troops observe damage
suffered by a building during the war.

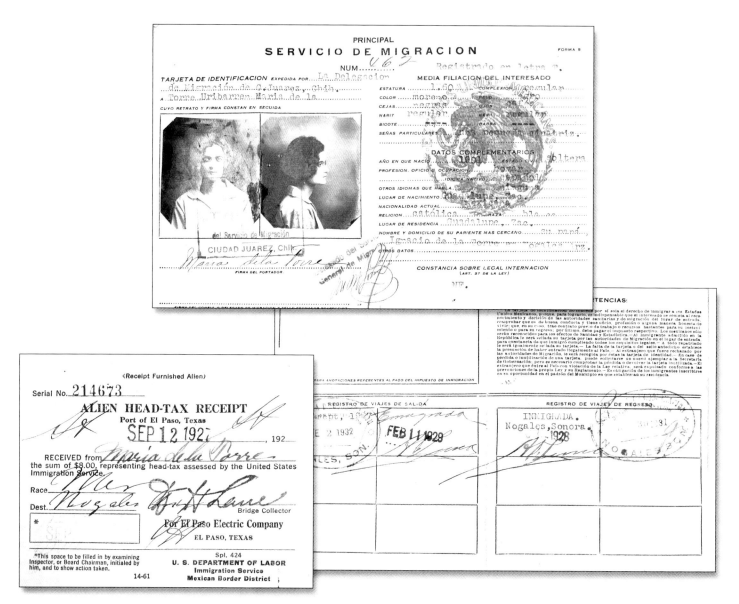

Uprooted families.
The immigration card and alien head-tax receipt of María de la Torre—one of the hundreds of thousands of Mexicans who came to the United States either permanently or temporarily during the war.

written in English, for each letter he received from the U.S. clergy that offered congratulations on the Accords and on his elevation to the Archbishopric. In one such note to Cardinal Dougherty of Philadelphia, we are reminded not only of the trials endured, but also of the sobering trials ahead:

> As I assume the heavy responsibility entrusted to me by the Holy See, my thoughts go back to the many good and true friends in the United States whose unfailing support and encouragement sustained us during the years of trial and expectation. . . . It was an inspiring demonstration of the universality and true Catholicity of our common faith. And I beg a continuance of the prayers of the Catholic population of Philadelphia for the difficult problems that lie before us all in Mexico.

As we shall see, few knew just what those "difficult problems" would entail like the Cristeros, who would feel forced to take up arms once more in defense of what they held most dear.

Cristiada Timeline 1929

THE STATE AND THE CHURCH	DIPLOMACY AND U.S. RELATIONS	CATHOLIC IDENTITY, PROTESTS, AND THE WAR

THE STATE AND THE CHURCH

January
Calles founds the Partido Nacional Revolucionario (PNR), later renamed the Institutional Revolutionary Party (PRI).

February
President Portes Gil sends emissary to Gorostieta to discuss peace terms.

March 3
Federal General Escobar issues the Plan of Hermosillo— a refusal to recognize the presidency of Portes Gil— initiating the Escobar rebellion.

June 5
Calles, Ambassador Morrow, Archbishop Ruiz y Flores, and Bishop Díaz meet in Mexico to continue peace negotiations.

June 12–21
Final negotiations are made. The Accords are signed and announced on June 21.

DIPLOMACY AND U.S. RELATIONS

March 19
Portes Gil tells Morrow that he wants peace before the presidential elections in the fall.

May
Pope Pius XI names Archbishop Ruiz y Flores as the apostolic delegate to negotiate with the Mexican government.

May 3
American report notes the dire state of Mexico's economic and financial situation.

CATHOLIC IDENTITY, PROTESTS, AND THE WAR

January
Gorostieta asks presidential candidate José Vansconcelos to publicly back the Cristero cause. The candidate refuses to do so before the election.

February 9
José de León Toral is executed after pleas for leniency are rejected. The next day, an unsuccessful assassination attempt is made against Portes Gil.

March–May
Federal troops go north in response to the Escobar rebellion, allowing Cristeros to go on the offensive. Guadalajara, Aguascalientes, Tepic, and Durango fall under Cristero control.

May 20
Gorostieta notes that the Cristeros have 2,000 civilian authorities and 300 schools.

June
The Cristero movement reaches its zenith, totaling 50,000.

June 2
General Gorostieta is killed in battle.

June–September
Cristeros return home after the Accords are signed.

A church in ruins.
People tour the inside of a church
in Oaxaca in 1932.

9.

The Second Cristiada

A DISEASED PEACE

When Calles and the bishops agreed to the Accords of 1929, the Cristeros returned to civilian life with some degree of peace. Worship was restored in newly re-opened churches, and the government offered amnesty, license, and money to anyone who would give up his weapon or horse. About one-third of the Cristeros took the offer, while others went home peacefully without bothering with paperwork they did not trust.

Some Cristeros found sympathy among those Federals who wanted to maintain the peace. For example, Don Ezequiel Mendoza, the Cristero leader in Coalcomán, Michoacán, recounted negotiations with Federal officials who sought men with leadership skills—skills shown in the success of the Cristero government. He said:

> Ramón and I were the last ones, and General Cárdenas came after us. He entered Colima and Coalcomán and asked who I was. They spoke well of me. And I met him in the road with five of my men at the Parotas ranch. He came with no illusions and said, "I think that you should stay in this area and the government will help you. In the end, your way of governing is in line with that of the government. Stay and care for that which you have cared for for so many years." He named me in writing as the chief of operations, and that was my post until 1942.

Peace without victory.
Cristeros in Tepatitlán mingle with Federal soldiers after laying down their weapons in return for amnesty and the assurance of safe conduct home.

AGIC

Friendliness between former enemies.
Cristero General Andrés Salazar (third from left) stands with Federal General Heliodoro Charis (center). After the war, Charis offered Salazar a safe position as his chief of staff. Unfortunately, Charis's leniency was not shared, and Salazar was killed soon after declining the offer.

General Cárdenas's friendship with the old Cristero leaders of Coalcomán lasted until his death. He recognized their military rank and allowed many of them to occupy official posts within the rural defense forces.

Unfortunately, examples like this were rare. For many former Cristeros, the peace turned out to be worse than the war. Although the Accords were supposed to end the persecution of Catholics, ill will still festered in government circles, endangering the former Cristeros, who were forced to continue the fight or take to the hills once again for refuge.

To their credit, more than one Federal general warned the Cristeros of the danger they faced. Heliodoro Charis, whose generosity and integrity were praised by all, went so far as to offer to make Cristero Andrés Salazar his own chief of staff in the Federal army so that Salazar might escape assassination, but Salazar turned down the offer—and was killed soon after. Likewise, General Andrés Figueroa, leader of the Federal military operations in Jalisco, warned some Cristeros:

> Go very far away. . . . They would kill you soon. It will do you no good to go around armed. I am here as a representative of the Federal gov-

ernment and I give you my word as a gentleman that you have no reason to fear me. But these little local politicians always think they are
doing Mexico a favor by committing outrages like these; they will also
satisfy their thirst for vengeance.

His words proved accurate. Immediately after the Accords were signed,
a more direct and personal form of persecution began—the systematic, pre-
meditated assassination of the Cristero leaders for the purpose of preventing any renewal of the movement. As Cristero Bernardo González from
Michoacán remembered, "The Accords fell apart and everyone went their
own way." Then began "the slaughter of my old companions by the secondary elements of the government."

The first victim fell just ten days after the Accords. Father Aristeo Pedroza,
general of the Altos Brigade, was executed on July 3, 1929, by order of the Secretary of War. That same month, Cristero leaders in Guanajuato were also executed. In Colima, half of the Cristero leaders were assassinated. Before the
year was out, nearly all of the Cristero leaders in Zacatecas were dead. Between 1929 and 1935, the manhunt claimed 5,000 victims—500 were officers
ranging in rank from lieutenant to general. Even lowly soldiers were not
spared. Among those killed in the government's manhunt were Primitivo
Jiménez, Pedro Quintanar, Vicente Cueva, Lorenzo Arreola, José María Gutiérrez Beltrán, and Carlos Bouquet (many are pictured in this book).

An assassinated leader.
General José María Gutierrez, shown
here, was assassinated in Jalpa, the place
of his celebrated military victory during
the first Cristiada.

AGICA

Two war veterans.
Heriberto Navarrete (smoking)
sits with Mario Guadalupe Valdéz
(behind him in vehicle) and other
fellow Cristeros in Mexico City
after the Cristiada. Later, Valdéz
would help Federal officials hunt
down Cristeros.

During the Cristiada, much changed for Calles and the Mexican presidency. Calles's second wife, Natalia Chacón (who was described as a devout Catholic), died on June 2, 1927, around the time that the Cristero revolt solidified. Shortly after the conflict ended, Calles married again, this time to twenty-four year-old performer Leonor Llorente. In addition to dealing with unexpected presidential challenges, including Obregón's assassination, Portes Gil's election, and various attempted coups, Calles impacted decades of presidential elections by founding the National Revolutionary Party (PNR), which would become the Institutional Revolutionary Party (PRI)—the political party that would dominate every presidential election until the year 2000.

Nevertheless, Calles was unwilling to withdraw entirely from presidential power, so he created a new position in government for himself: the *Jefe Maximo* ("Supreme Leader"). From 1928 to 1935, former President Calles was the strong man in Mexico and virtually controlled the presidency—a fact known to U.S. presidents and the Department of State. Through his own power, Calles selected (and dismissed) three consecutive Mexican presidents (Portes Gil, Pascual Ortiz Rubio, and Abelardo Rodríguez). The fourth one he elected—President Lázaro Cárdenas—proved to be even stronger than Calles (as we shall see). But until then, as long as Calles was present, still more persecution (and resistance) lingered in Mexico.

Knowing how fragile the peace was, Secretary of War Joaquín Amaro took every measure to prevent a revival of the Cristero movement. For this, he drew on the lessons of the war. Although the conflict had officially ended, he did not demobilize military units. Instead, he rejuvenated their commands by dismissing officers over age fifty-five. Garrisons were maintained in all the towns that had been occupied by the Cristeros. He also tailored the army to Mexico's needs. Before the war, the cavalry forces had been left to dwindle in favor of building a European-style army—a move that left the army vulnerable to the rebels, whose strong cavalry had made them masters of Mexico's inaccessible terrain. So Amaro began to build up the cavalry. In response to the poor infrastructure that had impeded mobility and communications during the war, he oversaw the construction of highways, the stringing of telegraph lines, and the installation of military detachments. With its renovated army, the government was prepared for any possible renewal of the Cristero insurrection—an insurrection that the government expected would arise sooner or later.

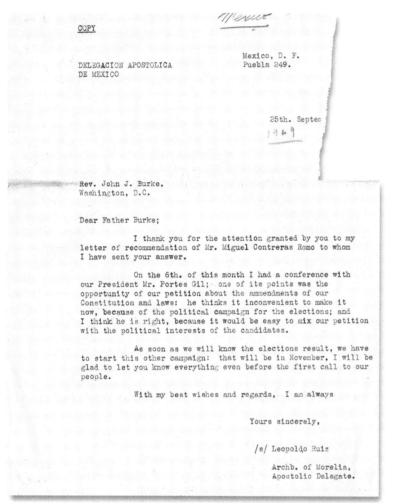

"Inconvenient" time for revisions.
In this 1929 letter to Father Burke, Bishop Leopoldo Ruiz describes a meeting he had with President Portes Gil. During that meeting, Portes Gil suggested that the upcoming presidential campaign season was not a good time for constitutional amendments. Ruiz apparently agreed, adding in the letter "I think he is right, because it would be easy to mix our petition with the political interests of the candidates."

Like their commander, Luis Ibarra, many of these Cristeros who fought in "The Second" were veterans of "The First."

THE REPRISE OF THE CRISTIADA

General Amaro's precautions proved wise—and necessary. The government's strong anticlerical lobby had hastily accepted the Accords of June 1929, because a truce was absolutely needed at that moment; but the agreement was quickly set aside. As soon as these government radicals—including Calles—felt that their forces were strong enough, they launched a new offensive in 1931 that contributed to the resignation of President Pascual Ortiz Rubio in 1932. From 1931 to 1935, the situation for Catholics grew steadily worse. Once again, the Church was subjected to a persecution that left it almost like the church of the catacombs: its doors were closed, its leaders were exiled, and its priests were forced to go underground.

As Catholics faced persecution again, rebellion reared its head for a second time. In 1932, despite the systematic executions of Cristero leaders and the disarming of others by the government, survivors of the first Cristiada and a new band of combatants joined forces. They took up arms in regions as distant as Veracruz and Sonora, places that were mostly quiet during the first Cristiada.

The rebels had implemented changes based on lessons learned during the first war. Aware of their small forces, the rebels did not fight on the front lines, but used even more guerilla warfare tactics. Despite all the Federal forts and garrisons in the mountains, the Cristeros were able to slip between the posts and surprise the Federal forces and the agrarians. They also turned to political terrorism, including the systematic slaughter of local officials such as teachers and agrarian leaders.

An unruly child.
In this political cartoon, Federal General Amaro is pictured as unpacifiable.
(Artist: Alfonso de la Torre)

Perhaps most important, remembering the desperate lack of food during the first war, this time the Cristeros stored enough corn for a year and planted crops before marching off to fight. This required the Federal army commanders to change their strategy as well, and it highlighted other inadequacies in the army. Federal General Anacleto López concluded that to reduce the rebel forces, it would be necessary to pursue a campaign without interruption for a full year so as to outlast the Cristeros' food reserves. Additionally, the army could not stop the Cristeros from harvesting the crops they had planted because the troops, though numerous, were not sufficient to do the job. Meanwhile, the Federal troops found it difficult to find enough food in the locations where they were posted due to the agricultural crisis.

With these conditions, how could the Federal army have any illusions of "pacifying" the countryside? Yet, the Federal government played down the rebels' tenacity and, like it did during the 1926 uprisings, hid the truth from the people about the Cristeros' persistence, offering assurances that everything was over. But in the memoirs of the Secretary of War, accounts of campaigns were recorded until 1941. Also included were discussions among the generals that involved strategies for reducing the rebels.

A prediction proved right.
In late 1929, Morrow turned in his resignation as ambassador to Mexico. In this letter, written to him by Calvin Coolidge (above), the former President commented on Morrow's decision, saying, "I think on the whole you are wise in retiring from Mexico. It would be unfair for you to stay there the rest of your life and any time that you might wish to come away, there would always be many unsolved problems."

CALVIN COOLIDGE
NORTHAMPTON
MASSACHUSETTS

December 7, 1929

Honorable Dwight W. Morrow,

Englewood, New Jersey.

My dear Mr. Ambassador:

When I first thought of going to Texas I entirely forgot about our city election which was held last Tuesday and as I have to be in New York on the eleventh to attend a New York Life meeting, I did not see how I could get away.

I think on the whole you are wise in retiring from Mexico. It would be unfair for you to stay there the rest of your life and any time that you might wish to come away there would always be many unsolved problems. I hope you will enjoy your work on the Naval Conference. It will be rather difficult. Still, I think that the English now understand that we do not intend to hold second place. I mistrust they thought we would not build a navy. I think the speech I made on the eleventh of November, 1928, and our passage of the bill for fifteen cruisers had a wholesome effect upon them.

I hope that I may see you.
With kindest regards, I am

Very truly yours,

Another young soldier.
The artist of numerous political cartoons included throughout this text, Alfonso de la Torre also fought as a Cristero. He is pictured here (at left) with fellow Cristero Luis Ibarra. In the log above, he recorded battle information and noted political events that took place during the Second Cristiada.

JUVENTUD

PUBLICACION QUINCENAL

ORGANO DEL GRUPO LOCAL "ALFONSO DE LA TORRE"

VOL. I. | Admor. ABELARDO FAVELA | N GALES, SONORA, NOV. 15 DE 1935 | Director: J. JESUS CORDOVA | NUM. 9

Loor eterno a nuestros Martires d' la ACJM

IN MEMORIAM

Es una consoladora realidad el hecho de que la juventud cuente siempre con corazones dispuestos a sacrificar, en aras de los ideales más sublimes, no solo las comodidades, (q ye ya sería algo) sino hasta la misma vida, considerada generalmente como el más precioso tesoro de que el hombre es poseedor.

En efecto, desde las épocas más remotas, contemplamos a través de la historia, como en la primavera de la existencia se han rebelado los corazones juveniles contra oprobiosas tiranías, han luchado en todos campos, conquistando el lauro inmarcesible, no de una fama caduca y perecedora fincada en el aplauso de los necios, sino el honor de servir de modelo a las juventudes, han conquistado una grandeza que no puede ser destruida por el juicio erróneo de los que por su apasionamiento, no pueden ser imparciales.

Haríamos interminable esta modesta semblanza si recorriéramos las páginas de la historia, para hacer desfilar las figuras venerables de jóvenes que con su vida pagaron su fidelidad por las causas santas.

Solo diremos, en general, que nuestro México ha contado con valerosos paladines de la verdad, que supieron morir como hombres y como cristianos, frente a los neronianos opresores.

Toca a la benemérita Asociación Católica de la Juventud Mexicana la gloria de haber formado a no pocos campeones de la fe, que en la tribuna, en la prensa y en la vida de campaña con el fusil en las manos lucharon por las libertades a que, como seres racionales, tenían derecho los mexicanos, y, proclamando el Reinado de

Cristo, ofrendaron su sangre generosa, que quiera Dios no haya sido derramada en vano.

Las consideraciones que anteceden, brotan espontáneamente de nuestra pluma, ante la proximidad de una fecha, gloriosa para la Juventud Católica de Sonora: el día 13 de noviembre, en que cayó fija

ALFONSO DE LA TORRE

Ex-Presidente de nuestro grupo local muerto "Por Dios y por la Patria" el 13 de Nov. de 1935 cerca de Agua Fría, Sonora.

la mirada en el cielo, bajo las balas de la tiranía, nuestro inclito compañero, el joven Alfonso de la Torre, cuyo retrato honra las páginas de este humilde periódico.

No es nuestro intento escribir una biografía completa, sino una breve semblanza de quien supo luchar siempre y morir; "Por Dios y por la Patria", que sintetiza las aspiraciones de la A. C. J. M.

La cuna de de la Torre se meció en la risueña ciudad de Aguascalientes. Miembro de una familia católica fervorosa, empezó su educación al amparo de las prácticas de piedad, y a los diez años lo encontramos convertido en un fervoroso entusiasta y fervoroso amante de las Vanguardias de la A. C. J. M.; poco tiempo después, y ya en Sonora, el entusiasmo y dotes oratorias de q' estaba dotado le valieron ocupar la Secretaría y la Presidencia de las Vanguardias, puestos que desempeñó con acierto comunicando su dinamismo a los que, como él se preparaban para la lucha.

Al celebrarse el primer Congreso Regional de la A. C. J. M., en Sonora, fué nombrado delegado.

Cuando cumplió los quince años, pasó a ser miembro activo de la A. C. J. M., en el grupo local de Magdalena, Sonora, y habiéndose visto obligado, por circunstancias

Pasa a la 4ta. Plana

In 1935, while serving as a soldier during the Second Cristiada, Alfonso de la Torre was killed in combat near Agua Fria, Sonora. After his death "under the bullets of tyranny," this local ACJM group adopted his name and praised his life and service "for God and for the Country" in its newsletter. (For more information on Alfonso and his family, see In Focus "The de la Torre Family" beginning on page 187.)

THE CHURCH: A LOST SUPPORT

For his book on the "Second Cristiada," journalist Antonio Estrada chose the title *Rescoldo*—the word for the embers left in a household fire, the ones that are never fully extinguished and never die. How well-chosen that title is!

This conflict was commonly called "The Second." Many people did not dare say its full name, "The Second *Cristiada*," for this time, the Church that the Cristeros fought to defend had become their enemy. Indeed, the Church condemned both the uprising and any support given to it. If the first Cristiada (1926–1929) was a war of the poor, this was a war of the miserable—people without means and without aid, confronted by a much more efficient army and a Church that was unwavering in its disapproval of violence.

The rebels represented a dangerous energy in a country like this—a country lacking peace, fraught with mistreatment and obstinate parties, and the victim of local politics and a terrible economic crisis. Like the zealous *raskolniki*, whose religious revolt afflicted seventeenth-century Russia, these indomitable men in Mexico had a similar zeal. For some, the rebellion was seen as a refusal to submit to "Caesar," and even to the Church (which condemned this insurgence) because they had given their word to Jesus Christ and the Virgin of Guadalupe. And as the State continued to prey upon the Church, even while the State declared the Church to be "free," these second Cristeros fought for greater religious freedom because, as one said, they did not want the Church to be "free like a prostitute in a brothel." Between 1930 and 1932, the bishops issued twenty-two statements condemning any resort to violence. This was reaffirmed with pontifical instructions in January 1932, as well as a papal encyclical entitled *Acerba Animi* issued by Pope Pius XI in September 1932. The encyclical condemned the breach of the Accords and lamented the grievous situation in Mexico, but nonetheless firmly maintained the ban on armed struggle.

A blow to the League. The ACJM, which formed the militant core of the League, was disbanded after the Cristiada and was later re-established. Yet, its impact during the 1930s remained comparatively small. Here, members in Zacatecas are shown during the Second Cristiada.

Indeed, the Church's categorical opposition to the insurrection was perhaps the force most hostile to the rebels; it dragged popular opinion and local clerical practice along with it. Bishop Valverde of León and his clergy, along with that of Michoacán, Querétaro, and all of the other dioceses, did what they could to disarm the insurrectionists and prevent new uprisings. Calling them bandits, rebels, proud, and intemperate, the clergy collaborated with the government and worked to convince the public not to continue helping the rebels. In retrospect, the bishops even condemned the first Cristiada.

In great contrast with the cessation of liturgies in 1926, this time the bishops permitted liturgies to be celebrated; but often, the rebels themselves were banned from receiving the sacraments. On May 31, 1932, after recalling the pope's prohibition on violence, Bishop Ignacio Placencia of Zacatecas banned priests from administering the sacraments to "the leaders of the agitators, who should consider themselves unfit to receive them because of their disobedience to the ecclesiastical authority. Those others committed to the armed movement could receive the sacraments if they promised to correct their insubordination."

The harshness of that statement, which the Cristeros jokingly called "the red and black," had terrible consequences. It was frequently seen as an invitation for clergy to make accusations against these new rebels. In one case in Colima, Father Covarrubias even ordered a penitent to go to the authorities to tell them what she had just confessed.

Thus, while ignoring the prohibitions of the Church, these new Cristeros launched a hopeless battle. As one Cristero song stated in its refrain, "Don't be afraid that no one will help you, that neither the rich nor the clergy will shield you." The same theme was repeated in a song that was composed in 1936 after the death of Cristero Ramón Aguilar:

Agrarian leader turned Cristero.
Ramón Aguilar (seated) joined the Cristero ranks after the assassination of Primo Tapia—his friend and founder of the Agrarian League of Michoacán. Gaining a reputation as the scourge of the Federal army during the first Cristiada, Aguilar took up arms in the Second Cristiada and died in combat.

> The rich in Michoacán
> And the clergy in Jalisco
> Had in Ramón Aguilar
> A lash at the ready.
> The clergy and the capital
> Walk now with trust
> Because in Tangamandapio
> The general has already been killed.

Nevertheless, the Church had good reasons for adhering to the "realistic" policy of banning violence: the Cristeros were now endangering the restoration of worship.

Despite their enthusiasm, the rebels faced great odds against the reformed and improved Federal army. This efficient foe wisely concentrated half its forces in one region and conducted a cleanup operation that lasted for months. The rise of aviation and the use of radio communication made these operations possible. In 1932 and 1933, the Cristero attacks subsided—although briefly.

CALLES AND THE LAST STRUGGLES FOR CONSCIENCE

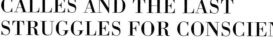

Just as the attacks were subsiding, the government pushed a new agenda: social education. In 1933 and 1934, Jefe Maximo Calles and the anticlerical lobby reformed Mexico's constitution, so that the country's educational system had to offer the children a "rational conception" of the world, far from "obscurantism and fanaticism" (a veiled reference to religion). On July 20, 1934, Calles declared, "It is necessary that we enter into a new phase of the Revolution which I shall call the psychological revolutionary period; we must enter into and take possession of the minds of the children, the consciences of the young, because they do belong and should belong to the Revolution." In a memorandum to Lázaro Cárdenas, Calles defended his views, stating that Soviet Russia, Nazi Germany, and Fascist Italy were doing the same.

The implementation of this so called "socialist education" provoked the resignation of thousands of teachers in the public schools. The Catholic schools had been closed by the authorities, of course, but many families refused to send their children to the public schools in a sort of "scholar strike" that lasted years.

The policy of "socialist education" also provoked the Church, and provided increased support to several thousand rebels who declared that they would not submit until the government kept the promise it had made in 1929. Another resurgence of Cristeros arose, lasting five more years, from 1935 to 1940. The teachers were primary targets during these years of the unpopular "socialist education" declared by the government. Many were victims of horrific cruelties, such as having their ears cut off by some Catholic *guerrilleros* who had become more terrorist than Catholic.

In 1935, "The Second" had reached its peak, but compared to the first Cristiada, it suffered from a marked scarcity of soldiers. In fact, at this "peak," the rebel forces numbered only 7,500, who remained unreachable in the mountains, declaring that they would never give in until the government abandoned all persecution of the Church.

A call for "liberation."
This article of propaganda from Mexico's National Executive Committee describes the government's socialist education agenda as a means of intellectual, moral, and economic freedom.

A staged scene.
As part of the government's effort to show public support for its religious and educational policies, a parade led by PNR President Carlos Riva Palacio was staged on October 28, 1928.

In Focus

The de la Torre Family

Much of the photographic and archival material in this book was preserved and passed down by members of the de la Torre family, whose lives were affected by the Cristiada in ways both tragic and inspirational.

The de la Torres provide just one example of how shared faith can be nurtured through familial bonds. They also demonstrate how the family itself can be a voice for religious liberty.

During this war of Mexico's struggle for religious freedom, several members of the family were active in a number of Catholic organizations, including the ACJM and the League.

The concept of this In Focus presentation was inspired by a photo album/scrapbook that was kept by María, the only daughter of the de la Torre family.

Ignacio de la Torre and his wife, María, were the parents of eight children—daughter María, and sons Ignacio, Francisco, Alfonso, Luis, Edmundo, Carlos, and Benjamin. With close ties to the Church and Catholic groups, the de la Torres (some who were targeted for protesting the government's religious restrictions) had to move several times, bringing the cause with them to northern Mexico.

Several family members left the country and spent time in the United States to avoid the persecution (and its economic fallout). They were forced to use pseudonyms even in their private correspondence.

Three of the de la Torre sons—Ignacio, Carlos, and Francisco—joined the priesthood. After both Cristiadas, they were instrumental in reopening a number of churches in Nogales that had been closed by the government. Carlos appears by himself in a photograph below, while Ignacio and Francisco are pictured in another photo with their mother.

The inscription on the photo of daughter María and her younger brother Luis reads: "To our favorite little grandmother with our affection."

Benjamin, the youngest de la Torre son, is seen here on the day of his First Holy Communion. Born in 1918, he was only eight years old at the start of the Cristiada.

During the war, María's boyfriend, Cristero soldier Fidel Muro (pictured below) was captured and held prisoner in the San Luis Potosi penitentiary. Muro was executed by the government in 1928. María kept his memory alive through the safekeeping of photos, postcards, flowers, and other meaningful memorabilia, some of which appear in this album.

Son Alfonso of the de la Torre family (pictured in the page at right) served as a soldier in the Cristero army, and was killed in combat during "The Second" in 1935. Alfonso was also a talented artist and responsible for many of the political graphics that are found throughout this book. (For more information on Alfonso, see page 183.)

Penitenciaria. - San Luis Potosi.   Arnoldo Kai

During those decades after the war when the Cristiada was neither taught nor discussed, the de la Torre family safeguarded numerous invaluable materials from the persecution and the resistance movement. These items are now housed at the University of Arizona.

In addition to their impact in Mexico, the de la Torre family is a reminder of how the conflict in Mexico shaped the United States through the many families who relocated there. And in their dedication to preserving relics of the era, they provide a rich glimpse into some of the events that shaped the lives of many who made the United States their new home.

Protests flare up again. Although churches began reopening again in 1936, it was a process that spread slowly across Mexico. In February of 1937, the protest against closed churches (pictured here in Orizaba) spread through the entire state of Veracruz. It eventually led people to reopen the churches themselves—something the government made no attempt to oppose.

THE BEGINNING OF A NEW ERA

While "The Second" approached its climax, the Mexican presidency entered a new era with the election of Lázaro Cárdenas in 1934. In a stroke of independence, Cárdenas decided to break away from Calles, his old protector and friend, for the good of the nation. In June 1935, he exiled Calles, ending the era of the *Maximato*. For the first time in over a decade, Mexico was free from Calles's political artistry as President Cárdenas slowly began to ease the pressure against the Church. In fact, he had been asked to do this unofficially by U.S. President Franklin D. Roosevelt, who badly needed the Catholic vote for the upcoming presidential election of 1936.

The "Jefe Maximo" was gone, now living in the United States, but damage remained in Mexico from both Calles's regime and the renewed rebel spirit. This country, which once had 4,000 priests, now had only 305 priests authorized by the State. (Seventeen states would not accept even one priest.) The losses suffered by the Cristeros were often worse than those during the first war. Practically all the Cristero leaders who had returned to take up arms had been killed. Indeed, with all the powers against them, the tenacity with which they undertook this hopeless war resembled a death wish.

In 1936, after Calles's exile, President Cárdenas promised that his administration would not make the same mistakes as his predecessors. Cárdenas ordered governors to give back churches and allow priests to return. Officials in Jalisco began taking troops to Mass, making support for the Cristeros more difficult to justify. Very slowly, the situation began to change for the better, first in Mexico City, then in the neighboring states, and finally, in 1938, in the most peripheral parts of southeastern Mexico. The new tactic adopted by Catholics—heavily attended peaceful demonstrations—made the task easier.

From then on, support for the Cristeros waned. There were so many forces against the rebels, including the total impoverishment of a hungry public that no longer saw the need to continue sustaining the Cristeros. By then, 80 percent of the public was against the rebels, and the struggle became desperate. Three-fourths of the combatants withdrew, leaving just 2,000 hard-core militants. Confronted by these hopeless developments, Federico Vázquez, a Cristero leader in Durango, expressed the desolation, saying, "Our situation is regrettable and sad," and "In our hands, it is over. We cannot bear this cross. Only God knows the agonies we have suffered. God have mercy on us."

Yet flare-ups still occurred. For example, in February 1937, a teenage girl who was attending a clandestine Mass was murdered by a policeman. This brought about a general mobilization of the common people in Orizaba, Veracruz, and eventually in all the cities of that state. Under pressure, Governor Miguel Alemán consulted with President Cárdenas, and then gave in, authorizing the reopening of all the churches in Veracruz. The same happened in Chiapas, and finally in Tabasco, land of the "red shirts" led by the anticlerical fanatic Tomás Garrido Canabal. And in 1937, the Federal army was able to quell the rebel forces one by one, concentrating thirteen regiments and 3,000 irregulars in Durango.

From then on, the Accords of 1929 were largely observed and respected. The year 1938 became a year of national reconciliation, when President Cárdenas suspended the application of the anticlerical legislation and extended to the entire republic the same mercy that had been shown in Michoacán in 1929. This second peace appeared to be more firm than the first.

Among some Federal officials, the anticlerical sentiment decreased in intensity, while among many Mexicans, the systematic opposition to the government gradually subsided. Although the price was high, the *modus vivendi* —the state of coexistence—had finally been achieved.

An unexpected casualty.
Like during the first Cristiada, clandestine Masses were also held during the 1930s—and sometimes with tragic consequences. Fourteen-year-old Lenor Sanchez, who is mourned here, was killed in a police raid of one clandestine gathering for worship in 1937.

Standing by the cross.
Perhaps more than anything else, it was the Cristeros'
identification with this symbol—the cross of
Christ—that infused their struggles and sacrifices
with meaning, pointing toward a greater purpose.

Epilogue

MEMORY AND RECONCILIATION

In the course of history, large crosses are lifted up from time to time—like the ones old Mexico placed on its borders—where continuity is at a crossroads with ruptures that either renew or destroy it. Such moments are often defined by a choice: a people can reclaim its identity against the threat posed by such a rupture, or be destroyed by it. For religious freedom in Mexico, the Cristiada was just such a crossroads.

In the 1910s and 1920s, there was an increasing awareness that Mexico would have to undergo important social and political transformations. Problematically, the State's push for modernization also politicized religious affiliations and religious practice. At the time, the question facing the State was this: for modernization, would it be necessary to throw away Mexico's religious heritage and traditions—indeed, everything that had been its *raison d'être*? Undoubtedly, the State's final answer—to sever Mexico from its Catholic roots—was terribly miscalculated. The Cristiada was not a struggle between revolutionary and counterrevolutionary forces. It was a reaction of legitimate defense of an assaulted people. Since a group of famous men could not keep the peace at that time, not knowing they would later lose it, other anonymous men had to take up the war and put it to the service of freedom of conscience, faith, and prayer—the freedom that includes all other freedoms. They fought for the truest ideals of their nation and faith. And as history shows, the faith of those who responded to this rupture was strengthened in many ways, although Mexico itself was weakened by persistent discrimination that continued in various forms.

Of course, it is not an easy task to come to grips with or to reconcile oneself to such a recent, controversial, and currently relevant history. Sometimes, reconciling oneself to history is as difficult as reconciling a country's people and its leaders. It is not easy to accept mistakes, offenses, and crimes (in this case, committed on *both* sides of the Cristiada), but it is a healthy and necessary thing to do.

Mexico has already lost too much of this history because of continued fear. As mentioned in the Introduction, making the Cristiada almost a taboo subject for so many years has caused a nearly irrevocable loss of testimonies, literature, and historical artifacts from that period—priceless information that should have been gathered, but was instead destroyed due to this long period of silence. We might rightly wonder whether such suppression, rather than resulting from fear, corresponds to a willingness to forget the horrors of history.

It would be a mistake, however, to think that in order to strengthen national identity, it is necessary to write a mythological history that glosses over any unpleasant chapters. Today's world has taught us about the dangers such a mythological history poses even to freedom. A strong national identity is compatible with a brand of history that remains true to the facts. Times may change, but our past will not disappear, and being truthful about it is invaluable, even if certain aspects are unpleasant. For this reason, the memory of the Cristiada should not be suppressed. Memory, so long as it does not contradict the truth or preach hatred and revenge, can be informative and enlightening. That is how this history should be recounted.

Consequently, we are obliged to express our appreciation to those who passed on this story with compassion, devotion, and absolute candor—they are the veterans of the Cristiada and their relatives, who, through the modest and beautiful channel of oral tradition, have kept the memories alive despite half a century of silence. Catholics in Mexico lived through this dreadful period of persecution, suffering from the actions of a government that despised them. They lived through and died in a war that cost their country over 200,000 lives, and much more. Theirs were memories of sacrifice and injustice, of accepted martyrdom, and of generously granted forgiveness.

At the same time, the history of the Cristiada, though distinctively part of Mexican history, has universal relevance. Indeed, it expresses something of the challenges of all religious people: to live their faith in an authentic way. Part of the unique tragedy of the Cristiada was that the Cristeros' struggle included deliberate persecution and armed conflict with their own government. (It is also notable that the temptation to suppress religious freedom was apparent in many places throughout the twentieth century, including Nazi Germany and Communist Russia.)

Today, the questions that were faced during the Cristiada by the State, the Church, and the Cristeros appear again everywhere in our world. Is religion subject to the whim of the State? Or is religious freedom such a basic human need that it constitutes a human right, a right that the State cannot abolish?

For this reason, the Cristiada should be of interest to more than just the historian. Today, more than ever, the Cristiada—with its courageous acts, trials, failed and successful negotiations, and men and women who strove to be both patriots and believers—deserves a place in our memory.

Most of all, we should consider not only the events of persecution and war, but also those brave events of reconciliation and peace, which continued even into the 1990s: the Accords of 1929; the move toward renewed freedom in the 1940s; the visit of Pope John Paul II to Mexico in 1979 (an event that would not have been permitted years earlier); and finally, Pope John Paul II's second visit in 1990, during which he celebrated Mass publicly outdoors. This papal visit prompted President Carlos Salinas de Gortari to pass a constitutional reform in 1992, revising the very articles whose promulgation and enforcement provoked the Cristiada.

Thus, the publication of this work is dedicated to friendship and goodwill among all Mexicans, and among all the people of North America who came to the assistance of those who were displaced and silenced by the conflict. Through them, millions of people in Mexico and the United States have been made heirs to the fruits of their acts of courage and dedication to religious freedom. The Cristiada was never forgotten by those who lived it; and by remembering their courage, their dedication, their lives, and even their deaths, we can help ensure that the sacrifices made for religious freedom then still count today and tomorrow.

Credits

The photographs, illustrations, and graphics that appear throughout this book have been used with permission by the sources listed below. Every reasonable effort has been made to determine copyright holders and to secure permission as needed. If any copyrighted material has been used without appropriate attribution, please notify the publisher in writing, so that future printings of this work may be corrected accordingly. The images in this book may not be reproduced without acquiring permission from the appropriate copyright holders. To facilitate identification, each image is listed with its caption and page number, and appears under the appropriate source.

ARCHIVO GENERAL DEL INSTITUTO CULTURAL DE AGUASCALIENTES (AGUASCALIENTES, AGUASCALIENTES, MEXICO).
Bullets and Bandoleers (p. i); A celebration in honor of Christ the King (p. 11); ACJM members (p. 12); Marching for the repeal of the Calles Law (p. 34); From far and wide (p. 35); Timeline (p. 36: middle right); Cristeros under General Elías Vergara (p. 38); Soldiers under General Lauro Rocha (p. 42); Retaliation photograph (p. 45); Battlefield photographer (p. 50); Guerilla cavalry (p. 50); Combat communication (p. 50); General Jesús Degollado Guízar (p. 51); Captain Alberto B. Gutiérrez (p. 52); Troops among the mountains (p. 54); Preparing for battle (p. 55); Newlyweds (p. 56); An elderly volunteer (p. 57); Cristeros in training (pp 58–59); Cristeros of the Huichol Indians (p. 60); A Cristero distinction (p. 61); Four young officers (p. 62); Troops of the Sahuayo zone, Michoacán (p. 62); Military supplies (p. 63); Cristero cavalrymen (p. 63); Camp accommodations (p. 64); Striking a pose (p. 65: at left); Family ties (p. 66); At the Hacienda de Tetapán (p. 67); Unpredictable leadership (p. 68); Cristeros kill a steer for food (p. 69); Leading women into the war (p. 72); Amparo Mireles (p. 73); Catalina de la Peña (p. 73); María del Carmen Robles (p. 75); Toñita

Castillo (p. 76); Carrying Christ (p. 79); Parish without borders (p. 83); Safety in secrecy (pp. 84–85); Father Pedroza, "The Pure One" (p. 90); Father Vega, "Pancho Villa in a Cassock" (p. 91); From Federal soldier to Cristero (p. 92); Martyrs of León (p. 93); Revered as a martyr (p. 94); A heavy burden (p. 95); Making an example (p. 95); Honoring the dead (p. 97); Mourners at a tomb (p. 98); Timeline (p. 99: middle right; bottom left); Christ at the center (p. 100); Two brothers, one funeral (p. 104); Another dire replacement (p. 105); A voice for order (p. 107); Double mission (p. 108); Internal conflict (p. 112); Disillusioned by a verdict (p. 112); Traitor, agitator—spy? (p. 113); Governor in overalls (p. 116); A moment of rest (p 118); An invaluable leader (p. 122); A military man (p. 123); Military excellence (p. 124); Beyond colleagues (p. 126); A father with his son (p. 131); Sending a message that backfires (p. 138); Timeline (p. 139: middle right; bottom left; bottom right); Putting down arms (p. 162); Proof of death (p. 165); Military succession (p. 165); A town greets its priest (p. 170); Isla Marías prisoners return (p. 170); A peace celebration (p. 171); Timeline (p. 175: bottom right); Peace without victory (p. 177); Friendliness between former enemies (p. 178); Two war veterans (p. 179); A blow to the League (p. 184).

THE ASSOCIATED PRESS (NEW YORK, NEW YORK).
In contrast (p. 64); Striking a pose (p. 65: at right); The once and future president (p. 129); Moments before the assassination (p. 130); Upturned chairs, peace talks tabled (p. 130); Courtroom theater (p. 131); Passing on the presidency (p. 132); War along the border (p. 135); After a victory (p. 136); Timeline (p. 139: middle left); Border control (p. 140); Overnight fame (p. 148: photo at right); Dr. Jose Manuel Puig Casauranc, Secretary of Education (p. 156); President Emilio Portes Gil (p. 156); A staged scene (p. 186); Protests flare up again (p. 192); An unexpected "casualty" (p. 193).

THE BANCROFT LIBRARY, UNIVERSITY OF CALIFORNIA, BERKELEY (BERKELEY, CALIFORNIA).
Armed and ready (p. 65); A harvest during the Cristiada (p. 120); Standing by the cross (p. 194).

CORBIS (NEW YORK, NEW YORK).
Building lines of communication—literally (p. 28); Timeline (p. 37: bottom left).

Bettmann/Corbis
Presidential duo (p. 13); San Luis Potosi, June 2, 1926 (p. 20); The United States—a new home for religious Catholics (p. 25); Meeting at the White House (p. 26); Timeline (p. 77: lower right; bottom center); Religious celebration (p. 80); Timeline (p. 99: middle center); A new president (p. 133); An unwilling ally (p. 134); Exhibition in Washington, DC (p. 142); Showing their strength (p. 144); Cause for celebration (p. 149); Cordial introductions (p. 154: photo at right); A last day in office (p. 161); Words of comfort from Pope Pius XI (p. 164: portrait); Timeline (p. 175: top center).

Hulton-Deutsch Collection/Corbis
Anti-Catholicism in America (p. 143).

International Newsreel/Corbis
Altar of Santa Dregeda Church (p. 9); Cathedral in Mexico City (p. 24); Volatile labor issues (p. 27); Demonstration in Mexico City (p. 32); "Propagandists" (p. 41); Pat down for pedestrians (p. 74); Bishop Pascual Díaz (p. 156).

DE LA TORRE FAMILY PAPERS, UNIVERSITY OF ARIZONA LIBRARIES, SPECIAL COLLECTION (TUCSON, ARIZONA).
In Defense of the Clergy (p. 8); ACJM membership card for Alfonso de la Torre (p. 12); "Catholics—Be Alert" (p. 15); An ex-patriot's take on Mexico's powerful labor union (p. 15); The League celebrates the Feast of Christ the King (p. 17); A relic of precarious religious freedom (p. 20); International notice, international inspiration (p. 29); Death of the Church? (p. 30); "Follow the Boycott" (p. 30); Praising the "resounding failure" of the boycott (p. 30); General José María Gutiérrez (p. 52); The Unión Pop-

ular's popularity (p. 102); Bonds from the League (p. 114); LNDL Stamps (p. 115); Lottery—for liberty! (p. 115); Military collaboration (p. 125); Cristero victory publicized (p. 126); "Viva Toral!" (p. 131); An early exit? (p. 132); A political perspective (pp. 150–151); Uprooted families (p. 174); An assassinated leader (p. 179); Cristero cavalry in Sonora, 1935 (p. 181); An unruly child (p. 181); Another young soldier (p. 183); Agrarian leader turned Cristero (p. 185); A call for liberation (p. 186); The de la Torre Family (pp. 187–191).

DWIGHT W. MORROW PAPERS, AMHERST COLLEGE ARCHIVES AND SPECIAL COLLECTIONS (AMHERST, MASSACHUSETTS).
Cordial introductions (p. 154: letter); American Embassy in Mexico (p. 155); Bishop Leopoldo Ruiz y Flores (p. 157); Ambassador Dwight W. Morrow (p. 157); In case of government overthrow (p. 158); Planning a diplomatic date (p. 159); Morrow's notes (p. 160); Words of comfort from Pope Pius XI (p. 164: letter); A presidential announcement (p. 166); Congratulations from an influential journalist (p. 167); Timeline (p. 175: middle right, Archbishop Ruiz y Flores); "Inconvenient" time for revisions (p. 180); A prediction proved right (p. 182: letter).

THE KNIGHTS OF COLUMBUS
(NEW HAVEN, CONNECTICUT)
Knights of Columbus Museum
Our Lady of Guadalupe (p. 6).
Supreme Council Archives
"Services end in Mexican Churches" (p. 22); Cathedral in Mexico City (p. 24); The pope's words on the Mexican situation (p. 33).
Multimedia Archives
The "Capitals" of Church and State (pp. 4–5); Altar of Santa Dregeda Church (p. 9); President Plutarco Elías Calles (p. 14); A Catholic Church in Cholula, Mexico (p. 23); Volatile labor issues (p. 27); Demonstration in Mexico City (p. 32); Timeline (p. 37: top left); Upholding the Constitution (p. 40); "Propagandists" (p. 41); Victim of Ortiz (p. 47); A group of agraristas (p. 48); Pat down for pedestrians (p. 74); Timeline (p. 99: top left); International brotherhood (p. 81); Relic of a raid (p. 82); Martyred Knights (pp. 86–87); Father Miguel Pro (p. 87, 88); Humberto Pro (p. 88); Juan Antonio Tirado (p. 88); Luis Segura Vilchis (p. 88); The executioner (p. 88); The personal side of a priest's execution (p. 88); Incognito (p. 89); A last prayer (p. 89); Imitation of Christ (p. 89); Crowds of Mourners (p. 89); Artistic memory (p. 96); "El Maestro" (p. 102); A blow to the Unión Popular (p. 103); "Table of honor" (p. 128); Passing on the presidency (p. 132); Disillusioned officer (p. 136); On the international stage (p. 145); Part of the Knights of Columbus campaign (p. 147);

Shifting priorities in Washington (p. 146); "Lovers of Liberty, Stay Out of Mexico!" (p. 152); Banned reading (p. 153); Bishop Pascual Díaz (p. 156); William F. Montavon (p. 157); Church services resumed (p. 169); Pilgrims to the Virgin's shrine (p. 170); Protests flare up again (p. 192).

LIBRARY OF CONGRESS PRINTS AND PHOTOGRAPHS DIVISION (WASHINGTON, DC).
A prediction proved right (p. 182: photograph).
National Photo Company Collection
A full agenda (p. 141).

MUSEO NACIONAL CRISTERO (ENCARNACIÓN DE DÍAZ, JALISCO, MEXICO).
Bullets and Bandoleers (p. i).

NATIONAL CATHOLIC WELFARE COUNCIL (NCWC)/OFFICE OF THE GENERAL SECRETARY (OGS) COLLECTION, THE AMERICAN CATHOLIC HISTORY RESEARCH CENTER AND UNIVERSITY ARCHIVES, THE CATHOLIC UNIVERSITY OF AMERICA (WASHINGTON, DC).
Timeline (p. 139: top center); Father John J. Burke (p. 157).

NATIONAL PARK SERVICE PHOTO, NATIONAL PARK SERVICE, THOMAS EDISON NATIONAL HISTORICAL PARK, NEW JERSEY, EDIPHONE GALLERY.
Timeline (p. 175: middle left, Pope Pius XI).

SINAFO – FOTOTECA NACIONAL DEL INSTITUTO NACIONAL DE ANTROPOLOGÍA E HISTORIA (PACHUCA, HIDALGO, MEXICO). ARCHIVO CASASOLA.
Archive inventory control numbers are included below and appear after the page numbers.

State expropriation (p. 8) #5149; New president, renewed anticlericalism (p. 10) #32603; Three presidents, three revolutionaries (p. 11) #5403; Pro-CROM labor rally (p. 16) #5925; Luis Morones (p. 16) #22792; Protest of Catholic workers, Mexico City, 1926 (p. 17) #5907; Demonstration at the Zócalo (p. 18) #45690; Silenced—at least for the moment (p. 18) #45590; Quenching resistance (p.19) #45687, 45596, 45598; Ceaseless search for resolution (p. 21) #45692; Monsignor Caruana with Bishop Diaz (p. 21) #45681; Mexican clergy with Archbishop Mora y del Rio (p. 24) #45699; "Government inventory" (p. 23) #45705; Bishop Pascual Díaz Barreto, Mexico City, 1925 (p. 31) #13982; Timeline (p. 36: top center, #18548; bottom left, #5013; bottom right, #5217); Timeline (p. 37: top right, #186381; middle left, #22792; middle center, #32603; bottom center, #174520; bottom right, #45741); More than collateral damage (p. 39) #2581; The face of judgment (p. 40) #45709; General Vega's train raid (p. 44) #45748; Reforming Mexico's Military College (p. 46) #44460; Off to War (p. 47) #5590; Attacks on railroad trains and infrastructure (p. 53) #32256, 33277; Federal infantry and their weapons (p. 65) #45723; Motivating resistors (p. 70) #45126; Execution of General Manuel Reyes (p. 71) #45737; Timeline (p. 77: top center, #50946; middle left, #45699; upper right, #45699); Receiving Christ in Communion (p. 78) #45720; Timeline (p. 99: bottom center, #128892); The army comes to town (p. 117) #45710; From monument to memorial (p. 127) #45741; A friendly "enemy" (p. 135) #14505; Chaos at the rails (p. 137) #33271; Overnight fame (p. 148: photo at left) #128892; Unconventional diplomacy (p. 149) #128931; A "hero" for Anne (p. 149) #128948; President Plutarco Elías Calles (p. 156) #364925; Celebrating his return (p. 168) #45603; Ready to return home (p. 172) #45740; Urban disrepair (p. 173) #45725; Timeline (p. 175: top left, #14505; bottom left, #128931); A church in ruins (p. 176) #82380.

Special thanks is extended to the following institutions for granting permission to use affiliated/related images held elsewhere:
Eastman Kodak Company (Rochester, NY).
United States Conference of Catholic Bishops (Washington, DC).
Walter Lippmann Papers, Manuscripts and Archives, Sterling Memorial Library, Yale University (New Haven, Connecticut).

About the Author

Jean Meyer, PhD, was born in the south of France in 1942 to Alsatian parents who had fled the Nazi invasion. Until 1959, he lived in the beautiful town of Aix en Provence at the foot of Mont Sainte-Victoire, the subject of a number of paintings by Cézanne. Meyer studied history at the École Normale Supérieure and at the Sorbonne before travelling to Mexico in 1965 to study the Mexican Revolution. This resulted in his first book, *La Cristiada,* which was published in 1973. Meyer has been a researcher-teacher at the Colegio de México, the Sorbonne, the Université de Peripignan, and the Colegio de Michoacán. He is Professor Emeritus at Mexico City's CIDE (Centro de Investigación y Docencia Económica—Center of Economic Investigation and Teaching), where he has worked since 1993. There, he started his own history division and the quarterly magazine *ISTOR* in 2000.

Meyer's books on Mexico and Latin America have been published in North America and Europe. They include: *The Cristero Rebellion; La Révolution Mexicaine (The Mexican Revolution) 1910–1940; Problemas Campesinos y Revueltas Agrarias (Peasant Problems and Agrarian Revolts) 1821–1910; Historia de los Cristianos en America Latina, Siglos XIX y XX (History of Christians in Latin America, 19th and 20th Centuries);* and *El Sinarquismo, el Cardenismo y la Iglesia (Sinarquism, Cardenism and the Church) 1937–1947.* His 2008 title, *La Cruzada por México (The Crusade for Mexico),* focuses on North American Catholics and the Cristiada.

Until 1987, Meyer published exclusively on topics related to Mexico and Latin America; but in 1988, not forgetting his first love, he also began writing about the history of Russia and the USSR. Titles he has published on this subject include *La Perestroika; El Campesino en la Historia Rusa y Soviética (The Peasant and Russian-Soviet History); La Gran Controversia entre las Iglesi-*

as *Católica y Ortodoxa* (*The Great Controversy between Catholic and Orthodox Churches*); *and Rusia y Sus Imperios* (*Russia and Her Empires*) *1894–2006*, which was published in 2008.

In 2009, Meyer's *El Celibato Sacerdotal: Su Historia en la Iglesia Católica* (*Priestly Celibacy: Its History in the Catholic Church*) was published. And in June 2012, he received the Doctorate Honoris Causa from the University of Chicago.

Since 1988, Meyer has written a weekly column on international and national current affairs for *El Universal,* a daily newspaper in Mexico City. A dual French and Mexican citizen since 1979, he is married to historian Beatriz Rojas; they have five children and several grandchildren.

Index

and appointment of Portes Gil, 132
and dealings with the Church,
   14–17, 20–24
and diplomacy issues with United
   States, 26–28
effect of Obregón's assassination
   on, 130, 132
exile of, 192
and formation of the Calles Law, 22
and initial view of Cristero
   rebellion, 45
as Jefe Maximo, 180, 186
and Mexican labor movement, 26,
   27
overview of achievements, 13–14
and railway system, 26, 28
role in peace negotiations, 156,
   158, 159, 160–161
role in post-Cristiada government,
   180, 181
as self-appointed secretary of war,
   135
and socialist education, 186
See also Calles Law.
Calles Law
   about, 22–24
   effect on clergy, 83, 85, 86–87
   protestors/opposers of, 32, 34, 35
   suspension of, 167
   Vatican's reaction to, 22
Callistas, 132
Caloca, Agustín, 97
Caloca, Lauro, 32, 132–133
Camarena, Lupe, 62
Camarena, Salvador, 62
Cárdenas, Lázaro, 177, 178–179, 180,
   186, 192–193
Caro, Esteban, 91
Carrancistas, 42
Carranza, Venustiano, 9–11, 42, 46,
   123, 124
Carrillo, General, 94
Caruana, Jorge José, 21
Castillo, Toñita, 76
Catholic Association of Mexican
   Youth (ACJM), 35, 161, 184
   and formation of National
   League for the Defense of
   Religion, 16
   founding of, 12
Catholic Church. *See* Roman
   Catholic Church.

"Catorce, El." *See* Ramírez, Victoriano.
Cedillo, Saturnino, 108, 135, 163
Charis, Heliodoro, 178
Church, schismatic, 14–15
Church of the Virgin of Guadalupe, 70
Clergy
   Calles Law's effect on, 83, 85, 86–87
   canonized by Pope John Paul II,
   83, 86–87
   in support of Cristeros, 86–87
Coalcomán region and Cristero
   government, overview of, 111
Colima region and Cristero
   government, overview of, 111
Columbia, 33, 147, 151, 153
"Conchita, Madre." *See* de la Llata
   Acevedo, Concepción.
Confederacion Regional Obrera
   Mexicana (CROM)
   and attempts to weaken the
   Church, 14–16,
   membership (1922), 17
   and railway strike, 28
Constitution of 1917
   articles of, 9, 11
   See also Calles Law.
Constitutionalists, 123, 124
Coolidge, Calvin, 26, 143, 150, 158,
   182
   and dealings with the Knights of
   Columbus, 145, 146
   and support of Mexican
   government, 126
Cordero, Pedro, 68
Córdoba, Treaty of, 8
"Coronela, La." *See* Montes,
   Agrippina.
Correa Magallanes, Mateo, 47, 83, 86
Covarrubias, Father, 185
Cristero army
   differences from Federal army,
   42–43, 51, 64–65
   early victories, 49
   and guerilla warfare, 50, 51, 52
   strengthening of during the war,
   126, 132–133
   strengths and weaknesses, 66–69
   See also Cristero soldiers; Cristero
   War.
Cristero government
   administrative capital of, 109
   commissions of, 105

creation of, 101
early aspirations for, 101
and economic mobilization,
   116–117, 119–121
educational system of, 113
funding of, 114–115
General Ordinance for, 106,
   108–109
growth of, 104–105
important locations of, 110–111
and Joan of Arc Women's Brigade,
   105
judicial system of, 112–113
and responsibility of leaders, 103
and role of Unión Popular, 102–104
in Zacatecas, 106, 108–109, 110–111
See also Acevedo, Aurelio.
Cristero soldiers
   and agraristas, 48, 49
   and banditry, 69, 91
   characteristics of, 44–45, 57, 60–61,
   64, 66–69
   differences from Federal soldiers,
   42, 51–52, 64–65
   immoral behavior of, 91–92
   moral instructions for, 92
   resources of, 61–63
   uniforms of, 61, 62
   See also Cristero army; Cristero War.
Cristero War
   aftermath of, 171–174, 177–180
   cost of, 172–173
   and effect on clergy, 83, 86–87
   name origin, 42, 80
   official start of, 41
   preliminary uprisings of, 39–40, 41
   significance of, 60–61
   and strengthening of Cristero
   army, 126, 132–133, 163
   See also Accords of 1929; Cristero
   army; Cristero soldiers; Escobar
   rebellion; Gorostieta Velarde,
   Enrique; Peace negotiations;
   Second Cristiada; Serrano-
   Gómez rebellion.
Cristiada. *See* Cristero war.
CROM. *See* Confederacion Regional
   Obrera Mexicana.
Cruz, Roberto, 88, 136
Cubilete Hill, 127
Cueva, Vincente, 179
Cuevas, Mariano, 151–152

D

Daughters of Mary, 75, 96
de Alba, Josefina, 74
de Dios Robledo, Juan, 133
de la Castañeda, Félix, 87
de la Huerta, Alberto, 46
de la Huerta rebellion. *See* Huerta
    rebellion.
de la Llata Acevedo, Concepción
    ("Madre Conchita"), 70, 71
de la Luz Laraza, María, 73
de la Mora de la Mora, Miguel, 20,
    83–84, 86, 159
de la Peña, Catalina, 73
de la Torre, Alfonso, 12, 150–151,
    183, 188, 190
de la Torre, Benjamin, 188, 189
de la Torre, Carlos, 188, 189
de la Torre, Edmundo, 188
de la Torre, Francisco, 188, 189
de la Torre, Ignacio, 188, 189
de la Torre, Jesús, 112
de la Torre, Luis, 188, 189
de la Torre, María, 174, 187, 188,
    189, 190
de la Torre Family, about, 187–191
de León Toral, José. *See* Toral, José
    de León.
Degollado Guízar, Jesús, 51, 54, 58,
    67, 91, 104, 126, 163, 165
del Carmen Robles, María. *See*
    Robles, María del Carmen.
Diario Oficial, 22
Díaz, Adolfo, 28
Díaz Barreto, Pascual, 21, 31, 141,
    151, 156, 160, 161, 169, 173–174
Díaz, Porfirio, 9
"Doña Petrita." *See* Cabral, Petra.
Durán, Yocundo, 82

E

Economic mobilization of Cristero
    government, 116–117, 119–121
*Economists' Report for International
    Bankers,* 129, 132
Education, socialist, 186
Educational system of Cristero
    government, 113
"El Catorce." *See* Ramírez,
    Victoriano.
El Espinazo del Diablo, 52

"El Maestro." *See* González Flores,
    Anacleto.
El Primero Cristero. See Navarro
    Origel, Luis.
El Universal, 20
Emigration, Mexican
    during the Cristiada, 173
    restriction of, 140
Episcopal Committee, Mexican, 161
    formation of, 21
    and response to the Second
        Cristiada, 185
    and suspension of worship,
        23–24
Escobar, José Gonzalo, 134, 135
Escobar rebellion, 135–136
Espinosa, José María, 95
Estrada, Antonio, 184
Estrada, Enrique, 28
Estrada, Florencio, 121

F

Federal army. *See* Armed Forces of
    the Federation.
Federal soldiers
    characteristics of,
    differences from Cristeros, 42, 51,
        64–65
    difficulties of, 51–55
    uniforms of, 61
    See also Armed Forces of the
        Federation.
Federales. *See* Federal soldiers.
Federation, the. *See* Armed Forces
    of the Federation.
Ferreira, General, 45
59th Regiment, 39
Figueroa, Andrés, 178–179
Figueroa Figueroa, Rubén, 13
"First Cristero, The." *See* Navarro
    Origel, Luis.
Flaherty, James A., 145
Flores, Anacleto González. *See*
    González Flores, Anacleto.
Flores, Luis, 71
Flores, Sara, 74
Franco, Jesús, 112
Frías, Manuel, 76
Fumasoni-Bondi, Pietro, 160
Funding of Cristero government,
    114–115

G

Garrido Canabal, Tomás, 193
Gladium, 105, 111
Goldstein, David, 146
Gómcz, Arnulfo, 46, 126, 129
Gómez, Celia. *See* Goyaz, María.
Gómez Loza, Miguel, 74, 103–104
    beatification of, 104
    as governor, 104, 105, 110,
        114–115, 116
Gompers, Samuel, 150
González, Bernardo, 179
González, Brigido, 97
González, Toribio Romo, 97
González Flores, Anacleto ("El
    Maestro"), 43, 70, 71, 126
    beatification of, 104
    death of, 102, 103
    as founder of Unión Popular, 102
Gorostieta Velarde, Enrique
    background of, 122, 123–124
    as Cristero commander-in-chief,
        122, 124–125, 126, 136, 163
    death of, 165
    and Escobar rebels, 135, 136
    and Joan of Arc Women's
        Brigade, 73, 125
    as leader of Jalisco, 104, 105
    and peace negotiation concerns,
        163, 165
    and proposal for José
        Vasconcelos, 134
Government, Cristero. *See* Cristero
    Government.
Goyaz, María ("Celia Gómez,"
    "Celia Ortiz,"), 72, 73
Green, William, 150–151
Guadalupe, Our Lady of. *See* Our
    Lady of Guadalupe.
Guadalupe Regiment, 90, 94
Guadalupe Valdéz, Mario, 113, 179
Guerilla warfare, 50, 51, 52, 69
    and leadership of Gorostieta,
        124, 125
Guillén, J. Rosario, 91
Gutiérrez, Alberto B., 52
Gutiérrez, Chema, 68
Gutiérrez, José María, 52, 91, 125, 179
Gutiérrez, Luis, 42
Gutiérrez, María, 74

H

Hayes, Patrick, 147, 151
Hefflin, James Thomas, 153
Hermosillo, Plan of. *See* Plan of Hermosillo.
Hernández, Miguel, 50, 112
Herrera Valencia, Cosme, 94
Hidalgo, Miguel, 136
Hoover, Herbert, 144, 161
    and support of Mexican government, 126–127
Huejuquilla el Alto, 109, 110
Huerta, Victoriano, 123
Huerta rebellion, 47, 80, 126
Huichol Indians, 60

I

Ibarra, Bonafacio, 112
Ibarra, Luis, 181, 183
In Defense of the Clergy, 8
Iniquis Afflictisque, 35
Institutional Revolutionary Party. *See* Partido Revolucionario Institucional.
Islas Marías prisoners, 170

J

Jalisco region and Cristero government, overview of, 110
Jefe Maximo, 180, 186
Jiménez, Jesús, 62
Jiménez, Primitivo, 179
Joan of Arc Women's Brigade, 71–75, 105, 125
Judge, minor. *See* Juez menor.
Judge of studies. *See* Juez de letras.
Judicial system of Cristero government, 112–113
Juez de letras, 112
Juez menor, 112

K

K of C. *See* Knights of Columbus.
Kauffman, Christopher J., 153
Kellogg, Frank, 143, 145
KKK. *See* Ku Klux Klan.
Knights of Columbus (K of C)
    early presence in Mexico, 12, 81, 145
    and efforts toward U.S. involvement, 145–147, 153

founding of, 145
    impact during the Cristiada, 81–82, 145–147
    membership dangers in Mexico, 82
    and raising of U.S. public awareness, 146–147, 150
    reputation of, 81
    See also Mexican Fund.
Knights of Guadalupe, 15
Knights of San Cristobal. *See* Knights of Columbus.
Ku Klux Klan (KKK), 142, 143–144, 153

L

La Bombilla restaurant, 129
"La Coronela." *See* Montes, Agrippina.
La Merced Market, 73
La Sagrada Familia Church, 20
Lady of Guadalupe, Our. *See* Our Lady of Guadalupe.
Lamas, Honorio, 94–95
Lamas, Manuel, 95
Land distribution policy, 119
Langarrica, Colonel, 68
Lara y Torres, Leopoldo, 159
Law for Reforming the Penal Code. *See* Calles Law.
League, the. *See* National League for the Defense of Religion.
Ledvina, Emmanual B., 166
Lindbergh, Charles, goodwill tour of, 148–149
Lippman, Walter, 17, 167
Llorente, Leonor, 180
LNC. *See* National Peasants League.
Lopes, Jesús, 95
López, Anacleto, 182
López, Nemesio, 91
López, Norberto, 94
López, Víctor, 115
Los Altos Brigade, 90, 105, 179
Loza Márquez, Ildefonso, 108
Loza, Miguel Gómez. *See* Gómez Loza, Miguel.
Lucatero, Refugio, 69

M

Macías, Carmen, 74
Madero, Francisco, 9, 123

"Madre Conchita." *See* de la Llata Acevedo, Concepción.
Magallenes, Cristóbal, 86, 97
Maldonado Lucero, Pedro de Jesús, 86, 87
Manrique, Aurelio, 32, 35
Manzo, Francis, 134
Map of Mexico
    central region of, 43
    entire country, vi–viii
    with significant Cristero locations, 111
María Gutiérrez, José. *See* Gutiérrez, José María.
Martínez, José María, 105
Martyrs, 83, 86–87, 88–89, 93–98
    canonization of, 83, 86–87, 97
Martyrs of León, 93
Mayfield, Earle Bradford, 144
Maximato. See Jefe Maximo.
Mendoza Barragán, Ezequiel, 32, 52, 93–94, 95, 105, 177–178
Mexican Catholic Apostolic Church. *See* Church, schismatic.
Mexican Fund, 146, 151, 153
Mezquitic Congress, 110
Michel, Guadalupe, 87
Michel, Manuel, 61, 87, 110, 125
Miller, George, 23
Minor judge. *See* Juez menor, 112
Minutillo bulletin, 126
Mireles, Amparo, 73
Montavon, William F., 150, 157, 159
Montes, Agrippina ("La Coronela"), 76
Mora y del Río, José, 20, 24, 31, 45, 161
Moreno Aldrete, Manuel, 56
Morones, Luis, 14, 15, 16, 21, 22–23, 29, 150–151
Morrow, Anne, 148, 149
Morrow, Dwight W., 127, 129, 133, 135, 148, 149, 153, 154–155, 157, 158–161, 166–167, 182
Mújica, Francisco, 170
Muñoz, Pedro, 94
Muro, Fidel, 190

N

National Catholic Labor Confederation, 17
National Catholic Party, 8

Sánchez, Ignacio, 62
Sánchez, Lenor, 193
Sandoval, Pedro, 69
Santa Dregeda Church, 9
Schismatic church. *See* Church,
    schismatic.
Scorched earth policy, 116
Second Cristiada
    differences from the first
        Cristiada, 182, 184
    and election of Lázaro Cárdenas,
        192–193
    initial uprisings of, 181
    and opposition of the Church,
        184–185
Sedano, Gumersindo, 95
Segura Vilchis, Luis. *See* Vilchis,
    Luis Segura.
Serrano, Francisco, 126, 129
Serrano-Gómez rebellion, 126
Sheffield, James, 141, 143, 153, 154,
    158
Smith, Al, 144
Socialist education, 186
Soldiers. *See* Cristero soldiers;
    Federal soldiers.
Sons and Daughters of Washington,
    143
Studies, judge of. *See* Juez de letras.

T

Taft, William, 26
Tajeda, Adalberto, 20, 22–23, 31
Tapia, Primo, 185
Tertullian (theologian), 95
3rd Regiment, 61
Time magazine, 24
Tirado, Juan Antonio, 88
Toral, José de León, 70, 115, 129,
    130, 131

Treaty of Córdoba, 9
Treviño, Ricardo, 15

U

Unión Popular, 43, 70
    and affiliation with Knights of
        Columbus, 81
    purpose of, 102
    and role in Cristero government,
        102–104,
    See also González Flores,
        Anacleto.
United States
    and diplomacy issues with
        Mexico, 26–28, 143
    obstacles to involvement in
        Cristiada, 143–144
    in peace negotiations, 154–155
    role in promoting education in
        Cristero government, 113
    and support of Federal army,
        61–62
    and support of Mexican
        government, 62, 126–127, 135
    supporters of involvement in
        Mexico, 150–151, 152
    See also Knights of Columbus;
        Morrow, Dwight W.
University of Arizona, 191

V

Valenzuela, Gilberto, 20
Valles, General, 82
Valparaíso Regiment, 67, 76, 94,
    106, 116
Valverde of León, Bishop, 185
Vargas, Carlos, 98
Vargas, Jorge, 104
Vargas, Ramón, 104
Vasconcelos, Jóse, 134

Vázquez, Federico, 63, 193
Vega, José Reyes, 90, 91, 92, 105,
    110, 124, 163
    and train raid, 44, 45
Velasco, David Uribe, 97
Vera, Francisco, 40
Vilchis, Luis Segura, 88
Villa, Francisco "Pancho," 42, 90,
    124
Villistas, 42
Viramontes, Colonel, 112
Virgin of Guadalupe, Church of
    the, 70
Viva Cristo Rey!, 42–43

W

Women, role of
    and Daughters of Mary, 75
    during the Cristiada, 70–76
    and Joan of Arc Women's
        Brigade, 71–75
    prior to Cristiada, 70
Women's Brigade. *See* Joan of Arc
    Women's Brigade.
World, The, 167

Y

Yaqui Indians, 28, 53, 55

Z

Zacatecas region and Cristero
    government, overview of,
    110–111
Zapata, Emiliano, 42, 123
Zapatistas, 42
"Zarco, the." *See* Zepeda, Jesús.
Zepeda, Jesús ("the Zarco"), 91
Zócalo, the, 4–5, 18–19